ETHICS IN THE REAL WORLD

ETHICS IN THE REAL WORLD

90 Essays on Things That Matter

A FULLY UPDATED AND EXPANDED EDITION

Peter Singer

PRINCETON UNIVERSITY PRESS

PRINCETON & OXFORD

Published by Princeton University Press
41 William Street, Princeton, New Jersey 08540
99 Banbury Road, Oxford OX2 6JX

press.princeton.edu

All Rights Reserved

Library of Congress Control Number 2022948600
ISBN 978-0-691-23787-9
ISBN (pbk.) 978-0-691-23786-2
ISBN (e-book) 978-0-691-23788-6

British Library Cataloging-in-Publication Data is available

Editorial: Rob Tempio and Chloe Coy
Production Editorial: Jill Harris
Text Design: Karl Spurzem
Cover Design: Katie Osborne
Production: Erin Suydam
Publicity: Maria Whelan
Copyeditor: Karen Verde

This book has been composed in Arno

Printed on acid-free paper. ∞

Printed in the United States of America

10 9 8 7 6 5 4 3 2 1

CONTENTS

LIFE AND DEATH

PUBLIC HEALTH AND PANDEMIC ETHICS

SEX AND GENDER

DOING GOOD

HAPPINESS

POLITICS

GLOBAL PROBLEMS

INTRODUCTION

We all make ethical choices, frequently without being aware
that we are doing so. Too often we assume that to live ethically,
all one needs to do is obey the generally accepted rules that
begin with "You must not . . ." If that were all there is to living
ethically, then as long as we were not violating one of those
rules, we would be living an ethical life. That view of ethics,
however, is incomplete. It fails to consider the good we can—
and should—do to others less fortunate than ourselves, not
only in our own community, but anywhere within the reach of
our help. We ought also to extend our concern to future generations, and to sentient beings beyond our own species including
nonhuman animals and, should we ever encounter them, conscious artificial intelligence and aliens.

Another important ethical responsibility applies to citizens
of a democratic society: to participate in the decisions our society makes. Many of these decisions involve ethical choices. In
public discussions of these ethical issues, people with training
in ethics, or moral philosophy, can play a valuable role. Today
that is not an especially controversial claim, but when I was
a student, philosophers themselves proclaimed that it was a
mistake to think that they have any special expertise that would

qualify them to addresses substantive ethical issues. The accepted understanding of the discipline, at least in the English-speaking world, was that philosophy is concerned with the analysis of words and concepts, and is neutral on substantive ethical questions.

I doubt that I would have continued in philosophy if that view had prevailed. Fortunately for me, at least, the radical student movement of the late 1960s and early 1970s transformed the way moral philosophy is practiced and taught. In the era of the Vietnam War, with other struggles against racism, sexism, and for a cleaner, safer environment, students demanded that university courses should be relevant to the important issues of the day.

Philosophers responded by returning to their discipline's origins. They recalled the example of Socrates questioning his fellow Athenians about what it takes to live justly, and they summoned up the courage to ask similar questions of their students, and eventually, of the wider public.

My first book, written against the background of civil, and sometimes not so civil, disobedience against racism, sexism, and the war in Vietnam, asks when disobedience is justified in a democracy.[1] Since then, I've continued to address issues that matter to people outside departments of philosophy. Some academics still think that writing a book aimed at the general public is beneath them, and writing an opinion piece for a newspaper is sinking lower still. In the pages that follow you will find a selection of my shorter writings. Newspaper columns are often ephemeral, but the ones I have selected here discuss enduring

---

1. *Democracy and Disobedience* (Oxford: Clarendon Press, 1973).

issues, or address problems that are still with us. The pressure of not exceeding 1,000 words demands a style that is clear and concise. Granted, in such essays it is impossible to present one's research in a manner that can be assessed adequately by other scholars, and inevitably some of the nuances and qualifications that could be explored in a longer essay have to be omitted.

It's nice when your colleagues in philosophy departments appreciate what you are doing, but I also judge the success of my work by the impact my books, articles, and talks have on people who are interested in thinking about how to live ethically, irrespective of where they work or live. The average article in a peer-reviewed journal is, according to one study, read in full by just ten people.[2] An opinion piece for a major newspaper or a syndicated column may be read by tens of thousands or even millions, and some of these readers will change their minds on an important issue, and may even change the way they live. I know that happens, because people have told me that my writing has led them to stop eating animal products, changed what they donate to charity, or, in at least one case, to donate a kidney to a stranger. Beyond such anecdotal evidence, as I describe below in "Can Ethics Be Taught?" I took part in the first randomized controlled studies showing that what students discuss in a philosophy class can change their behavior outside the class.

The essays in the opening section will shed some light on my approach to ethics, but it may be useful to say a little more here. Moral judgments are not purely subjective, in that they

---

2. Asit Biswas and Julian Kirchherr, "Prof, No One Is Reading You," *Straits Times*, April 11, 2015, http://www.straitstimes.com/opinion/prof-no-one-is-reading-you.

are different from judgments of taste. If they were merely subjective, we would not think it was worth arguing about ethical issues, any more than we think that it is worth arguing about which ice cream flavor to choose. We recognize that tastes differ, and there is no "right" amount of garlic to put in a salad dressing; but we do think it is worth arguing about the legalization of voluntary assisted dying, or whether it is wrong to eat meat.

Nor is ethics just a matter of expressing our intuitive responses of repugnance or approval, even if these intuitions are widely shared. We may have innate "yuck" reactions that helped our ancestors to survive, at a time when they were social mammals but not yet human. Those reactions will not always be a reliable guide to right and wrong in the much larger and more complex global community in which we live today. For that, we need to use our ability to reason.

There was a time when I thought this kind of reasoning could only unravel the implications of a more basic ethical stance that is, ultimately, subjective. I no longer think this. There are, as Derek Parfit argued in his major work *On What Matters* (which I describe in the pages below in an essay entitled "Does Anything Matter?"), objective ethical truths that we can discover through careful reasoning and reflection.[3] But for those who reject the idea of objective ethical truths, the essays that follow can be read as attempts to work out the implications of accepting

---

3. Derek Parfit, *On What Matters*, 2 vols. (Oxford: Oxford University Press, 2013). Peter Singer (ed.), *Does Anything Really Matter* (Oxford: Oxford University Press, 2017) is a collection of commentaries on this work, to which Parfit responded in a third volume of *On What Matters* (Oxford: Oxford University Press, 2017). For my own views on the objectivity of ethics, see Katarzyna de Lazari-Radek and Peter Singer, *The Point of View of the Universe* (Oxford: Oxford University Press, 2014).

the ethical commitment espoused by many philosophers in different terms, and perhaps best put by the great nineteenth-century utilitarian philosopher Henry Sidgwick:

> the good of any one individual is of no more importance, from the point of view (if I may say so) of the Universe, than the good of any other; unless, that is, there are special grounds for believing that more good is likely to be realised in the one case than in the other.[4]

Sidgwick was a utilitarian, and so am I. Once we start to question our evolved and culturally transmitted intuitive responses to moral issues, utilitarianism is, I believe, the most defensible ethical view, as I have argued at much greater length in *The Point of View of the Universe*, written jointly with Katarzyna de Lazari-Radek.[5] Nevertheless, in the essays that follow, I do not presuppose utilitarianism, and some are written with a co-author who is not a utilitarian. That is because on many of the issues I discuss, my conclusions follow from non-utilitarian positions as well as from utilitarianism. Given the practical importance of these issues, as a good utilitarian I ought to aim to write for the broadest possible audience, and not merely for a narrow band of committed utilitarians.

Some of the following essays address topics for which I am well known: the ethics of our relations with animals, questions of life and death, and the obligations of the rich to those in extreme poverty. Others explore topics on which my views are

---

4. Henry Sidgwick, *The Methods of Ethics*, 7th edition (London: Macmillan, 1907), p. 382.
5. See fn3.

likely to be less familiar: the ethics of selling kidneys, or of growing genetically modified crops, the moral status of conscious robots, and whether incest between adult siblings is wrong. Happiness, and how to promote it, plays a key role in my ethical view, so that is the topic of one group of articles. Among the more personal essays is a reflection on surfing, which provides me with a refreshing break from thinking about the other topics discussed in this book.

This edition also differs from the previous one, in part because the world in which it is appearing is different from the world of 2016. Of the 90 essays in this book, 37 are new to this edition, and many of these cover recent ethical issues, such as the genetic modification of human embryos, limits to freedom of expression, the ethics of artificial intelligence, extending the human life span, the lockdowns and vaccine mandates that aimed to mitigate the impact of the COVID-19 pandemic, racism, and the riots that followed the murder of George Floyd, colonizing outer space, and Russia's invasion of Ukraine, which has once again raised the risk of a larger conflict and even a nuclear war. Some of these essays have been grouped in a special new section, "The Future," in which I address issues that I expect to become increasingly important over the next decade or two. Others are distributed throughout the book.

This edition differs from the previous one not only because it has new essays, but because all of the essays, irrespective of when they were originally written, have been fully updated. So, for example, the essay on "How Much Should Sex Matter?" was first written and published in response to the disqualification of Jenna Talackova from the 2012 finals of Miss Universe Canada, because she was not a "natural-born" female. Now the essay follows the issue right up to the 2022 success of Lia Thomas, also not a "natural-born" female, in US college women's swimming events.

Readers who already know my thoughts on some topics may be surprised by my views on others. I try to keep an open mind, to be responsive to the evidence, and not simply to follow a predictable political line. If you are not already persuaded that philosophers do have something to contribute to issues of broad general interest, I hope that this volume will convince you of that. Even more important, I hope it will convince you that if we are to solve the many problems we face, we need to discuss the ethical aspects of these problems in a manner that can reach across partisan political divides, and find the best solutions for all those affected by them.

ACKNOWLEDGMENTS

Many, though by no means all, of these pieces were written for Project Syndicate, a news service that provides a broad range of commentaries to more than 500 media outlets in 156 countries. At the instigation of Andrzej Rapaczynski, I have been writing a monthly column for Project Syndicate since 2005, so my greatest debt is to him for recruiting me as a member of his team of columnists. Over all these years, Agata Sagan has brought to my attention topics that have led to columns, and has also assisted by carrying out research on which I have drawn, and making helpful comments on drafts. On several occasions, as this text shows, she has been my co-author. I thank Project Syndicate for permission to reproduce the columns I wrote for them, and I thank Project Syndicate's editors, Ken Murphy and Jonathan Stein, for showing me that even my best efforts to write clearly can be improved upon.

Other articles come from the *New York Times*, the *Washington Post*, the *Los Angeles Times*, the *New York Daily News*, the *Sydney Morning Herald*, *The Age*, *Free Inquiry*, *New Statesman*, *Bioethics*, *Nautilus*, and www.effective-altruism.com. Some of them are co-authored, and I acknowledge the important contributions to my thinking and to this book made by my co- authors: Nick Beckstead, Katarzyna de Lazari-Radek, Frances Kissling, Jotham Musinguzi, Michael Plant, Julian Savulescu, Agata Sagan, and Matt Wage.

The idea for this book, as well as the encouragement to prepare a fresh edition, came from Rob Tempio of Princeton University Press, so an especially big thank you, Rob, for your continuing enthusiasm for the project. I am also grateful to two anonymous reviewers for the Press for their many constructive comments and their helpful suggestions, to Jill Harris for overseeing the production process, to Kathleen Strattan for compiling the index, and to Karen Verde of Green Pelican Editorial Services for copyediting the book with a light but deft touch.

For both the first and this edition, Agata Sagan went through my shorter writings and made suggestions—most of which I accepted—about which of them should be included in this book. The final shape of the book therefore owes a lot to her.

Finally, the University Center for Human Values at Princeton University has provided me, for the past 23 years, with an ideal working environment, and I thank all of my colleagues and the many visitors to the Center during this period for stimulating me to think about a wider range of issues than I would have been likely to think about in a department focused on a single discipline.

Peter Singer, Princeton University

BIG QUESTIONS

A Pale Blue Dot at the
Hinge of History

The eighteenth-century German philosopher Immanuel Kant wrote: "Two things fill the heart with ever renewed and increasing awe and reverence, the more often and more steadily we meditate upon them: the starry firmament above and the moral law within."

Today, we know a lot more about "the starry firmament above than Kant knew. By expanding our grasp of the vastness of the universe, science has, if anything, increased the awe and reverence we feel when we look up on a starry night (assuming, that is, that we have got far enough away from air pollution and excessive street lighting to see the stars properly). But we may feel that greater knowledge forces us to acknowledge that our place in the universe is not particularly significant.

In his essay "Dreams and Facts," the philosopher Bertrand Russell wrote that our entire Milky Way galaxy is a tiny fragment of the universe, and within this fragment our solar system is "an infinitesimal speck," and within this speck "our planet is a microscopic dot." The truth of this was vividly demonstrated in 1990 when the astronomer Carl Sagan suggested that the *Voyager* space probe capture an image of Earth as it reached the outer limits of our solar system. Earth shows up in a grainy image as a pale blue dot. If you go to YouTube and search for "Carl Sagan—Pale Blue Dot," you can see it, and hear Sagan himself telling us that we must cherish our world because everything humans have ever valued exists only on that pale blue dot.

That is a moving experience, but what should we learn from it?

Russell sometimes wrote as if the fact that we are a mere speck in a vast universe showed that we don't really matter all that much: "On this dot, tiny lumps of impure carbon and water, of complicated structure, with somewhat unusual physical and chemical properties, crawl about for a few years, until they are dissolved again into the elements of which they are compounded."

But no such nihilistic view of our existence follows from the size of our planetary home, and Russell himself was no nihilist. He thought that it was important to confront the fact of our insignificant place in the universe, because he did not want us to live under the illusory comfort of a belief that somehow the world had been created for our sake, and that we are under the benevolent care of an all-powerful creator. "Dreams and Facts" concludes with these stirring words: "No man is liberated from fear who dare not see his place in the world as it is; no man can achieve the greatness of which he is capable until he has allowed himself to see his own littleness."

After World War II, when the world was divided into nuclear-armed camps threatening each other with mutual destruction, Russell did not take the view that our insignificance, when considered against the vastness of the universe, meant that the end of life on Earth did not matter. On the contrary, he made nuclear disarmament the chief focus of his political activity for the remainder of his life.

Sagan took a similar view. While seeing the Earth as a whole diminishes the importance of things like national boundaries that divide us, he said, it also "underscores our responsibility to deal more kindly with one another, and to preserve and cherish the pale blue dot, the only home we've ever known."

Thirty years later, the Oxford philosopher Derek Parfit gave that idea even greater significance when he wrote, near the end of the second volume of his magisterial work *On What Matters*: "We live during the hinge of history." Parfit was thinking of the fact that our species is living through "its most dangerous and decisive period," but if we can survive the hazards we face, the development of new technologies will enable our descendants to spread through our galaxy. Over the next few centuries, Parfit suggested, we will be able to live independently on other planets. Those centuries will then be only a sliver of time compared to what is to come, for we may populate the Milky Way galaxy, or spread even further in this section of the universe. As Parfit put it in the penultimate paragraph of the third and final volume of *On What Matters*:

> Life can be wonderful as well as terrible, and we shall increasingly have the power to make life good. Since human history may be only just beginning, we can expect that future humans, or supra-humans, may achieve some great goods that we cannot now even imagine. In Nietzsche's words, there has never been such a new dawn and clear horizon, and such an open sea.

The most significant contribution our generation can make to reaching this open sea is to ensure the survival of intelligent life on our planet.

Could this idea that we are essential to this process be merely the latest version of the self-important delusion that humans are the center of existence? Surely, in this vast universe, there must be other forms of intelligent life, and if we don't populate the Milky Way galaxy, someone else will.

The physicist Enrico Fermi once asked some fellow scientists with whom he was having lunch at Los Alamos National Laboratory: "Where is everybody?" He wasn't commenting on empty tables in the lab's dining room, but on the absence of a visit, or at least a message, from extraterrestrials. The thought behind that "Where is everybody?" is now known as the Fermi Paradox: If the universe is so stupendous, and has existed for 13.7 billion years, why haven't other intelligent forms of life made contact?

According to a 2018 paper by researchers at the University of Oxford's Future of Humanity Institute, the most likely answer is that intelligent life is *extremely* rare. It is so rare that we may be the only intelligent beings in our galaxy, and perhaps in the much larger Virgo supercluster to which our galaxy belongs.

It is an extraordinary thought that we, the inhabitants of this pale blue dot at this particular moment, are making choices that will determine whether billions of stars are populated, for billions of years. It may not be true, but it could be. Granting that, what should we do about it?

Clearly, we should take all reasonable steps to reduce the risk that we will become extinct. We should seek to prevent nuclear war, of course, and future pandemics, whether natural or the result of bioterrorism. We should track asteroids and comets that might collide with our planet, and develop means for deflecting any that we might detect. That does not mean that we should neglect present problems, though, because we should acknowledge that we do not always know what will best reduce extinction risks. If we are at the hinge of history, enabling people to escape poverty and get an education is as likely to move things in the right direction as almost anything else we might do; and those are good things to do anyway.

Does Anything Matter?

Can moral judgments be true or false? Or is ethics, at bottom, a purely subjective matter, for individuals to choose, or perhaps relative to the culture of the society in which one lives?

Among philosophers, the view that moral judgments state objective truths went out of fashion in the 1930s, when logical positivists asserted that, because there seems to be no way of verifying the truth of moral judgments, they cannot be anything other than expressions of our feelings or attitudes. So, for example, when we say, "You ought not to hit that child," all we are really doing is expressing our disapproval of your hitting the child, or encouraging you to stop hitting the child. There is no truth to the matter of whether or not it is wrong for you to hit the child.

Although this view of ethics has often been challenged, many of the objections have come from religious thinkers who appealed to God's commands. Such arguments have limited appeal in the largely secular world of Western philosophy. Other defenses of objective truth in ethics made no appeal to religion, but for a long time they made little headway against the prevailing philosophical mood. That began to change in the early years of this century, boosted in part by the circulation, among philosophers, of drafts of a major work by Derek Parfit.

Parfit was born in 1942 and died in 2017. Just a year before, in a poll on a popular philosophy website, he had been voted the most important living Anglophone philosopher. He had received great acclaim for *Reasons and Persons*, which appeared in 1984, but that book did not tackle the question of the objectivity of ethics. That was, however, the subject of his second book, a two-volume work called *On What Matters*, published in 2011. (A third volume, consisting largely of replies to critics, appeared in 2017, shortly after Parfit's death.) The publication of this book, which makes no appeal to any religious beliefs, put those who reject objectivism in ethics on the defensive.

On What Matters is a book of daunting length, totaling more than 1,800 pages, of densely argued text. But the core of the argument comes in the first 400 pages, which is not an insurmountable challenge for the intellectually curious—particularly given that Parfit, in the best tradition of English-language philosophy, always strove for lucidity, never using obscure words where simple ones will do. Each sentence is straightforward, the argument is clear, and Parfit often uses vivid examples to make his points. Thus, the book is an intellectual treat for anyone who wants to understand not so much "what matters" as whether anything really *can* matter, in an objective sense.

Many people assume that rationality is always instrumental: reason can tell us only how to get what we want, but our basic wants and desires are beyond the scope of reasoning. Not so, Parfit argues. Just as we can grasp the truth that $1 + 1 = 2$, so we can see that I have a reason to avoid suffering agony at some future time, regardless of whether I now care about, or have desires about, whether I will suffer agony at that time. We can also have reasons (though not always conclusive reasons) to prevent others from suffering agony. Such self-evident normative truths provide the basis for Parfit's defense of objectivity in ethics.

One major argument against objectivism in ethics is that people disagree deeply about right and wrong, and this disagreement extends to philosophers who cannot be accused of being ignorant or confused. If great thinkers like Immanuel Kant and Jeremy Bentham disagree about what we ought to do, can there really be an objectively true answer to that question?

Parfit's response to this line of argument leads him to make a claim that is perhaps even bolder than his defense of objectivism in ethics. He considers three leading theories about what we ought to do—one deriving from Kant, one from the social-contract tradition of Hobbes, Locke, Rousseau, and the contemporary philosophers John Rawls and T. M. Scanlon, and one from Bentham's utilitarianism—and argues that the Kantian and social-contract theories must be revised in order to be defensible.

Then he argues that these revised theories coincide with a particular form of consequentialism, which is a theory in the same broad family as utilitarianism. If Parfit is right, there is much less disagreement between apparently conflicting moral theories than we all thought. The defenders of each of these theories are, in Parfit's vivid phrase, "climbing the same mountain on different sides."

Readers who go to *On What Matters* seeking an answer to the question posed by its title might be disappointed. Parfit's real interest is in combating subjectivism and nihilism. Unless he can show that objectivism is true, he believes, nothing matters.

When Parfit does come to the question of "what matters," his answer might seem surprisingly obvious. He tells us, for example, that what matters most now is that "we rich people give up some of our luxuries, ceasing to overheat the Earth's atmosphere, and taking care of this planet in other ways, so that it continues to support intelligent life."

Many of us had already reached that conclusion. What we gain from Parfit's work is the possibility of defending these and other moral claims as objective truths.

Is There Moral Progress?

In the nineteenth century, in Europe, North America, and Australia, belief in moral progress was widespread. Indeed, in Europe the century that passed from the end of the Napoleonic wars, in 1815, saw no major wars. Against that background, the first half of the twentieth century was a shock, containing, as it did, two world wars, the Nazi Holocaust, and Stalin's Gulag. The belief that we are progressing morally became difficult to defend, and the killing fields of Cambodia, and the atrocities in Rwanda and Darfur, did nothing to re-establish it.

Nevertheless, as Steven Pinker pointed out in *The Better Angels of Our Nature*, in the 13th century, the brutal Mongol conquests caused the deaths of an estimated 40 million people—not so far from the 55 million who died in the Second World War—in a world with only one-seventh the population of the mid-20th century. The Mongols rounded up and massacred their victims in cold blood, just as the Nazis did, though they had only battle-axes instead of guns and gas chambers. A longer perspective enables us to see that the crimes of Hitler and Stalin were, sadly, less novel than we thought.

After 1945, we saw a new phenomenon known as the "long peace": For more than 75 years the great powers and the most technologically advanced countries did not fight wars against one another. This was not, of course, an absolute peace, because there were many other wars, some killing millions of people and causing widespread destruction. Nevertheless, Pinker's *The Better Angels of Our Nature*, published in 2011, indicated that since the end of World War II, there had been a decline in all kinds of organized conflicts, including civil wars, genocides, repression, and terrorism. At the time of writing, it remains to be seen whether Russia's aggression against Ukraine will prove to be an isolated exception to the rule that technologically advanced countries do not go to war with other technologically advanced countries or will signal the end of this decline.

The revulsion against violence inflicted on ethnic minorities, women, children, homosexuals, and animals that has developed over the past half-century is also, Pinker argues, an important indicator of moral progress. He is not, of course, suggesting that these movements have achieved their goals, but he reminds us how far we have come in a relatively short time from the days when lynchings were commonplace in the South; domestic violence was tolerated to such a degree that a 1950s ad could show a husband with his wife over his knees, spanking her for failing to buy the right brand of coffee

In 1948, the United Nations General Assembly adopted the Universal Declaration of Human Rights which, in response to the crimes committed during World War II, sought to establish the principle that everyone is entitled to the same basic rights, irrespective of race, color, sex, language, religion, or other status. On the 60th anniversary of the adoption of the declaration, WorldPublicOpinion.org conducted polls to test support for these basic rights. The polls involved nearly 15,000 respondents in 16 countries representing 58% of the world's population: Azerbaijan, China, Egypt, France, Great Britain, India, Indonesia, Iran, Mexico, Nigeria, the Palestinian Territories, Russia, South Korea, Turkey, Ukraine, and the United States. In 11 of these countries, most people believe that, over their lifetimes, people of different races and ethnicities have come to be treated more equally.

On average, 59% say this, with only 19% thinking that people are treated less equally, and 20% saying that there has been no change. People in the United States, Indonesia, China, Iran, and Great Britain are particularly likely to perceive greater equality. Palestinians are the only people of whom a majority sees less equality for people of different racial or ethnic groups, while opinion is relatively evenly divided in Nigeria, Ukraine, Azerbaijan, and Russia.

An even stronger overall majority, 71%, regards women as having made progress toward equality, although once again, the Palestinian territories are an exception, this time joined by Nigeria. Russia, Ukraine, and Azerbaijan again have significant minorities saying that women are now treated less equally than they once were. In India, although only 53% say that women have gained greater equality, an additional 14% say that women now have more rights than men!

Overall, it seems likely that these opinions reflect real changes, and thus are signs of moral progress toward a world in which people are not denied rights on the basis of race, ethnicity, or sex. That view is backed up by the polls' most striking results: very widespread rejection of inequality based on race, ethnicity, or sex. On average, 90% of those asked said that equal treatment for people of different races or ethnic origins is important, and in no country were more than 13% of respondents prepared to say that equal treatment is not important.

When asked about equal rights for women, support was almost as strong, with an average of 86% rating it important. Significantly, these majorities also existed in Muslim countries. In Egypt, for example, 97% said that racial and ethnic equality is important, and 90% said that equality for women is important. In Iran, the figures were 82% and 78%, respectively.

Compared to just a decade before the Universal Declaration of Human Rights, this represents a significant change in people's views. Equal rights for women—not simply suffrage, but also working outside the home or living independently—was still a radical idea in many countries. Openly racist ideas prevailed in Germany and the American South, and much of the world's population lived in colonies ruled by European powers. Today, no country openly accepts racist doctrines, and equality for women is much more widely, if still not universally, accepted.

What factors have brought about this progress? In my 1981 book *The Expanding Circle*, I argued that our capacity to reason has played an important role in expanding the moral circle, that is, the circle of beings to whom our actions are subject to moral constraints. To indicate that reason can take us to places that we might not expect to reach, I wrote of an "escalator of reason" that can take us to a vantage point from which we see that our own interests are similar to, and from the point of view of the universe do not matter more than, the interests of others. Pinker adds to this argument by pointing to the "Flynn effect"—the remarkable finding by the philosopher James Flynn that ever since IQ tests were first administered, the scores achieved by those taking the test have been rising. The average IQ is, by definition, 100; but to achieve that result, raw test scores have to be standardized. If the average teenager today could go back in time and take an IQ test from 1910, he or she would have an IQ of 130, which would be better than 98% of those taking the test then.

Nor is it easy to attribute this rise to improved education, because the aspects of the tests on which scores have risen most do not require a good vocabulary or even mathematical ability, but instead test powers of abstract reasoning. One theory is that we have gotten better at IQ tests because we live in a more symbol-rich environment. Flynn himself thinks that the spread of the scientific mode of reasoning has played a role.

Pinker argues that enhanced powers of reasoning give us the ability to detach ourselves from our immediate experience and from our personal or parochial perspective, and frame our ideas in more abstract, universal terms. This in turn leads to better moral commitments, including avoiding violence. It is just this kind of reasoning ability that has improved during the 20th century. He therefore suggests that the 20th century has seen a "*moral* Flynn effect, in which an accelerating escalator of reason carried us away from impulses that lead to violence," and that this lies behind the long peace, the new peace, and the rights revolution. Among the wide range of evidence he produces in support of that argument is the tidbit that since 1946, there has been a negative correlation between an American president's IQ and the number of battle deaths in wars involving the United States.

Reason, Pinker suggests, also moves us away from forms of morality more likely to lead to violence, and toward moral advances that, while not eschewing the use of force altogether, restrict it to the uses necessary to improve social welfare, like utilitarian reforms of the savage punishments given to criminals in earlier times. For reason does, Pinker holds, point to a particular kind of morality. We prefer life to death, and happiness to suffering, and we understand that we live in a world in which others can make a difference to whether we live well or die miserably. Therefore we will want to tell others that they should not hurt us, and in doing so we commit ourselves to the idea that we should not hurt them. (Pinker quotes a famous sentence from the 18th-century philosopher William Godwin: "What magic is there in the pronoun 'my' that should justify us in overturning the decisions of impartial truth?") That morality can be grounded in some commitment to treating others as we would like them to treat us, an ancient idea, expressed in the golden rule and in similar thoughts in the moral traditions of many other civilizations. The escalator of reason leads us to it.

The God of Suffering

A few years ago, the conservative commentator Dinesh D'Souza was on a mission to debate atheists on the topic of the existence of god, challenging all the prominent nonbelievers he could find. I was happy to accept his invitation.

Given that I was debating an experienced and evidently intelligent opponent, I wanted to stake my position on firm ground. So I argued that while I cannot disprove the existence of every possible kind of deity, we can be sure that we do not live in a world that was created by a god who is all-powerful, all-knowing, and all good. Christians, of course, think we do live in such a world. Yet a powerful reason for doubting this confronts us every day: the world contains a vast amount of pain and suffering. If god is all-knowing, he knows how much suffering there is. If he is all-powerful, he could have created a world without so much suffering. If he is all-good, he surely would have created a world without so much suffering.

Christians usually respond that god bestowed on us the gift of free will, and so is not responsible for the evil we do. This response fails to deal with the suffering of those who drown in floods, are burned alive in forest fires caused by lightning, or die of hunger or thirst during a drought.

Sometimes Christians attempt to explain this suffering by saying that all humans are sinners, and so deserve their fate, even if it is a horrible one. But infants and small children are just as likely as adults to suffer and die in natural disasters, and it seems impossible that they could deserve to suffer and die. Yet, according to traditional Christian doctrine, since they have descended from Eve, they inherit the original sin of their mother, who defied god's decree against eating from the tree of knowledge. This is a triply repellant idea, for it implies, first, that knowledge is a bad thing, second, that disobeying god's will is the greatest sin of all, and third, that children inherit the sins of their ancestors, and may justly be punished for them.

Even if one were to accept all this, however, the problem remains unresolved. For humans are not the only victims of floods, fires, and droughts. Animals, too, suffer from these events, and since they are not descended from Adam and Eve, they cannot have inherited original sin.

In earlier times, when original sin was taken more seriously than it generally is today, the suffering of animals posed a particularly difficult problem for thoughtful Christians. The seventeenth-century French philosopher René Descartes solved it by the drastic expedient of denying that animals can suffer. They are, he maintained, merely very ingenious mechanisms, and we should not take their cries and struggles as a sign of pain any more than we take the noise of an alarm clock as a sign that it has consciousness. That claim is unlikely to convince anyone who lives with a dog or a cat.

Surprisingly, given his experience debating with atheists, D'Souza struggled to find a convincing answer to the problem. He first said that, given that humans can live forever in heaven, the suffering of this world is less important than it would be if our life in this world were the only life we have. That still fails to explain why an all-powerful and all-good god would permit it. Relatively insignificant as it may be, from the perspective of all eternity, it is still a vast amount of suffering, and the world would be better without it, or at least without most of it. (Some say that we need to have some suffering to appreciate what it is like to be happy. Maybe—but we surely don't need as much as we have.)

Next, D'Souza argued that since god gave us life, we are not in a position to complain if our life is not perfect. He used the example of being born with one limb missing. If life itself is a gift, he said, we are not wronged by being given less than we might want. In response I pointed out that we condemn mothers who cause harm to their babies by taking alcohol or cocaine when pregnant. Yet since they have given life to their children, it seems that, on D'Souza's view, there is nothing wrong with what they have done.

Finally, D'Souza fell back, as many Christians do when pressed, on the claim that we should not expect to understand god's reasons for creating the world as it is. It is as if an ant should try to understand our decisions, so puny is our intelligence in comparison to the infinite wisdom of god. (This is the answer given, in more poetic form, in *The Book of Job*.) But once we abdicate our own powers of reason in this way, we may as well believe anything at all.

Moreover, the assertion that our intelligence is puny in comparison with god's presupposes just the point that is under debate—that there is a god who is infinitely wise, as well as all-powerful and all-good. The evidence of our own eyes makes it more plausible to believe that the world is not created by a god at all. If, however, we insist on divine creation, the god who made the world cannot be all-powerful and all-good. He must either be evil or a bungler.

Postscript: In 2014, D'Souza pleaded guilty to using a "straw donor" to make illegal campaign contributions, a felony for which he was sentenced to eight months' detention in a halfway house, fined $30,000, and placed on probation for five years. In 2018, then-president Trump pardoned him.

Do You Have a Moral Plan?

(with Agata Sagan)

Many people make New Year's resolutions. The most common ones, at least in the United States, are to exercise more, eat healthier, save money, lose weight, or reduce stress. Some may resolve to be better to a particular person—not to criticize their partner, to visit their aging grandmother more often, or to be a better friend to someone close to them. Yet few people—just 12%, according to one US study—resolve to become a better person in general, meaning better in a moral sense.

One possible explanation is that most people focus on their own well-being, and don't see being morally better as something that is in their own interest. A more charitable explanation is that many people see morality as a matter of conforming to a set of rules establishing the things we should *not* do.

That is not surprising in societies built on the Jewish and Christian traditions, in which the Ten Commandments are held up as the core of morality. But, today, traditional moral rules have only limited relevance to ordinary life. Few of us are ever in situations in which killing someone even crosses our mind. Most of us don't need to steal, and to do so is not a great temptation—most people will even return a lost wallet with money in it.

For those who take this view of morality, and can make an honest living sufficient to meet their own essential needs, being a good person hardly seems worthy of a special resolution. This is suggested in a survey of US adults that found that only 23% report that they often think about or research the ethical aspect of a choice in their life.

Most people can just live as they have always been living, and as their friends and co-workers live. In the same survey, another 31% reported that they sometimes think about ethical aspects of choices in their lives, suggesting that moral choices arise only in unusual circumstances, and many people thus simply cross those bridges when they come to them. What of the remaining 46%? It seems that they never think about ethics at all!

These findings could be interpreted as indicating that nearly half of Americans don't regard ethics as important. But in the same survey, 87% said that it is important to teach ethics to children, from kindergarten through high school. The correct interpretation, therefore, seems to be that at least three-quarters of Americans think that ethics is important, but they don't believe that it requires much thought or research.

We reject this view. Being a good person today requires thought and work. The moral intuitions that evolved during many millennia of living in small, face-to-face societies are no longer adequate. Our actions now—or our failure to act—affect people all over the world and people who will live on this planet for many centuries to come.

That means we face moral choices all the time. Global problems like climate change, extreme poverty, the cruel confinement of billions of animals in factory farms, overfishing of the oceans, and of course the pandemic raise complex questions about how we should spend our money, how much of it we should give to help others, what we should eat, and how we should use our abilities to influence others and our governments. Moral codes written thousands of years ago are silent about climate change, and usually say nothing, or very little, about protecting the environment, the treatment of animals, and how we should exercise our responsibilities as citizens in a democracy.

No short set of rules can possibly deal with the variety of circumstances in which individuals find themselves today. To be a good person today requires time and thought. We need to inform ourselves about problems like those just mentioned, decide on our priorities, and consider where we can make the most difference. That's why this is an appropriate area for the kind of commitment involved in making a resolution.

We must consciously direct our attention to living ethically. It's a mistake to think that we can wait until life puts us in a situation requiring us to make a difficult moral choice. Anyone sufficiently affluent to have choices about how to live, and what to do with their time and money, is already there.

For these reasons, a resolution to be a morally better person would not be a matter of sticking to rules, like not smoking or eating sweets. Such resolutions are rarely kept anyway.

Setting goals works better, especially if the goals are incremental, steps along a path. So make a moral plan. Think about your values, and choose one or two issues that are important to you. Then you can affirm those values by living in a way that addresses the issues you care about, whether it is by reducing your personal contribution to climate change, or animals' suffering, or finding the most effective organizations helping people in extreme poverty, and supporting them with your time or money.

When you do this, make a note of what you have done, and the progress you have made. You will not be perfect. There are few saints, and for most people, aspiring to sainthood is bound to be self-defeating. But take pride in your achievements, and aim to build on them in the months and years to come.

Are We Ready for a "Morality Pill"?

(with Agata Sagan)

In 2011, in Foshan, China, a two-year-old girl was run over by a van. The driver did not stop. Over the next seven minutes, more than a dozen people walked or bicycled past the injured child. A second truck ran over her. Eventually, a woman pulled her to the side, and her mother arrived. The child died in a hospital. The entire scene was captured on video and caused an uproar when it was shown by a television station and posted online. A similar event occurred in London in 2004, as have others, far from the lens of a video camera.

Yet people can, and often do, behave in very different ways.

A news search for the words "hero saves" will routinely turn up stories of bystanders braving oncoming trains, swift currents, and raging fires to save strangers from harm. Each year, around the world, hundreds of people donate one of their kidneys to a stranger, knowing that their act can save a life. Acts of extreme kindness, responsibility, and compassion are, like their opposites, nearly universal.

Why are some people prepared to risk their lives to help a stranger when others won't even stop to dial an emergency number?

Scientists have been exploring questions like this for decades. In the 1960s and early '70s, famous experiments by Stanley Milgram and Philip Zimbardo suggested that most of us would, under specific circumstances, voluntarily do great harm to innocent people. During the same period, John Darley and C. Daniel Batson showed that even some seminary students on their way to give a lecture about the parable of the Good Samaritan would, if told that they were running late, walk past a stranger lying moaning beside the path. More recent research has told us a lot about what happens in the brain when people make moral decisions. But are we getting any closer to understanding what drives our moral behavior?

Here's what much of the discussion of all these experiments missed: some people did the right thing. An experiment (about which we have serious ethical reservations) at the University of Chicago seems to shed new light on why.

Researchers there took two rats who shared a cage and trapped one of them in a tube that could be opened only from the outside. The free rat usually tried to open the door, eventually succeeding. Even when the free rats could eat up all of a quantity of chocolate before freeing the trapped rat, they mostly preferred to free their cage-mate. The experimenters interpret their findings as demonstrating empathy in rats. But if that is the case, they have also demonstrated that individual rats vary, for only 23 of 30 rats freed their trapped companions.

Sadly, such experiments—and many that cause even more severe stress to their animal subjects—are still continuing. We refer to this one reluctantly, because it does show clearly that the causes of the difference in the behavior of the rats must lie in the rats themselves. It seems plausible that humans, like rats, are spread along a continuum of readiness to help others. There has been considerable research on abnormal people, like psychopaths, but we need to know more about relatively stable differences (perhaps rooted in our genes) in the great majority of people as well.

Undoubtedly, situational factors can make a huge difference, and perhaps moral beliefs do as well, but if humans are just different in their predispositions to act morally, we also need to know more about these differences. Only then will we gain a proper understanding of our moral behavior, including why it varies so much from person to person and whether there is anything we can do about it.

Research on the brains of people who have donated one of their kidneys to a stranger indicates that their amygdalas are above average size and, when they see someone in distress, more active than that of the average person. It is possible that the amygdala is responding to oxytocin, which is known to motivate care for others, including strangers. There are also many other studies linking biochemical conditions to mood and behavior, and there are drugs that modify these biochemical factors in order to change behavior.

Hence the idea of a "morality pill"—a drug that makes us more likely to help others—is not far-fetched. Would people choose to take it, in order to become better people? Could criminals be given the option, as an alternative to prison, of a drug-releasing implant that would make them less likely to harm others? To ensure that they take the drug, it could be combined with a so-called smart pill or digital pill containing a sensor that transmits data when swallowed.

Similarly, governments could begin screening people to discover those most likely to commit crimes. They too could be offered a drug to make this less likely, and if they refused, they might be required to wear a tracking device that would show where they had been at any given time, so that they would know that if they did commit a crime, they would be detected.

Fifty years ago, Anthony Burgess wrote *A Clockwork Orange*, a futuristic novel about a vicious gang leader who undergoes a procedure that makes him incapable of violence. Stanley Kubrick's 1971 movie version sparked a discussion in which many argued that we could never be justified in depriving someone of his free will, no matter how gruesome the violence that would thereby be prevented. No doubt any proposal to develop a morality pill would encounter the same objection.

But if our brain's chemistry does affect our moral behavior, the question of whether that balance is set in a natural way or by medical intervention will make no difference in how freely we act. If there are already biochemical differences between us that can be used to predict how ethically we will act, then either such differences are compatible with free will, or they are evidence that at least as far as some of our ethical actions are concerned, none of us have ever had free will anyway. In any case, whether or not we have free will, we may soon face new choices about the ways in which we are willing to influence behavior for the better.

The Empathy Trap

Soon after Barack Obama was elected President of the United States, he told a young girl: "We don't have enough empathy in our world today, and it is up to your generation to change that." Obama expressed a widespread view, so the title of a 2016 book, *Against Empathy*, by Yale University psychologist Paul Bloom, came as a shock. How can anyone be against something that enables us to put ourselves in others' shoes and feel what they feel?

To answer that question, we might ask another: for whom should we have empathy? As Donald Trump prepared to succeed Obama, analysts were suggesting that Hillary Clinton lost the election because she lacked empathy with white Americans, particularly Rust Belt voters yearning for the days when the United States was a manufacturing powerhouse. The problem is that empathy for American workers is in tension with empathy for workers in Mexico and China, who would be even worse off without jobs than their American counterparts are.

Empathy makes us kinder to people with whom we empathize. That's good, but it also has a darker side. Trump, in his campaign speeches, made use of the tragic murder of Kate Steinle by an undocumented immigrant to stoke support for his anti-immigrant policies. He did not, of course, offer any similarly vivid portrayals of undocumented immigrants who have saved the lives of strangers, although such cases have been reported.

Animals with big round eyes, like baby seals, arouse more empathy than chickens, on whom we inflict vastly more suffering. People can even be reluctant to "harm" robots that they know can feel nothing at all. On the other hand, fish—cold, slimy, and unable to scream—arouse little sympathy, although, as Jonathan Balcombe argues in *What a Fish Knows*, there is plenty of evidence that they feel pain just as birds and mammals do.

Likewise, empathy with a handful of children who are, or are believed to be, harmed by vaccines largely drives popular resistance to vaccinating children against dangerous diseases. As a result, millions of parents do not have their children vaccinated, and hundreds of children become ill, with many more affected, sometimes fatally, by the disease than would have suffered adverse effects from the vaccine.

Empathy can make us act unjustly. Subjects in an experiment listened to an interview with a terminally ill child. Some were told to try to be as objective as possible, while others were told to imagine what the child feels. All were then asked if they wanted to move the child up the waiting list for treatment, ahead of other children who had been assessed as having higher priority. Three-quarters of those told to imagine what the child feels made this request, compared to only one-third of those told to try to be objective.

"One death is tragedy; a million is a statistic." If empathy makes us too favorable to individuals, large numbers numb the feelings we ought to have. The Oregon-based nonprofit

Decision Research has a website, ArithmeticofCompassion .org, aimed at enhancing our ability to communicate information about large-scale problems without giving rise to "numerical numbness." In an age in which vivid personal stories go viral and influence public policy, it's hard to think of anything more important than helping everyone to see the larger picture.

To be against empathy is not to be against compassion. In one of the most interesting sections of *Against Empathy*, Bloom describes how he learned about differences between empathy and compassion from Matthieu Ricard, the Buddhist monk sometimes described as "the happiest man on earth." When the neuroscientist Tania Singer (no relation to me) asked Ricard to engage in "compassion meditation" while his brain was being scanned, she was surprised to see no activity in the areas of his brain normally active when people empathize with the pain of others. Ricard could, on request, empathize with others' pain, but he found it unpleasant and draining; by contrast, he described compassion meditation as "a warm positive state associated with a strong pro-social motivation."

Singer has also trained non-meditators to engage in compassion meditation, by thinking kindly about a series of persons, starting with someone close to the meditator and then moving outward to strangers. Such training may lead to kinder behavior.

Compassion meditation is close to what is sometimes called "cognitive empathy," because it involves our thought and understanding of others, rather than our feelings. This brings us to the final important message of Bloom's book: the way in which psychological science proceeds has led it to downplay the role of reason in our lives.

When researchers show that some of our supposedly carefully considered choices and attitudes can be influenced by irrelevant factors like the color of the wall, the smell of the room, or the presence of a dispenser of hand sanitizer, their findings are published in psychology journals and may even make headlines in the popular media. Research showing that people make decisions based on relevant evidence is harder to publish, much less publicize. So psychology has an inbuilt bias against the view that we make decisions in sensible ways.

Bloom's more positive view of the role of reason fits with what I take to be the correct understanding of ethics. Empathy and other emotions often motivate us to do what is right, but they are equally likely to motivate us to do what is wrong. In making ethical decisions, our ability to reason has a crucial role to play.

Can Ethics Be Taught?

Can taking a philosophy class—more specifically, a class in practical ethics—lead students to act more ethically?

Teachers of practical ethics have an obvious interest in the answer to that question. The answer should also matter to students thinking of taking a course in practical ethics. But the question also has broader philosophical significance, because the answer could shed light on the ancient and fundamental question of the role that reason plays in forming our ethical judgments and determining what we do.

Plato, in the *Phaedrus*, uses the metaphor of a chariot pulled by two horses; one represents rational and moral impulses, the other irrational passions or desires. The role of the charioteer is to make the horses work together as a team. Plato thinks that the soul should be a composite of our passions and our reason, but he also makes it clear that harmony is to be found under the supremacy of reason.

In the eighteenth century, David Hume argued that this picture of a struggle between reason and the passions is misleading. Reason on its own, he thought, cannot influence the will. Reason is, he famously wrote, "the slave of the passions."

Hume spoke of "passions" in a wider sense than we understand that term today. Among what he called passions are our fellow-feeling or sympathy for others, and our concern for our own long-term interests. On Hume's view, what other philosophers take to be a conflict between reason and emotion is really a conflict between these "calm passions" and our more violent and often imprudent passions.

Something like Hume's view of reason is now influential in contemporary psychology. Jonathan Haidt, author of *The Happiness Hypothesis* and *The Righteous Mind*, uses a metaphor reminiscent of Plato, but in support of a view closer to Hume, to illustrate what he calls the social intuitionist perspective on ethics: "The mind is divided, like a rider on an elephant," he writes on the first page of *The Righteous Mind*, "and the rider's job is to serve the elephant." The rider, in Haidt's metaphor, is the mental process we control, mainly conscious reasoning, and the elephant is the other 99% of our mental processes, mostly our emotions and intuitions.

Haidt's research has led him to see moral reasoning largely as post hoc rationalization of our automatic, intuitive responses. As a result, he writes, "I therefore became skeptical of direct approaches to fostering ethical behavior—particularly direct teaching in the classroom. We can't just put moral knowledge into our students' heads, and expect them to implement that knowledge after they leave the classroom."

In *The Righteous Mind*, Haidt draws support for his views from research by the philosophers Eric Schwitzgebel of the University of California, Riverside, and Joshua Rust of Stetson University. On a range of ethical issues, Schwitzgebel and Rust show, philosophy professors specializing in ethics behave no better than professors working in other areas of philosophy; nor are they more ethical than professors who don't work in philosophy at all. If even professors working in ethics are no more ethical than their peers in other disciplines, doesn't that support the belief that ethical reasoning is powerless to make people behave more ethically?

Perhaps. Yet, despite the evidence, I was not entirely convinced. I had a lot of anecdotal evidence that my classes in practical ethics changed the lives of at least some students, and in quite fundamental ways. Some became vegetarian or vegan. Others began donating to help people in extreme poverty in low-income countries, and a few changed their career plans so that they could do more to make the world a better place.

In 2017, Schwitzgebel offered me an opportunity to test, more rigorously than had ever been done before, whether a class on the ethics of eating meat could change what students eat. Together with Brad Cokelet, a philosophy professor at the University of Kansas, we ran a study involving 1,143 students at the University of California, Riverside. Half the students were required to read a philosophical article defending vegetarianism, followed by a small group discussion with the option of watching a video advocating avoiding meat. The other half were a control group. They received similar materials and discussion on donating to help people in poverty.

We used information from campus dining cards to find out what food purchases the students in the two groups made before and after these classes. We had data on nearly 6,000 food purchases from 476 students. The purchases were identified with students who had, or had not, read and discussed the ethics of eating meat, but the data we received were made anonymous so that we could not identify any named student's purchases.

The result was a decline, from 52% to 45%, in meat purchases among students in the meat ethics group, and the lower rate of meat purchases was maintained for a few weeks after the class. There was no change in the level of meat purchases in the charitable giving group (and we had no way of discovering whether these students gave more to charity).

Our study was published in 2020, in *Cognition*, a leading peer-reviewed journal in psychology, but it gave rise to further questions. Could the results be replicated? How long would the effect last? To what extent did our results depend on having the students watch the video—which would have appealed to students' emotions more than their reason? To answer these questions we ran a further study, along similar lines, but this time the video was presented to only half the students, randomly selected.

This second study was published in *Review of Philosophy and Psychology*, in 2021. Again, there was a significant decline in meat-eating, from 51% to 42%, in the students in groups that had discussed the ethics of eating meat, while there was no change in meat-eating in students who discussed charitable giving. The decline did appear to be more marked in those groups that watched the video, but there was also a detectable change in those groups that discussed meat ethics without the video. Unfortunately, the outbreak of COVID-19 closed the campus before we could complete the section of the study designed to discover how long the effect lasted.

These two studies are, as far as we have been able to discover, the first properly controlled investigations, in the real world and not in a laboratory setting, of the impact of university-level philosophy classes on student behavior. The decline in meat-eating is not dramatic, but it is statistically significant. Ethical reasoning in the classroom can change what students eat.

Thinking about the Dead

My mother was proud of the fact that her father, David Oppenheim, had been a member of a discussion circle that was led by Sigmund Freud, the founder of psychoanalysis, and that he had even written a paper together with Freud. Once I was old enough to understand the significance of this fact, I developed an interest in my grandfather.

Sadly, I had never known him. My parents, who were Jewish, left their home in Vienna as soon as they could after the Nazi annexation of Austria. They found refuge in Australia. My grandparents, like many older people, were more reluctant to abandon their home and travel to a foreign country. Deported to the overcrowded, underfed ghetto of Theresienstadt, David soon died. Amalie, my mother's mother, survived Theresienstadt and came to join my parents after the war, around the time I was born.

David, a scholar of ancient Greece and Rome, had left his papers with a non-Jewish friend, and Amalie was able to retrieve them after her liberation and bring them to Australia. I had long wanted to read some of his work, but I always had more important things to do, and it was not until I was in my fifties that I finally made time to do it. One of the papers asks: What is a good life?—a question that, as a philosopher working mainly in ethics, I had already thought about a great deal. David discusses this question in the context of a classical text: the passage from the first book of Herodotus describing the visit of Solon, the wise lawgiver of Athens, to Croesus, the fabulously wealthy king of Lydia. After entertaining Solon and hearing about his travels, Croesus asks him: "Who is the happiest man you have ever seen?" Croesus expects to hear that he, Croesus, is the happiest of all—for who is richer, or rules over a greater and more numerous people, than he? Solon dashes Croesus's expectation by naming an Athenian called Tellus. Taken aback, Croesus demands to know the reason for this choice, and so Solon describes the key points of Tellus's life. He lived in a prosperous city, had fine sons, and lived to see each of them have children. He had wealth enough. And he had a glorious death, falling in battle just as the enemy were being routed. The Athenians paid him the high honor of a public funeral on the spot where he fell.

From this story my grandfather distills Solon's conception of a happy life as consisting in ten elements:

1. A period of peaceful prosperity for his country.
2. A life that stretches out far into the third generation.
3. One does not lose the complete vigor of a valiant man.
4. A comfortable income.
5. Well-brought-up children.
6. Assurance of the continuation of one's line through numerous thriving grandchildren.
7. A quick death.
8. Victorious confirmation of one's own strength.

9. The highest funeral honors.
10. The preservation of one's own name through glorious commemoration by the citizens.

As we can see from the last two points, Solon believed that what happens to people after they die—what kind of funeral they have, and how their name is remembered—makes a difference to how good their lives were. This was not because Solon imagined that, after you died, you could look down from somewhere and see what kind of a funeral you were given. There is no suggestion that Solon believed in any kind of afterlife, and certainly I don't. But does skepticism about a life after death force one to conclude that what happens after you die cannot make a difference to how well your life has gone?

In thinking about this issue, I vacillate between two incompatible positions: that something can only matter to you if it has an impact on your awareness, that is, if you experience it in some way; and that what matters is that your preferences be satisfied, whether or not you know of it, and indeed whether or not you are alive at the time when they are satisfied. The former view, held by classical utilitarians like Jeremy Bentham, is more straightforward, and in some ways easier to defend, philosophically. But imagine the following situation. A year ago a colleague of yours in the university department in which you work was told that she had cancer, and could not expect to live more than a year or so. On hearing the news, she took leave without pay and spent the year writing a book that drew together ideas that she had been working on during the ten years you had known her. The task exhausted her, but now it is done. Close to death, she calls you to her home and presents you with a typescript.

"This," she tells you, "is what I want to be remembered by. Please find a publisher for it." You congratulate your friend on finishing the work. She is weak and tired, but evidently satisfied just with having put it in your hands. You say your farewells. The next day you receive a phone call telling you that your colleague died in her sleep shortly after you left her house. You read her typescript. It is undoubtedly publishable, but not groundbreaking work. "What's the point?" you think to yourself, "We don't really need another book on these topics. She's dead, and she'll never know if her book appears anyway." Instead of sending the typescript to a publisher, you drop it in a recycling bin.

Did you do something wrong? More specifically, did you wrong your colleague? Did you in some way make her life less good than it would have been if you had taken the book to a publisher, and it had appeared, gaining as much and as little attention as many other worthy but not groundbreaking academic works? If we answer that question affirmatively, then what we do after a person dies can make a difference to how well their life went.

I read more of my grandfather's papers, as well as many personal letters he wrote to Amalie before they were married, and later letters written by him and Amalie to my parents after they had gone to Australia, and life became more and more difficult for my grandparents. The wealth of material led me to write a book about David's life, his work, and the dramatic times in which he lived, from Vienna's golden age before the First World War to the barbarity of Nazism. The book was published in 2003, under the title: *Pushing Time Away: My Grandfather and the Tragedy of Jewish Vienna.*

My own work, therefore, raised the question posed by David's account of Solon's view of a good life. Was I, in reading my grandfather's works and bringing his life and thought to a larger audience, doing something *for him*, and in some way mitigating, however slightly, the wrong that the Nazis did to him?

It is easy to imagine that a grandfather would like to be remembered by his grandchildren, and that a scholar and author would like to be read after his death. Perhaps this is especially so when he dies a victim of persecution by a dictatorship that sought to suppress the liberal, cosmopolitan ideas my grandfather favored, and to exterminate all members of his tribe. Do I have here an example of how, as Solon said, what happens after one dies does make a difference to how well one's life goes? You don't have to believe in an afterlife to give this question an affirmative answer—but is that the right answer?

Should This Be the Last Generation?

Have you ever thought about whether to have a child? If so, what factors entered into your decision? Was it whether having children would be good for you, your partner, and others close to the possible child, such as children you may already have, or perhaps your parents? For most people contemplating reproduction, those are the dominant questions. Some may also think about the desirability of adding to the strain that the eight billion people already here are putting on our planet's environment. But very few ask whether coming into existence is a good thing for the child itself. Most of those who consider that question probably do so because they have some reason to fear that the child's life would be especially difficult—for example, if they have a family history of a devastating illness, physical or mental, that cannot yet be detected prenatally.

All this suggests that we think it is wrong to bring into the world a child whose prospects for a happy, healthy life are poor, but we don't usually think the fact that a child is likely to have a happy, healthy life is a reason for bringing the child into existence. This asymmetry is not easy to justify. But rather than go into the justifications philosophers working on these issues have proffered, I want to raise a related problem. How good does life have to be to make it reasonable to bring a child into the world? Is the standard of life experienced by most people in developed nations today good enough to make this decision unproblematic, in the absence of specific knowledge that the child will have a severe genetic disease or other problem?

The nineteenth-century German philosopher Arthur Schopenhauer held that even the best life possible for humans is one in which we strive for ends that, once achieved, bring only fleeting satisfaction. New desires then lead us on to further futile struggle, and the cycle repeats itself.

Schopenhauer's pessimism has had few defenders over the past two centuries, but in 2006 the South African philosopher David Benatar published a book with an arresting title: *Better Never to Have Been: The Harm of Coming into Existence*. One of Benatar's arguments trades on something like the asymmetry just noted. To bring into existence someone who will suffer is, Benatar argues, to harm that person, but to bring into existence someone who will have a good life is not to benefit them. Few of us would think it right to inflict severe suffering on an innocent child, even if that were the only way in which we could bring many other children into the world. Yet everyone will suffer to some extent, and if our species continues to reproduce, we can be sure that some future children will suffer severely. Hence continued reproduction will harm some children severely, and benefit none.

Benatar also argues that human lives are, in general, much less good than we think they are. We spend most of our lives with unfulfilled desires, and the occasional satisfactions that are all most of us can achieve are insufficient to outweigh these prolonged negative states. If we think that this is a tolerable state of affairs it is because we are, in Benatar's view, victims of the illusion of Pollyannaism. This illusion may have evolved because it helped our ancestors survive, but it is an illusion nonetheless. If we could see our lives objectively, we would see that they are not something we should inflict on anyone.

Here is a thought experiment to test our attitudes to this view. Most thoughtful people are extremely concerned about climate change. Some stop eating meat, or flying abroad on vacation, in order to reduce their carbon footprint. But the people who will be most severely harmed by climate change have not yet been conceived. If there were to be no future generations, there would be much less for us to feel to guilty about.

So why don't we make ourselves the last generation on Earth? If we would all agree to have ourselves sterilized then no sacrifices would be required—we could party our way into extinction!

Of course, it would be impossible to get agreement on universal sterilization, but just imagine that we could. Then is there anything wrong with this scenario? Even if we take a less pessimistic view of human existence than Benatar, we could still defend it, because it makes us better off—for one thing, we can get rid of all that guilt about what we are doing to future generations—and it doesn't make anyone worse off, because there won't be anyone else to be worse off.

Is a world with people in it better than one without? Put aside what we do to other species—that's a different issue. Let's assume that the choice is between a world like ours and one with no sentient beings in it at all. And assume, too—here we have to get fictitious, as philosophers often do—that if we choose to bring about the world with no sentient beings at all, everyone will agree to do that. No one's rights will be violated—at least, not the rights of any existing people. Can non-existent people have a right to come into existence?

I do think it would be wrong to choose the non-sentient universe. In my judgment, for most people, life is worth living. Even if that is not yet the case, I am enough of an optimist to believe that, should humans survive for another century or two, we will learn from our past mistakes and bring about a world in which there is far less suffering than there is now. But justifying that choice forces us to reconsider the deep issues with which I began. Is life worth living? Are the interests of a future child a reason for bringing that child into existence? And is the continuance of our species justifiable in the face of our knowledge that it will certainly bring suffering to innocent future human beings?

ANIMALS

The Case for Going Vegan

We are members of the species *Homo sapiens,* living among a vast number of members of other species that have, like us, evolved on this planet. Among them are trillions of nonhuman animals who, like us, can feel pain and pleasure, whose lives can be full of suffering, or enjoyable. How should we act toward them? How much do their interests count, when they clash with our own interests?

Of all the ways in which we affect animals, the one most in need of justification today is raising them for food. Far more animals are affected by this than by any other human activity. Worldwide, more than 77 billion mammals and birds are produced for food each year. If we include fish farming, the number of vertebrate animals we raise more than doubles, and if we add wild fish, the total number killed may be more than a trillion.

Most of this unimaginable amount of suffering that we inflict on these animals in raising and killing them is unnecessary. In affluent countries, where we have a wide choice of foods, no one needs to eat meat. Many studies show that we can live as healthily, or more healthily, without it. We can also live well on a vegan diet, consuming no animal products at all. (Vitamin B12 is the only essential nutrient not available from plant foods, and it is easy to take a supplement obtained from vegan sources.)

Ask people what the main ethical problem about eating animals is, and most will refer to killing. That is an issue, of course, but at least as far as modern industrial animal production is concerned, there is a more straightforward objection. Even if there were nothing wrong with killing animals because we like the taste of their flesh, we would still be supporting a system of agriculture that inflicts prolonged suffering on animals.

Pigs are at least as intelligent as dogs, perhaps more so, but if someone treated a dog as factory-farmed pigs are treated, they would be guilty of a crime. Male piglets often have their testicles ripped out and their sensitive tails cut off without anesthesia. Pregnant sows are essentially breeding machines, confined for months in gestation crates too narrow for them to turn around. Then when they give birth they are shifted to farrowing crates that restrict the mother's movements even more tightly, to prevent them crushing their piglets in the unnatural situation of lying on bare concrete or metal slats (providing straw or other bedding materials would increase costs).

Beef cattle spend the last six months of their lives in feedlots, on bare dirt, eating grain that is not suitable for their digestion, and fed steroids to make them put on more muscle and antibiotics to keep them alive. They have no shade from the blazing summer sun, or shelter from winter blizzards.

Most egg-laying hens are crammed into small battery cages in which they are unable to express basic behaviors, such as spreading their wings fully, or laying an egg in a nest or similar protected space. To prevent the dominant birds pecking the weaker birds to death in these unnaturally crowded conditions, the end of their beaks—a sensitive part of their anatomy, filled with nerve tissue—are cut off with a hot blade, without anesthesia. Male chicks of the laying breeds have no commercial value and are ground up or suffocated immediately after birth.

Broiler chickens are bred to have voracious appetites so that they grow extremely rapidly, and are ready for slaughter just six weeks after hatching. This puts such stress on their immature legs that they are in chronic pain for the final weeks of their lives. The birds' droppings are allowed to accumulate until the atmosphere in the sheds has such high levels of ammonia that, should the chickens try to ease the stress on their legs by sitting down, they would get burns on their hocks. The parents of these birds have the same appetites as their offspring, of course, but if they were allowed to eat as much, they would be likely to collapse before reaching sexual maturity. To prevent this, they are kept half-starved, and spend their days desperately seeking food that is not there.

Farmed fish are also often packed into overcrowded nets or ponds, where they suffer from diseases, parasites, asphyxiation, and injuries. The mortality rate of fish before leaving their ponds or cages is typically 20–30% and can go as high as 50%. The fish that survive long enough to be killed by humans do not fare any better because in most countries there are no laws regulating their slaughter and the economic costs of handling them carefully are very high. Hence they are often killed brutally by being cut, descaled, and skinned while they are still alive.

But what, you may ask, is wrong with milk and other dairy products? Don't the cows have a good life, grazing on the fields? Nor do we have to kill them to get milk. But most dairy cows are now kept inside, and do not have access to pasture. Like human females, they do not give milk unless they have recently had a baby, and so dairy cows are made pregnant every year. The calf is taken away from its mother just hours after birth, so that it will not drink the milk intended for humans. If it is male, it may be killed immediately, or raised for veal, or perhaps for hamburger beef. The bond between a cow and her calf is strong, and she will often call for the calf for several days after it is taken away.

● ● ●

In addition to the ethical question of our treatment of animals, there are other powerful arguments for a vegan diet. Ever since Frances Moore Lappé published *Diet for a Small Planet* in 1971, we have known that modern industrial animal production is extremely wasteful. Pig farms use six pounds of grain for every pound of boneless meat they produce. For beef cattle in feed-lots, the ratio is 13:1. Even for chickens, the least inefficient factory-farmed meat, the ratio is 3:1.

Lappé was concerned about the waste of food and the extra pressure on arable land this involves, since we could be eating the grain and soybeans directly, and feeding ourselves just as well from much less land. Now global warming sharpens the problem. Emissions from farmed animals make up about 14.5% of all greenhouse gas emissions. If the production of animal products, especially beef, lamb, and dairy, continues to rise, eliminating emissions from fossil fuels will not be enough to prevent the Earth warming beyond the 2°C limit set by the Paris agreement on climate change, let alone the safer 1.5°C target that would be necessary to prevent the inundation of low-lying Pacific island nations.

Most Americans think that the best thing they could do to cut their personal contribution to global warming would be to swap their family car for a fuel-efficient hybrid like the Toyota Prius. Gidon Eshel and Pamela Martin, researchers at the University of Chicago, have calculated that while this would indeed lead to a reduction in emissions of about 1 ton of carbon dioxide per driver, switching from the typical US diet to a vegan diet would save the equivalent of almost 1.5 tons of carbon dioxide per person. Vegans are therefore doing significantly less damage to our climate than those who eat animal products.

● ● ●

Concerns about health, both one's own and that of people everywhere, are now increasingly significant reasons for avoiding meat. Authoritative medical reports such as that of the EAT-Lancet Commission have recommended that in order to reduce the risk of heart disease, cancer, and diabetes, we should avoid red and processed meats, and eat predominantly plant-based foods.

It isn't just your own health that you are imperiling by eating meat. For many years now, researchers have sounded the alarm about the routine feeding of antibiotics to animals, which has led to the development of strains of bacteria that are resistant to antibiotics used in fighting infection in humans.

The COVID-19 pandemic has brought new awareness of the links between eating animals and novel viruses to which we have no resistance. COVID-19 may have been caused by a virus present in bats, and brought to humans through a market in Wuhan where wild animals were sold for human consumption. These markets in the sale of wild animals should be closed down, both because of the cruelty involved in capturing, caging, and slaughtering wild animals, but also to protect our public health from pandemics.

A further, larger step is also imperative. As Dr. Michael Greger pointed out in *How to Survive a Pandemic,* if you wanted to create ideal conditions for the development of a virus that could cause a new pandemic, you would take thousands of animals and crowd them into a shed, stressing them enough to weaken their immune systems. Then you would have them handled by humans. That, of course, is what happens in factory farms. If we are serious about minimizing the risk of another pandemic, one perhaps far more lethal than COVID-19, factory farming must end.

• • •

Is there an ethical way of eating animal products? It is possible to obtain meat, eggs, and dairy products from animals who have been treated less cruelly, and allowed to eat grass rather than grain or soy. Limiting one's consumption of animal products to these sources also avoids some of the greenhouse gas emissions, although cows kept on grass still emit substantial amounts of methane, a particularly potent contributor to global warming. So *if* there is no serious ethical objection to killing animals, as long as they have had good lives, then being selective about the animal products you eat could provide an ethically defensible diet. It needs care, however. "Organic," for instance, says little about animal welfare, and hens not kept in cages may still be crowded into a large shed. Going vegan is a simpler choice that sets a clear-cut example for others to follow.

There is also another possibility of eating ethically without being vegan: eating real meat cultured from cells grown in a bioreactor. With an estimated 3% of the greenhouse gases of meat from a cow, and no living animal to suffer, meat produced in this way would be sustainable and cruelty-free. In 2020, a Singapore restaurant began offering chicken nuggets made by this method. The price of cultured meat is not yet competitive with animal products, but it is getting closer to that level.

In 2015, Charles Krauthammer, a conservative *Washington Post* columnist, asked what present practice, universally engaged in and accepted by people of great intelligence and moral sensitivity, will be seen by future generations as abominable, in the way that we now see slavery as abominable? Mr. Krauthammer's answer was: our treatment of animals. "I'm convinced," he wrote, "that our great-grandchildren will find it difficult to believe that we actually raised, herded and slaughtered them on an industrial scale—for the eating." With the recent surge in vegan eating and novel foods providing alternatives to meat from animals, perhaps we won't have to wait three generations for this change.

Why Loving Our Animals Is Not Enough

(with Agata Sagan)

There are about 184 million dogs and cats in the United States; two-thirds of all US households include an animal, popularly known as "pets." But animal advocates regard that term as demeaning, and prefer "companion animal." In fact, in many homes, dogs or cats are regarded as members of the family. They are provided with everything they might need or enjoy, and much else besides, including fancy treats and clothing.

Spending on companion animals in the United States alone has been growing rapidly over the past decade, rising from an already very substantial $43 billion in 2008 to an estimated $72 billion in 2022. And similar trends are evident elsewhere. Ownership of dogs and cats in China, for example, was estimated at 100 million in 2015, and rising.

Large as these numbers may seem, they are insignificant compared to the 77 billion birds and mammals raised for food in the world each year. In general, companion animals are treated far better than factory-farmed pigs, cows, and chickens.

Nevertheless, despite the more positive attitudes people have toward dogs and cats, many of them lead miserable lives. Dogs, unlike cats, are social animals, and generally do not do well without company. As Karen Dawn points out in her book *Thanking the Monkey*, solitary confinement is considered cruel punishment for humans. But it is even crueler for a pack animal. Too often our companion animals are, in her words, "slaves to love."

Dogs from breeds that were used to hunt or guard sheep often suffer from being unable to follow their instincts. Other breeds have been shaped to please us, often at severe cost to the animals themselves. Bulldogs suffer several health problems, including breathing difficulties, because of the way they have been bred, and Dalmatians often cannot hear, because the genes that produce their desirable spots also can produce deafness. One in every four dogs suffers from separation anxiety, most often from being left alone for long periods of time during the workweek.

Specific problems arise when more exotic animals become fashionable pets. Keeping birds in cages that prevent them flying scarcely merits comment. In China, a recent craze was having pet pygmy marmosets, also known as "finger monkeys" because they are small enough to sit on your finger. People may buy just one, as a novelty, but they are highly social animals, normally living in a group, and they will suffer and die if kept on their own, no matter how much attention they receive from humans. Even if these problems could be overcome, large populations of companion animals have other consequences.

High demand has led to the rise of large-scale commercial puppy breeders, who frequently keep dogs in horrible conditions.

Cute puppies and kittens bought on impulse may be abandoned when they grow older and become less appealing. Cats, whether abandoned or allowed outside, regularly kill birds and small mammals. One study estimated that cats, most of them without owners, kill 1–4 billion birds and 6–22 billion small mammals each year in the US alone. These figures have been challenged, but no one disputes that the number is large and that, in some areas, it is having an impact on the survival of other species.

Nor should we overlook the contribution of all these meat-eating companion animals to climate change. According to UCLA geography professor Gregory Okin, if all the dogs and cats in the U.S. comprised a separate country, that country would rank fifth in the world in meat consumption, behind only Russia, Brazil, the United States and China. Given the high level of greenhouse gas emissions caused by meat production, that is a very substantial additional contribution to climate change. Dogs can thrive on a vegetarian diet, so that's one option for people with canine companions, but it's more difficult for cats. Okin suggests that it would be desirable for people to switch to smaller, herbivorous pets. (From personal experience, we can recommend rats as lovable, clean companion animals who do well on a diet of grains.)

If you don't have a companion animal, but are thinking of getting one, we recommend you think not just twice, but three times. Ask yourself: will it be good for me? Will it be good for the animal? Will it be good for the environment?

If, on the other hand, you already have a companion animal, ask yourself whether you are taking her, his, or their real needs into account. You may think that you love them unconditionally, and that is good, but you may not know as much about their real nature and needs as you think you do. Uninformed love, no matter how good your intentions, may not be what your companion animal needs. And think about how you can lessen their harmful impact on the environment.

Find out more, and don't try to mold animals into what you want them to be. They have lives of their own to lead. They do not exist to please you.

Learning from Europe's More Ethical Eggs

Fifty years ago, I stood with a few other students on a busy Oxford street handing out leaflets protesting the use of battery cages to hold hens. We were part of what has now become known as "the Oxford Group." In 2020, we became the subject of a book, *The Oxford Group and the Emergence of Animal Rights*, by Robert Garner and Yewande Okuleye.

Most of those who took the leaflets did not know that their eggs came from hens kept in cages so small that even one bird—the cages normally housed four—would be unable to fully stretch and flap her wings. The hens could never walk around freely, or lay eggs in a nest.

Many people applauded our youthful idealism, but told us that we had no hope of ever changing a major industry. They were wrong.

On the first day of 2012, keeping hens in such cages became illegal, not only in the United Kingdom, but in all 27 countries of the European Union. Hens could still be kept in cages, but they had to have more space, and be provided with nest boxes and a scratching post. Then, in 2021, the European Commission, the governing body of the European Union, announced that by

2027 it would ban cages, not only for laying hens, but also for female breeding pigs, calves raised for veal, rabbits, ducks, and geese.

For anyone interested in the process of moral progress, this change is worth studying. In the early 1970s, when the modern animal liberation movement began, no major organization was campaigning against the battery cage. In the United Kingdom, the early radicalism of the Society for the Prevention of Cruelty to Animals—which under Queen Victoria's patronage became the Royal Society for the Prevention of Cruelty to Animals, and can rightly be regarded as the mother of all animal protection organizations—was long past. The RSPCA focused on isolated cases of abuse and failed to challenge well-established ways of mistreating animals on factory farms or in laboratories. It had fox hunters on its council, the governing body of the organization. Some of the new animal radicals of the 1970s made a concerted effort to stir the RSPCA from its conservatism. Richard Ryder, another member of the Oxford Group, whose early work protecting animals included sabotaging hunts, successfully stood for election to the RSPCA council, and eventually be came its Chair.

The new animal movement used the media to reach the broader public. Consumers responded by buying eggs from free-ranging hens. Some supermarket chains even ceased to carry eggs from battery hens.

In Britain and several European countries, animal welfare became politically salient, and pressure on parliamentary representatives mounted. The European Union established a scientific committee to investigate animal welfare issues on farms, and the committee recommended banning the battery cage, along with some other forms of close confinement of pigs and calves. A ban on battery cages in the EU was eventually adopted in 1999, but, to ensure that producers would have plenty of time to phase out the equipment in which they had invested, its implementation was delayed until January 1, 2012.

To its credit, the European egg industry accepted the situation, and developed new and less cruel methods of keeping hens. At least 300 million hens who would have been living miserable lives in standard battery cages are now in significantly better conditions, and if the European Commission carries out its plans, those conditions will become better still from 2027.

With the ban on cages for other farmed animals too, Europe will confirm its place as the world leader in animal welfare, a position also reflected in its restrictions on the use of animals to test cosmetics. But why is Europe so far ahead of other countries in its concern for animals?

In the United States, there are no federal laws about how egg producers house their hens. On the other hand, when Californian citizens initiated state referenda on the issue in 2008 and again in strengthened form in 2020, Californian voters overwhelmingly supported proposals requiring that all farm animals have room to stretch their limbs fully and turn around without touching other animals or the sides of their cage. That suggests that the problem may not be with US citizens' attitudes, but rather that, at the federal level, the US political system allows industries with large campaign chests too much power to thwart the wishes of popular majorities.

The amelioration of the suffering of farmed animals in Europe, in California, and some other states of the United States, is a major advance in animal welfare, and a step toward becoming a more civilized and humane society that shows its concern for all beings capable of suffering. It is also an occasion for celebrating the effectiveness of democracy, and the power of an ethical idea. We must hope that somehow this concern for animals will spread to other countries where it is so far less evident. In China, which confines the largest number of hens and pigs in factory farms, an animal welfare movement is only beginning to emerge, and its progress over the past decade has been disappointingly slow.

The anthropologist Margaret Mead is reported to have said: "Never doubt that a small group of thoughtful, committed citizens can change the world. Indeed, it is the only thing that ever has." The last part may not be true, but the first part surely is. The end of the battery cage began with a small group of thoughtful and committed people.

If Fish Could Scream

When I was a child, my father used to take me for walks, often along a river or by the sea. We would pass people fishing, perhaps reeling in their lines with struggling fish hooked at the end of them. Once I saw a man take a small fish out of a bucket and impale it, still wriggling, on an empty hook to use as bait.

Another time, when our path took us by a tranquil stream, I saw a man sitting and watching his line, seemingly at peace with the world, while next to him, fish he had already caught were flapping helplessly and gasping in the air. My father told me that he could not understand how anyone could enjoy an afternoon spent taking fish out of the water and letting them die slowly.

In most of the world, it is accepted that if animals are to be killed for food, they should be killed without suffering. Regulations for slaughter generally require that animals be rendered instantly unconscious before they are killed, or death should be brought about instantaneously, or, in the case of ritual slaughter, as close to instantaneously as the religious doctrine allows.

Not for fish. There is no humane slaughter requirement for wild fish caught and killed at sea, nor, in most places, for farmed fish. Fish caught in nets by trawlers are dumped on board the ship and allowed to suffocate. In the commercial fishing technique known as longline fishing, trawlers let out lines that can be 50–100 kilometers long, with hundreds or even thousands of baited hooks. Fish taking the bait are likely to remain fully conscious while they are dragged around for many hours by hooks through their mouths, until eventually the line is hauled in.

Likewise, commercial fishing frequently depends on gill nets—walls of fine netting in which fish become snared, often by the gills. They may suffocate in the net, because, with their gills constricted, they cannot breathe. If not, they may remain trapped for many hours before the nets are pulled in.

On how many fish do humans inflict these awful deaths? It's not easy to estimate, because the official figures ignore the fact that each fish is an individual, and instead report the tonnages of the various species of fish caught. To obtain the number of sentient beings brutally killed, one has to know the average weight of the fish, of varying species, killed, and then divide the reported tonnage by the estimated average weight for each species. Alison Mood and Phil Brooke have done this for their website, fishcount.org.uk. They estimate that, in round figures, each year somewhere between *one and two trillion fish* are killed.

To put this in perspective, the United Nations Food and Agriculture Organization estimates that 77 billion birds and mammals are killed each year for human consumption—the equivalent of about ten animals for each human being on the planet. If we take Mood and Brooke's lower estimate of one trillion, the comparable figure for fish is 125. This does not include billions of fish caught illegally nor "bycatch"—unwanted fish accidentally caught and discarded, nor the live fish impaled on hooks as bait in longline fishing.

Many of these fish are consumed indirectly—ground up and fed to factory-farmed chicken or fish. A typical salmon farm churns through at least 1.5 kilos of wild fish for every kilo of salmon that it produces. In terms of sentient individual lives, the ratio is much worse, because the fish used for feed are typically smaller than the fish sold for consumption. So fishcount .org.uk estimates that in 2019, approximately 100 billion farmed fish were raised and killed, while the estimate for the number of fish caught to be ground up into fishmeal and fish oil, most of which goes to feed farmed fish and crustaceans, is between 500 billion and 1 trillion. If we take the most favorable—for the fish farming industry—estimates of these ranges, and include the killing of the fish who is the end product of the process, 627 billion fish were killed so that 167 billion fish could be sold.

Let's assume that all this fishing is sustainable, though of course it is not. It would then be reassuring to believe that killing on such a vast scale does not matter, because fish do not feel pain. But the nervous systems of fish are sufficiently similar to those of birds and mammals to indicate that they do. When fish experience something that would cause physical pain to other animals, they behave in ways suggestive of pain, and the change in behavior may last several hours. (It is a myth that fish have short memories.) Fish learn to avoid unpleasant experiences, like electric shocks. And painkillers reduce the symptoms of pain that they would otherwise show.

Victoria Braithwaite, a professor of fisheries and biology at Pennsylvania State University, has probably spent more time investigating this issue than any other scientist. Her book *Do Fish Feel Pain?* shows that fish not only are capable of feeling pain, but also are a lot smarter than most people believe. In

2009, a scientific panel to the European Union concluded that the preponderance of the evidence indicates that fish do feel pain.

Fish may even be aware of themselves, as a distinct being. In 2022, a team of researchers led by Masanori Kohda, of Osaka City University, showed that cleaner wrasse, a fish that eats parasites off the skin of other animals, and so is attuned to looking for colored patches on fish, can recognize themselves in a mirror—the classic test of self-recognition. The researchers injected colored patches into the throats of 18 anesthetized cleaner fish. When the fish recovered from the anesthetic, they were shown a mirror. After seeing their reflection with the colored patch, all but one of them scraped their own throats, rather than seeking to scrape the throats of their reflection.

Why are fish the forgotten victims on our plate? Is it because they are cold-blooded and covered in scales? Is it because they cannot give voice to their pain? Whatever the explanation, the evidence is now accumulating that commercial fishing and fish farming both inflict unimaginable quantities of pain and suffering. We have many less cruel and more sustainable foods to eat.

The Nation of Kangaroos

The red kangaroo, the largest of all kangaroo species, is Australia's national animal. Kangaroos appear on the country's coat of arms, on its coins, on its sporting uniforms, and on the aircraft flown by Australia's most popular airline. On a hike in Australia, seeing these magnificent animals bound across the landscape awakens my sense that I am in a unique country, with its distinctive flora and fauna. Yet Australia's relationship with kangaroos has a much darker side.

Every year, millions of kangaroos are shot, in the largest commercial slaughter of terrestrial wildlife anywhere in the world. No one really knows how many are killed. Australia's state governments issue quotas, which in recent years have allowed for the killing of more than five million kangaroos, but the quotas are not a reliable indication of the number actually shot. On one hand, the quotas are not fully taken up, so the number killed may be less than five million. On the other hand, hundreds of thousands of joeys inside the pouches of female kangaroos who are shot are not counted, though they will invariably die. In addition, no one knows how many kangaroos are killed illegally, outside the quota system.

There are two main reasons why so many kangaroos are killed. First, there is money to be made from the sale of their meat, skin, and fur. Kangaroos were hunted and eaten by indigenous Australians, but among urban Australians, the meat is not popular—one survey found only 14% eat kangaroo four times or more per year. Tourists coming to Australia often try it, and there is a modest export trade as well, but much of it ends up as pet food. Kangaroo skin is used for leather and the fur for souvenirs.

The other major reason for killing kangaroos is that farmers regard them as a pest, eating grass that the farmers want to use to feed more profitable cattle and sheep.

There is some evidence that, because graziers have put water into dry areas for their cattle or sheep, there are more kangaroos in Australia now than there were when Europeans first arrived. These estimates, however, are controversial. There are many parts of Australia where kangaroos were once plentiful, but now are rare. Some kangaroo species are endangered, but the Australian government asserts that the four species that can legally be hunted—which includes the red kangaroo—are not. Some wildlife ecologists challenge that assertion, but even if it is true, this fact would not end the controversy about killing kangaroos, which is not limited to the danger of extinction. In its simplest form, the controversy is about the inhumane way in which many kangaroos die.

The kangaroo shooting industry's code of practice states that the animals must be killed with a single shot to the head, which would lead to a death that is instantaneous, or close to it. But a report commissioned by the Australian government showed that at least 100,000 kangaroos die each year after shots to other parts of the body. Their deaths are not likely to be humane. Then there are the joeys; as many as 800,000 die each year, usually clubbed to death by shooters who don't want to waste another bullet. Older joeys who are outside the pouch when their mothers are shot are likely to hop away into the darkness— commercial kangaroo shooters work at night—and starve to death.

Given the remote areas in which kangaroo shooting takes place, enforcement of humane slaughter is not practical. Nor can kangaroos be farmed and taken to slaughterhouses—they are wild animals, and cannot be herded or induced to board a truck. Their ability to jump standard fences with ease means that barricading them into a field, or keeping them out of the vast cattle ranches typical of outback Australia, would be prohibitively expensive.

There is, however, a deeper ethical question about the large-scale slaughter of kangaroos. Should we be giving precedence to sheep and cattle, and the money they earn for the community, over native animals who have little commercial value but are not environmentally damaging in the way that cattle and sheep are in Australia's arid interior?

The underlying issue is played out all over the world. We do not have to shoot an animal to bring about their death. We can do it just as cruelly when we take over, for our own purposes, the land that wild animals use. The displacement and killing of orangutans by palm oil plantations in Borneo has received extensive publicity because we readily identify with animals so closely related to us, and with such demonstrable intelligence. But everywhere, as the human population expands, the space we leave for wild animals is steadily shrinking.

We rightly oppose the invasion of one country's territory by another. In *The Outermost House*, the American naturalist Henry Beston wrote, of nonhuman animals, "They are not brethren, they are not underlings; they are other nations, caught with ourselves in the net of life and time, fellow prisoners of the splendor and travail of the earth." We should take seriously the idea that appropriating land from wild animals is like invading another country, even if its inhabitants are of a different species.

Who Is a Person?

Tommy, a chimpanzee, spent years in solitary confinement in a wire cage in upstate New York. In 2013, the Nonhuman Rights Project invoked the ancient legal procedure of habeas corpus (Latin for "you have the body") to bring his imprisonment before a state appeals court.

The writ is typically used to get a court to consider whether someone's detention is lawful. The Nonhuman Rights Project application on behalf of Tommy sought to have him transferred to a sanctuary in Florida, where he could live with other chimps on a three-acre island in a lake. The application was rejected by the court that first heard it, and the Nonhuman Rights Project sought leave to appeal from the New York Court of Appeals. There five appellate judges listened to the case put by Nonhuman Rights Project founder Steve Wise and then asked him the obvious question: isn't legal personhood just for human beings?

Wise cited legal precedents to show that it is not. In civil law, to be a person is to count as an entity in one's own right. A corporation can be a legal person, and so, too, can a river, a holy book, and a mosque. Although the Court denied Tommy's advocates leave to appeal, Judge Eugene Fahey clearly had doubts about this decision. He filed a separate opinion in which he said: "The issue whether a nonhuman animal has a fundamental right to liberty protected by the writ of habeas corpus is profound and far-reaching. It speaks to our relationship with all the life around us. Ultimately, we will not be able to ignore it. While it may be arguable that a chimpanzee is not a 'person,' there is no doubt that it is not merely a thing."

In fact, difficult as it may be for a court to interpret the law as holding that a chimpanzee is a person, there is a strong philosophical case for saying that a chimpanzee really is a person, in the proper sense of that term. The word "person" has Roman origins, and was never limited to human beings. It was used by early Christian theologians in their debates about the doctrine of the Trinity—that God is "three persons in one," namely, the father, the son, and the holy spirit. If "person" meant "human being," that doctrine would be plainly contrary to Christian belief, for Christians hold that only one of those "persons" was ever a human being.

In more contemporary usage, in science fiction movies, we have no difficulty in grasping that aliens like the extraterrestrial in *E.T.*, or the Na'vi in *Avatar*, are persons, even though they are not members of the species *Homo sapiens*. Similarly, in reading the work of scientists like Jane Goodall or Dian Fossey, we can recognize that the great apes they describe are persons. They have close and complex personal relationships with others in their group. They grieve for lost loved ones. They are self-aware beings, capable of thought. Their foresight and anticipation enable them to plan ahead. We even see the rudiments of ethics in the way they respond to other apes who fail to return a favor.

Contrary to the caricatures of some opponents of these lawsuits, declaring a chimpanzee a person would not mean giving them the right to vote, attend school, or sue for defamation. It simply means giving them the most basic, fundamental right of having legal standing, rather than being considered a mere object.

European laboratories have, in recognition of the special nature of chimpanzees, freed them from research labs, and in 2015 the National Institutes of Health announced that it was also ending the use of chimpanzees in medical research. If the nation's leading medical research agency has decided that it will not use chimpanzees as research subjects, why are we allowing individuals to lock them up for no good reason at all?

Tommy, sadly, can no longer be found. His owner says he sold him to a zoo, but the zoo has no record of him. He may have died, but as he was not a human being, there is no record of his death. The Nonhuman Rights Project, however, continued to press its case for the rights of nonhuman animals. In 2022, the New York Court of Appeals heard their arguments on behalf of Happy, an elephant who since 1977 has been in the Bronx Zoo, in New York, where she lives alone in a one-acre enclosure. This was the first time that the highest court of an English-speaking jurisdiction heard a habeas corpus case on behalf of someone other than a human being. Again, the court denied the application, and Happy remains in the Bronx Zoo; but remarkably, it was not a unanimous verdict. Two of the seven judges voted to set Happy free.

Elsewhere, however, there has been greater recognition of the rights of nonhumans. In 2015, as a result of a habeas corpus action on behalf of Sandra, an orangutan kept in the Buenos Aires Zoo, a court in Argentina declared that "great apes are legal persons, with legal capacity." In 2018, the High Court of

Uttarakhand, a state in northern India, ruled that "The entire animal kingdom, including avian and aquatic ones, are declared as legal entities having a distinct persona with corresponding rights, duties and liabilities of a living person."

The Constitutional Court of Colombia recognizes animals as having standing. In 2021, that led to some involvement from a US court when authorities from Colombia asked a US court to take evidence from two wildlife experts in a case involving methods of sterilization of wild hippopotamuses in Colombia. In doing so, the US court applied legislation leading it to accept that the country making such a request decides who is recognized as able to bring a case. Hence the US court accepted, though only for the purposes of taking evidence in this case, that "the community of hippopotamuses living in the Magdalena River" were litigants.

Whether it comes through the courts, through legislation, through constitutional amendment, or through international treaties, it is time for the law to recognize that many animals are persons entitled to legal standing.

The Cow Who . . .

In January 2016, a steer escaped from a slaughterhouse in the New York City borough of Queens. Video of the animal trotting down a busy street was soon featured on many media outlets. For those who care about animals, the story has a happy ending: The steer was captured and taken to a sanctuary, where he will live out the remainder of his natural life.

To me, however, the most interesting aspect of the story was the language that the media used to refer to the animal. The *New York Times* had a headline that read: "Cow Who Escaped New York Slaughterhouse Finds Sanctuary." Animal advocates have long struggled against the convention of reserving "who" for people, and using "that" or "which" for animals. Not all languages make this distinction, but in English, to refer to "the cow that escaped" seems to deny the animal's agency. We would all say "the prisoner who escaped" but "the rock that rolled down the hill."

It would be premature to conclude that the *New York Times* article indicates a shift in usage. Rather, it seems to show uncertainty, for the first line of the article refers to "A cow that was captured by police."

I asked Philip Corbett, the standards editor for the *New York Times*, if the use of "cow who" reflected a change of policy. He told me that the *Times* style manual, like that of the Associated Press, suggested using "who" only for a named or personified animal. The manual gives the example "The dog, which was lost, howled" and contrasts this with "Adelaide, who was lost, howled."

Corbett added that the editors may have been caught between the two examples. The cow, or rather steer, did not have a name at the time of the escape, but was given one—Freddie—by Mike Stura, the founder of Freddie's new home, Skylands Animal Sanctuary & Rescue.

Among media reporting the story, some used "who" and others "that." A little searching on Google also shows mixed usage. In February 2022, I put in "cow who" and got 876,000 hits, whereas I got almost three times as many for "cow that." I then substituted "dog" for "cow," and the numbers got closer—more than 11 million for "dog who" as compared with 16 million for "dog that."

This could be because most of the dog stories are about people's pets, who have names. Yet, if Google is any indication, chimpanzees, who are rarely pets, are referred to as "who" almost twice as often as they are referred to as "that." Their similarity to us, and their undeniable individuality, must be playing a role. For gorillas and orangutans, too, "who" is more common than "that."

Google Ngram, which charts the frequencies of words or phrases in printed sources in different years, provides another interesting perspective. Whereas there were more than ten references to "cow that" for every reference to "cow who" in 1920, by 2000 the ratio had dropped to less than five to one. It seems that we are personifying cows more, despite the fact that many family-run dairy farms, in which the farmer knows every cow, have been replaced by corporate-run factory farms with thousands of nameless animals.

More surprising, perhaps, is that using "who" apparently is becoming more acceptable even for animals who are not pets and are less likely than great apes to be thought of as individuals. It's hard to connect canned tuna with an individual fish, let alone to think of that fish as a person, but the writer Sean Thomason has tweeted about "the tuna who died to get put in a can that wound up in the back of my cabinet until past expiration and which I just threw away."

Many social movements recognize that language matters because it both reflects and reinforces injustices that need to be remedied. Feminists have provided evidence that the supposedly gender-neutral use of "man" and "he" to include females has the effect of making women invisible.

Several remedies have been proposed, the most successful of which may be the use of the plural "they" in contexts like "Each person should collect their belongings." Terms used for members of racial minorities, and for people with disabilities, have also been challenged, to such an extent that it can be hard to keep up with the terms preferred by those in these categories.

The use of "who" for animals ranks alongside these other linguistic reforms. In most legal systems today, animals are property, just as tables and chairs are. They may be protected under animal welfare legislation, but that is not enough to prevent them being things, because antiquities and areas of natural beauty are also protected. English usage should change to make it clear that animals are fundamentally more like us than they are like tables and chairs, paintings and mountains.

The law is starting to show signs of change. In 1992, Switzerland became the first country to include a statement about protecting the dignity of animals in its constitution; Germany followed ten years later. In 2009, the European Union amended its fundamental treaty to include a statement that because animals are sentient beings, the EU and its member states must, in formulating policies for agriculture, fisheries, research, and several other areas, "pay full regard to the welfare requirements of animals."

In a language like English, which implicitly categorizes animals as things rather than persons, adopting the personal pronoun would embody the same recognition—and remind us who animals really are.

The Measure of Moral Progress

"The greatness of a nation and its moral progress," Mahatma Gandhi said, "can be judged by the way its animals are treated." If we apply that test to the world as a whole, how much moral progress have we made over the past two millennia?

That question is suggested by *The Golden Ass*, arguably the world's earliest surviving novel, written around 170 CE, when Emperor Marcus Aurelius ruled the Roman Empire. Apuleius, the author, was an African philosopher and writer, born in what is now the Algerian city of M'Daourouch. He learned Latin and Greek, completing his education in Athens and visiting Rome before returning to the region of his birth.

The Golden Ass is a first-person narrative told by Lucius, whose interest in magic takes him to Thessaly, a province of Greece renowned for the ability of its sorcerers. But his quest to learn the dark arts ends badly when he is turned into a donkey. In that guise, Lucius describes, from the animal's viewpoint, the life of a lowly working animal in Roman times.

The various forms of mistreatment inflicted on the donkey fall into three categories. There is sadism: a slave boy for whom he carries wood gathered from the mountainside loves to torment him by beating him with clubs, adding rocks to make his load even heavier, tying stinging thorns to his tail, and finally, when he has a load of dry kindling on his back, dropping a live coal into it and igniting an inferno from which the donkey barely escapes with his life.

There is also brutality: he falls into the hands of a band of robbers who beat him mercilessly, not because they enjoy making him suffer, but to compel him to carry their stolen silver up endless rough and steep mountain paths to their hideout.

Finally, there is exploitation, ruthless but economically rational for the donkey's new owner, a miller. In the mill, 24 hours a day, donkeys and horses turn the wheel that grinds the grain into flour. They are released from their exhausting labor only long enough to eat and sleep so that they will live to work another day. Overseeing their work, and beating them if they slacken off, are similarly exploited human slaves, clad in rags, with tattooed foreheads and shackled feet.

All of this makes *The Golden Ass* a remarkably progressive text. We have to jump forward 17 centuries before we find, in Anna Sewell's *Black Beauty*, a comparably vivid and empathetic presentation of the life of an animal mistreated by humans. But what can we learn from this Roman work about moral progress since it was written?

In many countries, the sadistic cruelty of the slave boy and the brutality of the bandits would be illegal. That is progress, but it is far from universal. If Apuleius were to return today to the area where he was born, he would not find laws to protect animals from cruelty. Across North Africa, only Egypt has such legislation.

In West and Central Africa, animals are protected by law only in Ghana and Nigeria. Saudi Arabia, Iran, and China have no national animal welfare laws. In contrast, there is at least some level of legislative protection for animals across the whole of Europe (with the sole exception of Belarus), on the Indian subcontinent, in Japan, much of Southeast Asia (where Vietnam is the major exception), Australia and New Zealand, and most of the Americas.

Typically, these laws prohibit both sadistic cruelty and brutal beatings, although there is wide variation in enforcement. And because attitudes to animals also vary widely, animals may be better treated in some countries with no legal protection than they are in other countries where cruelty is illegal.

Consider developed countries, where the exploitation of animals for commercial purposes is a far larger problem. Worldwide, more than 70 billion land-based vertebrates are killed for food each year, and 90% of them live their entire lives inside factory farms. Although a few jurisdictions, especially the European Union, do prohibit the most extreme forms of confinement, in most of the world there are no barriers to treating animals in whatever manner maximizes profit. A proposed United Nations Convention on Animal Health and Protection would help to remedy that situation.

In the mill that Apuleius describes, profits were maximized by working donkeys, horses, and human slaves nearly to death—but stopping just short of that point. If some of the animals (or slaves) did drop dead, well, it was cheaper to replace them than to ameliorate the working conditions that killed them.

Similarly, when giant agribusiness corporations decide how many animals to crowd inside their huge sheds, they know that the level of crowding that causes the fewest animals to die before reaching market weight will not be the most profitable level—and it is the latter benchmark that they will choose. As a result, more than 60 billion animals a year live miserable lives crowded into factory farms before being trucked to slaughter.

Gandhi's criterion for judging the greatness of a nation and its moral progress is not limited to maltreatment of animals that is sadistic or brutal. It refers only to the way that the nation's animals are treated. By that standard, as long as we keep most of the animals whose lives we control from birth to death in such appalling conditions, we cannot claim to have made much moral progress since Apuleius's time.

Are Insects Conscious?

Last summer, a cabbage white butterfly laid its eggs on an arugula I was growing. Before long, the plant was swarming with green caterpillars, well disguised against the green leaves. I had other arugula plants, some distance away, that would give me plenty of leaves for our salads, and I didn't want to use an insecticide, so I just left the caterpillars alone. Soon, every leaf was eaten down to the stalk. With nothing left to eat, the caterpillars, not ready to begin the next stage of their life cycle, all starved to death.

I had just been shown in microcosm something I had long accepted intellectually: Evolution is an impersonal natural process that has no regard for the well-being of the individual creatures it has produced. How, I sometimes wonder, can theists reconcile the world they observe with the belief that the world has been created by a being who is omniscient—and therefore saw that all this would happen—and yet is also good and worthy of being worshipped?

Christians have traditionally explained human suffering as the result of Adam's original sin, which we have all supposedly inherited. But caterpillars are not descended from Adam. Descartes' solution to that problem was to deny that animals are capable of feeling pain. When it comes to dogs or horses, however, few people could accept Descartes' view, even in his own time. Today, scientific investigations of the anatomy, physiology, and behavior of mammals and birds count against it. But can't we at least hope that caterpillars are incapable of feeling pain?

Scientists used to describe insects as not having a central brain. Rather, it was said, independent ganglia controlled different segments of the insect's body. If this were the case, it would be difficult to imagine how insects could be conscious.

But a recent article in *Proceedings of the National Academy of Sciences* rejects this model. Macquarie University's Andrew Barron, a cognitive scientist, and Colin Klein, a philosopher, argue that subjective experience could be more widespread in the animal kingdom—and older, in evolutionary terms—than we realize.

Subjective experience is the most basic form of consciousness. If a being is capable of having subjective experiences, then there is something that it is like to be that being, and this "something" could include having pleasant or painful experiences. In contrast, a driverless car has detectors capable of sensing obstacles that could collide with it, and of taking action to avoid such collisions, but there is nothing that it is like to be that car.

In humans, subjective experience is distinguishable from higher levels of consciousness, such as self-awareness, which requires a functioning cortex. Subjective experience involves the midbrain rather than the cortex and can continue even after massive damage to the cortex.

Insects have a central ganglion that, like a mammalian midbrain, is involved in processing sensory information, selecting targets, and directing action. It may also provide a capacity for subjective experience.

Insects are a very large and diverse category of beings. Honeybees have about a million neurons, which isn't many compared to our roughly 20 billion neocortical neurons, let alone the 37 billion recently found in the neocortex of a pilot whale. But it is still enough to be capable of performing and interpreting the famous "waggle dance" that conveys information about the direction and distance of flowers, water, or potential nest sites. Caterpillars, as far as we know, have no such abilities. But they may still be conscious enough to suffer as they starve.

In contrast, Barron and Klein say, plants have no structures that allow for awareness. The same is true of simple animals like jellyfish or roundworms; on the other hand, crustaceans and spiders, like insects, do have such structures.

If insects have subjective experiences, there is much more consciousness in the world than we may have thought, because there are, according to an estimate from the Smithsonian Institution, some ten quintillion (10,000,000,000,000,000,000) individual insects alive at any one time.

How we are to think about that depends on what we believe their subjective experiences could be like, and here the comparative structures don't tell us much. Perhaps the caterpillars gained so much pleasure from feasting on my arugula that their lives were worth living, despite their miserable deaths.

But the opposite is at least equally probable. With species that reproduce so prolifically, many of their offspring will starve from the moment they are hatched.

In the West, we tend to smile at Jain monks who sweep ants from their paths to avoid treading on them. We should, instead, admire the monks for carrying compassion to its logical conclusion.

That does not mean that we should launch a campaign for insect rights. We still do not know enough about insect subjective experiences to do that; and, in any case, the world is far from being ready to take such a campaign seriously. We need first to complete the extension of serious consideration to the interests of vertebrate animals, about whose capacity for suffering there is much less doubt.

Plant Liberation?

"Every day thousands of innocent plants are killed by vegetarians. Help end the violence. Eat meat." These words, written by an Edinburgh butcher on a blackboard outside his shop in January 2022 and shared on a vegan Facebook group, led to a heated online discussion. Some condemned the butcher for seeking to blur an important line between beings capable of suffering and those that are not. Others took it as a joke, as the butcher said he had intended it. But jokes can make serious points.

"How do you know that plants can't feel pain?" I was often asked when I stopped eating meat. In 1975, in the first edition of *Animal Liberation*, I offered two distinct responses. First, I argued, we have three strong reasons for believing that many nonhuman animals, especially vertebrates, can feel pain: They have nervous systems similar to our own; when subjected to stimuli that cause pain to us, they react in ways similar to how we react when in pain; and a capacity to feel pain confers an obvious evolutionary advantage on beings able to move away from the source of the pain. None of these reasons applies to plants, I claimed, so the belief that they can feel pain is unjustified.

My second response was that if plants could feel pain, even if they were as sensitive to it as animals, it would still be better to eat plants. The inefficiency of meat production means that by eating it we would be responsible not only for the suffering of the animals bred and raised for that purpose but also for that of the vastly larger number of plants they eat.

That second response clearly still stands. Estimates of the ratio of the food value of the plants we feed to animals to the food value of the edible meat produced range from 3:1 for chickens to 25:1 for beef cattle. I don't know if anyone has ever tried to calculate how many plants a cow eats before being sent to market, but it must be a *very* large number.

Increasing interest in plant sentience, however, has cast some doubt on my first response. Peter Wohlleben's 2015 worldwide bestseller, *The Hidden Life of Trees*, sparked popular attention to the issue. Wohlleben, a German forester, writes that trees can love, fear, make plans, worry about future events, and scream when they are thirsty—claims that have been repudiated by many scientists, some of whom signed a petition headed, "Even in the forest, it's facts we want instead of fairy tales." When questioned, Wohlleben himself often backs away from his attributions of mental states to plants.

That plants are sentient, in the literal meaning of the word— able to sense something—is obvious from the fact that they grow toward sunlight. Some are also sensitive in other ways. As a child, I enjoyed touching the leaves of a *Mimosa pudica*, or "touch-me-not" bush that my father had planted in our garden, to see the leaves close in response. And the carnivorous Venus Flytrap has sensitive hairs that trigger the closing of the trap when an insect lands on them.

But is there *something that it is like to be* a plant, in the sense that there is something that it is like to be a chicken, or a fish, or (possibly) a bee? Or is being a plant like being a rock—in other words, there is no subject of experience?

In *Animal Liberation*, I argued that plants are like rocks, and not like chickens or fish. (I was agnostic about bees, though I have not been indifferent to the question.) Isn't it possible that my argument there—that we frequently underestimate the awareness, needs, and cognitive abilities of animals, especially those we want to use for our own ends—applies to plants, too?

Consider the three reasons I gave for believing that animals can feel pain, which I claimed do not apply to plants. Both the fact that plants do not show pain behavior, and the apparent absence of an evolutionary advantage to consciousness for stationary organisms, could be met by the claim that they *do* respond to stresses, but on a much longer timescale than animals. They may not have a central nervous system, nor the neurons that form the physical basis of consciousness in animals, but they have substances like dopamine and serotonin, which function as neurotransmitters in animals.

We still have much to learn about both plants and consciousness. At this stage of that learning process, it would be foolish to exclude the possibility that plants have some physical basis for consciousness that we do not know about.

This does not vindicate the Scottish butcher's justification for eating meat. Not only does the second of the responses I made in *Animal Liberation* still stand; we now know that eating plant-based foods will significantly reduce our contribution to climate change. But it is a reason for thinking about plants a little differently, keeping in mind the possibility that more may be going on than we are aware of, and acting accordingly by minimizing the harm we do to them, when the costs of changing our behavior are not significant. On a larger scale, of course, we also know that forests and other forms of vegetation are essential for preserving biodiversity, not only for ourselves but for other animals as well.

(Agata Sagan contributed to this essay)

LIFE AND DEATH

The Real Abortion Tragedy

In 2018, just a week after the Argentine Senate refused to decriminalize abortion during the first 14 weeks of pregnancy, a 34-year-old woman died as a result of attempting to terminate her own pregnancy. Abortion receives extensive media coverage in the United States, where the first question asked of justices nominated for the Supreme Court is about their position on abortion. But much less attention is given to the 86 percent of all abortions that occur in the developing world. Although a majority of countries in Africa and Latin America have laws prohibiting abortion in most circumstances, official bans do not prevent high abortion rates. According to a 2018 report by the Guttmacher Institute, unsafe abortions lead to the deaths of 22,000 women every year, with almost all of these deaths occurring in developing countries. A further five million women are injured each year, sometimes permanently.

Bad as they are, these figures are coming down. They could be brought down almost to zero if we could meet the need for sex education and information about family planning and contraception, and provide safe, legal induced abortion, as well as follow-up care to prevent or treat medical complications. An estimated 220 million sexually active women in the developing world say that they want to prevent pregnancy, but are not using modern contraception. That is a huge tragedy for individuals and for the future of our already heavily populated planet. Yet when, in July 2012, the London Summit on Family Planning, hosted by the British government's Department for International Development and the Gates Foundation, announced commitments to reach 120 million of these women by 2020, the Vatican newspaper responded by criticizing Melinda Gates, whose efforts in organizing and partly funding this initiative were estimated to lead to nearly three million fewer babies dying in their first year of life, and to 50 million fewer abortions. One would have thought that Roman Catholics would see these outcomes as desirable. (Gates is herself a practicing Catholic who has seen what happens when women cannot feed their children, or are maimed by unsafe abortions.)

Restricting access to legal abortion leads many poor women to seek abortion from unsafe providers. The legalization of abortion on request in South Africa in 1998 saw abortion-related deaths drop by 91 percent. And the development of the drugs misoprostol and mifepristone, which can be provided by pharmacists, makes relatively safe and inexpensive abortion possible in developing countries, as well as in developed countries. In the United States, there has been a swing back toward more restrictive laws in some states. Thanks to Women on Web and Aid Access, both initiatives of the feminist activist Dr. Rebecca Gomperts, however, women in many jurisdictions where abortion is prohibited can obtain these drugs by mail, as thousands of Texas women did after abortion was drastically restricted there in 2021.

Opponents will respond that abortion is, by its very nature, unsafe—for the fetus. They point out that abortion kills a unique, living human individual. That claim is difficult to deny, at least if by "human" we mean "member of the species *Homo sapiens.*"

It is also true that we cannot simply invoke a woman's "right to choose" in order to avoid the ethical issue of the moral status of the fetus. If the fetus really did have the moral status of any other human being, it would be difficult to argue that a pregnant woman's right to choose includes the right to bring about the death of the fetus, except perhaps when the woman's life is at stake.

The fallacy in the anti-abortion argument lies in the shift from the scientifically accurate claim that the fetus is a living individual of the species *Homo sapiens* to the ethical claim that the fetus therefore has the same right to life as any other human being. Membership of the species *Homo sapiens* is not enough to confer a right to life on a being. Nor can something like self-awareness or rationality warrant greater protection for the fetus than for, say, a cow, because the mental capacities of the fetus are inferior to those of cows. Yet "pro-life" groups that picket abortion clinics are rarely seen picketing slaughterhouses.

We can plausibly argue that we ought not to kill, against their will, self-aware beings who want to continue to live. We can see this as a violation of their autonomy, or a thwarting of their preferences. But why should a being's potential to become rationally self-aware make it wrong to end its life before it actually has the capacity for rationality or self-awareness?

We have no obligation to allow every being with the potential to become a rational being to realize that potential. If it comes to a clash between the supposed interests of potentially rational but not yet even conscious beings and the vital interests of actually rational women, we should give preference to the women every time.

Abortion, Democracy, and the Reversal of *Roe*

Every person capable of bearing a child should have the legal right safely to terminate a pregnancy that they do not wish to continue, at least until the very late stage of pregnancy when the fetus may be sufficiently developed to feel pain—and even then, I would not oppose ending the pregnancy by a method that avoids causing pain to the fetus. That has been my firm view since I began thinking about the topic as an undergraduate in the 1960s. None of the extensive reading, writing, and debating I have subsequently done on the topic has given me sufficient reason to change my mind.

Yet I find it hard to disagree with the central line of reasoning of the majority of the US Supreme Court in *Dobbs v. Jackson Women's Health Organization*, the decision overturning *Roe v. Wade*, the landmark 1973 case that established a constitutional right to abortion. This reasoning begins with the indisputable fact that the US Constitution makes no reference to abortion, and the admittedly disputable, but still very reasonable, claim that the right to abortion is also not implicit in any constitutional provision, including the due process clause of the Fourteenth Amendment.

The reasoning behind the decision in *Roe v. Wade* to remove from state legislatures the power to prohibit abortion was clearly on shaky ground. Justice Byron White was right: The *Roe* majority's ruling, he wrote in his dissenting opinion in the case, was "the exercise of raw judicial power."

The Supreme Court exercised that power in a way that gave US women a legal right that they should have. *Roe* spared millions of women the distress of carrying to term and giving birth to a child whom they did not want to carry to term or give birth to. It dramatically reduced the number of deaths and injuries occurring at that time, when there were no drugs that reliably and safely induced abortion. Desperate women who were unable to get a safe, legal abortion from properly trained medical professionals would try to do it themselves or go to back-alley abortionists, all too often with serious, and sometimes fatal, consequences.

None of that, however, resolves the larger question: Do we want courts or legislatures to make such decisions? Here I agree with Justice Samuel Alito, writing the majority opinion for the Supreme Court in *Dobbs*, when he approvingly quotes Justice Antonin Scalia's view that: "The permissibility of abortion, and the limitations upon it, are to be resolved like most important questions in our democracy: by citizens trying to persuade one another and then voting."

There is, of course, some irony in the majority of the Supreme Court saying this the day after it struck down New York's democratically enacted law restricting the use of handguns. The Court would no doubt say that, in contrast to abortion, the US Constitution does explicitly state that "the right of the people to bear arms shall not be infringed." But that much-quoted phrase is preceded by the rationale that "a well-regulated militia" is "necessary to the security of a free state." The supposed right of individuals to carry handguns has absolutely nothing to do with the security of the United States, so a sensible application of Scalia's comment on how the question of abortion should be resolved would have been to leave the regulation of guns to democratic processes.

There is an even more radical implication of the view that courts should not assume powers that are not specified in the Constitution: The Supreme Court's power to strike down legislation is not in the Constitution. Not until 1803, 15 years after the ratification of the Constitution, did Chief Justice John Marshall, in *Marbury v. Madison*, unilaterally assert that the Court can determine the constitutionality of legislation and of actions taken by the executive branch. If the exercise of raw judicial power is a sin, then Marshall's arrogation to the Court of the authority to strike down legislation is the Supreme Court's original sin. *Marbury* utterly transformed the Bill of Rights. An aspirational statement of principles became a legal document, a role for which the vagueness of its language makes it plainly unsuited.

Undoubtedly, the US Supreme Court has issued some positive and progressive decisions. *Brown v. Board of Education*, in which the Court unanimously ruled that racial segregation in public schools violated the Fourteenth Amendment's equal protection clause, is perhaps the foremost among them. But it has also handed down disastrous decisions, such as the notorious Dred Scott case, which held that no one of African ancestry could become a US citizen, and that slaves who had lived in a free state were still slaves if they returned to a slave state.

More recently, in *Citizens United v. Federal Election Commission*, the Court invalidated federal laws restricting political donations, thus opening the floodgates for corporations and other organizations to pour money into the campaigns of their favored candidates or political parties. And the decision on handguns seems likely to cost more innocent people their lives.

Supreme Court decisions cannot easily be reversed, even if it becomes clear that their consequences are overwhelmingly negative. Striking down the decisions of legislatures on controversial issues such as abortion and gun control politicizes the courts and leads presidents to focus on appointing judges who will support a particular stance on abortion, guns, or other hot-button issues.

The lesson to draw from the Court's decisions on abortion, campaign finances, and gun control is this: Don't allow unelected judges to do more than enforce the essential requirements of the democratic process. Around the world, democratic legislatures have enacted laws on abortion that are as liberal, or more so, than the United States had before the reversal of *Roe v. Wade*. It should come as no surprise that these democracies also have far better laws on campaign financing and gun control than the United States has now.

Treating (or Not) the Tiniest Babies

In 2007, newspapers hailed the "miracle baby" Amillia Taylor, claiming that she was then the most prematurely born surviving baby ever recorded.. Born in October with a gestational age of just 21 weeks and six days, she weighed only 280 grams, or 10 ounces, at birth. Previously no baby born at less than 23 weeks had been known to survive, so doctors did not expect Amillia to live. But after nearly four months in a neonatal intensive care unit in a Miami hospital, and having grown to a weight of 1800 grams, or 4 pounds, doctors judged her ready to go home.

There was a certain amount of hype in all this. Amillia was conceived by in vitro fertilization, so the day on which conception took place could be known precisely. Usually this is not possible, and gestational age is calculated from the first day of the mother's last menstrual period. Since babies are usually conceived around the middle of the menstrual cycle, this adds about two weeks to the date of conception, and Amillia should therefore have been regarded as being born in the 23rd week of pregnancy. It is not uncommon for such babies to survive. Nevertheless, Amillia was certainly a very premature, and very tiny, baby (according to one source, the fourth-smallest baby to survive).

Amillia is now a teenager and reported to be doing fine. We should, of course, be delighted for her and for her parents that everything has worked out so remarkably well. But the use of all the resources of modern medicine to save smaller and smaller babies raises issues that need to be discussed.

In 2022, the *New England Journal of Medicine* published a "Case Vignette" with accompany articles debating whether all babies born at 22 weeks should routinely be resuscitated.

Dr. Leif Nelin, arguing for resuscitation of all babies delivered at 22 weeks, reported on one study indicating that at a hospital in Iowa that resuscitated all infants born at 22–23 weeks gestation, 70% survived, and 55% had no, or only mild, neurodevelopmental impairment. A Swedish study found a survival rate of 52% in infants born at 22 weeks gestation, with half the survivors having no impairment when checked 2.5 years later.

In contrast, Dr. Elizabeth Foglia argued that parents should, if circumstances permit, be given counseling before an extremely premature birth, and invited to decide whether they wish their baby to be resuscitated, or to be given only "comfort care" rather than invasive and possibly futile interventions. She referred to a meta-analysis of data from more than 2,000 infants born at 22 weeks gestation, all of whom received active treatment. This analysis reported a survival rate of only 29%, and only 11% survived without major in-hospital complications. The higher survival rates in the studies to which Dr. Nelin referred were, she said, likely to be due to these hospitals being better resourced than most. In general, she said, "Extremely preterm newborns who survive spend months in the neonatal intensive care unit, undergo hundreds of painful procedures, and are at high risk for subsequent neurodevelopmental impairment."

The journal invited readers to indicate whether they favor routinely resuscitating infants born at 22 weeks gestation. By the time the poll closed, 1,870 readers had voted, with 28% in favor of routine resuscitation for all infants born at 22 weeks gestation, and 71% recommending selective resuscitation. (This is not, of course, a scientific survey of physician opinion.)

On this question, I am with the majority of those polled. The parents should be involved in the decision. If the child survives, but with a severe disability—and even the Iowa study that Dr. Nelin quotes indicates that 45% of the surviving infants have an impairment that is not merely "mild"—the parents are the ones who will have to care for that child. It is wrong for doctors to impose that burden on parents without seeking their views. On the other hand, if the parents understand the situation, and are ready to welcome a severely disabled child into their family, should that be the outcome, then the hospital should be prepared to resuscitate the child, although even then, if the cost of treatment is coming from government funds, difficult policy issues will arise about how best to spend the available health-care budget.

Pulling Back the Curtain on the Mercy Killing of Newborns

In 2005, the *New England Journal of Medicine* published an article in which two doctors from the University Medical Center Groningen in the Netherlands outlined the circumstances in which doctors in their hospital had, in 22 cases over seven years, carried out euthanasia on newborn infants. All of these cases were reported to a district attorney's office in the Netherlands. None of the doctors were prosecuted.

In the article, Eduard Verhagen and Pieter Sauer divide into three groups the newborns for whom decisions about ending life might be made. The first consists of infants who would die soon after birth even if all existing medical resources were employed to prolong their lives. In the second group are infants who require intensive care, such as a respirator, to keep them alive, and for whom the expectations regarding their future are "very grim." These are infants with severe brain damage. If they can survive beyond intensive care, they will still have a very poor quality of life. The third group includes infants with a "hopeless prognosis" and who also are victims of "unbearable suffering." For example, in the third group was "a child with the most serious form of spina bifida," the failure of the spinal cord to form and close properly. Yet infants in group three may no longer be dependent on intensive care.

It is this third group that creates the controversy, because their lives cannot be ended simply by withdrawing intensive care. Instead, at the University Medical Center Groningen, if suffering cannot be relieved and no improvement can be expected, the physicians will discuss with the parents whether this is a case in which death "would be more humane than continued life." If the parents agree that this is the case, and the team of physicians also agrees—as well as an independent physician not otherwise associated with the patient—the infant's life may be ended.

American "pro-life" groups saw this as just another example of the slippery slope that, in their view, the Netherlands began to slide down in the 1980s, when it became the first country in which voluntary euthanasia could be openly practiced. But in fact the open practice of infant euthanasia in the Netherlands has contracted, rather than expanded: since 2005, there have only been three more cases. The likely explanation for this reduction is that in 2007 the Dutch government began offering free prenatal diagnosis to all pregnant women. This increased the number of abortions of babies with spina bifida, and hence there were fewer infants born with conditions that met the requirements for infant euthanasia in the Netherlands.

In any case, before any Americans denounce the Groningen doctors, they should take a look at what is happening in their own country's hospitals. Infants with severe problems are allowed to die in the United States. These are infants in the first two of the three groups identified by Verhagen and Sauer. Some of them—those in the second group—can live for many years if intensive care is continued. Nevertheless, US doctors, usually in consultation with parents, make decisions to withdraw intensive care. This happens openly, in Catholic as well as non-Catholic hospitals.

I have taken my Princeton students to St. Peter's University Hospital, a Catholic facility in nearby New Brunswick, New Jersey, that has a major neonatal intensive care unit. There, Dr. Mark Hiatt, the unit director, has described to my students cases in which he has withdrawn intensive care from infants with severe brain damage.

Among neonatologists in the United States and the Netherlands, there is widespread agreement that sometimes it is ethically acceptable to end the life of a newborn infant with severe medical problems. Even the Roman Catholic Church accepts that it is not always required to use "extraordinary" means of life support and that a respirator can be considered "extraordinary."

The only serious dispute is whether it is acceptable to end the life of infants in Verhagen and Sauer's third group, that is, infants who are no longer dependent on intensive care for survival. To put this another way: the dispute is no longer about whether it is justifiable to end an infant's life if that life won't be worth living, but whether that end may be brought about by active means, or only by the withdrawal of treatment.

I believe the Groningen protocol to be based on the sound ethical perception that the means by which death occurs is less significant, ethically, than the decision that it is better that an infant's life should end. If it is sometimes acceptable to end the lives of infants in group two—and virtually no one denies this—then it is also sometimes acceptable to end the lives of infants in group three.

On the basis of comments made to me by some physicians, I am sure that the lives of infants in group three are sometimes ended in the United States. But this is never reported or publicly discussed, for fear of prosecution. That means that standards governing when such actions are justified cannot be appropriately debated, let alone agreed upon.

In the Netherlands, on the other hand, as Verhagen and Sauer write, "obligatory reporting with the aid of a protocol and subsequent assessment of euthanasia in newborns help us to clarify the decision-making process." There are many who will think that the existence of 22 cases of infant euthanasia over seven years at one hospital in the Netherlands shows that it is a society that has less respect for human life than the United States. But I'd suggest that they take a look at the difference in infant mortality rates between the two countries.

The CIA World Factbook shows that the United States has an infant mortality rate of 5.22 per 1,000 live births, and the Netherlands, 3.45. Building a health-care system in the United States as good as that in the Netherlands—as measured by infant mortality—would save the lives of thousands of infants each year. That is far more worthy of the attention of those who value human life than the deaths of 22 tragically afflicted infants.

Should Children Have the Right to Die?

Since 2002, Belgium has permitted terminally or incurably ill adults to request and receive euthanasia from a doctor. In 2014, the Belgian parliament removed the provision of the country's law on euthanasia that restricted the law's use to adults. That led to an outcry.

Predictably, the uproar resumed when the first minor received euthanasia. Cardinal Elio Sgreccia, speaking on Radio Vatican, said that the Belgian law denies children the right to life. But the circumstances of the case, and the fact that it took two and a half years for this to happen, show just the opposite: The Belgian law respects the right to life—and, in carefully defined circumstances, the right to die.

Although Belgium's euthanasia law now has no specific age requirement, it does require the person requesting euthanasia to have a demonstrable capacity for rational decision-making. This effectively excludes very small children from the law's scope. The request must be examined by a team of doctors and a psychiatrist or psychologist, and requires the approval of the minor's parents. The minor has to be "in a hopeless medical situation of constant and unbearable suffering that cannot be eased and which will cause death in the short term."

In announcing the first use of the law by a minor, Wim Distelmans, the head of Belgium's federal euthanasia commission, pointed out that there are very few children for whom the question of euthanasia is raised. He added that this is not a reason for refusing a dignified death for those who request it and meet the law's stringent requirements.

Although no details about the minor were initially provided, it was subsequently revealed that he or she was 17 years old. If Cardinal Sgreccia had responded to the teenager's death by saying that the Belgian law denies that children have a duty to live, he might have begun a useful debate that would have clarified differences between those who believe that there is such a duty and those who do not. Thomas Aquinas, still an influential figure in the Catholic tradition, thought that we have a duty not to end our own life because to do so is a sin against God.

Aquinas illustrated this claim by drawing an analogy between ending one's own life and killing a slave belonging to someone else, which means that one "sins against that slave's master." Putting aside that grotesquely insensitive analogy, it is obvious that this argument provides no reason against suicide for people who do not believe in the existence of a god. Even theists will struggle to understand why a benevolent deity should want someone who is dying to remain alive until the last possible moment, no matter how severe the pain, discomfort, or loss of dignity may be.

There is a further reason why even Cardinal Sgreccia might hesitate to assert that there is a duty to live. The Catholic Church has long accepted that it is not obligatory for a doctor or a patient to continue all means of life support, irrespective of the patient's condition or prognosis.

In Catholic hospitals everywhere, respirators and other forms of life support are withdrawn from patients when the burdens of continuing the treatment are judged "disproportionate" to the benefits likely to be achieved. That surely indicates that any duty to live is subject to the benefits of continued life outweighing the burdens of treatment. Patients requesting euthanasia judge that the benefits of continued life do not outweigh the burdens of treatment, or of continuing to live, with or without treatment.

A right, however, is different from a duty. I have a right to freedom of expression, but I may remain silent. I have a right to my body parts, but I may donate a kidney to a relative, a friend, or a complete stranger who is suffering from kidney failure. My right gives me a choice. I can choose to exercise it or to waive it.

Age limits are always to some extent arbitrary. Chronological age and mental age can diverge. For some activities for which a mental age limit may be relevant, the number of people engaging in the activity is very large: voting, obtaining a driving license, and having sex, for example. But it would be very costly to scrutinize whether every person interested in those activities has the capacity to understand what is involved in voting, driving responsibly, or giving informed consent to sex. That is why we rely on chronological age as a rough indication of the relevant mental capacity.

This is not true of minors requesting euthanasia. If the number of those who meet the requirements of the law is so small that Belgium has had only one case over the past two years, it is not difficult to carry out a thorough examination of these patients' capacities to make such a request.

For these reasons, Belgium's extension of its law on euthanasia to minors with a demonstrable capacity for rational decision-making does not deny anyone's right to life. On the contrary, it grants a right to die to those who may reasonably choose to exercise that right.

No Diseases for Old Men

Pneumonia used to be called "the old man's friend" because it often brought a swift and relatively painless end to a life that was already of poor quality and would otherwise have continued to decline. But in 2008, a study of severely demented patients in US nursing homes around Boston, Massachusetts, showed that the "friend" is often being fought with antibiotics. Are doctors routinely treating illnesses because they can, rather than because doing so is in the best interests of the patient?

The study, carried out by Erika D'Agata and Susan Mitchell and published in the *Archives of Internal Medicine*, showed that over 18 months, two-thirds of 214 severely demented patients in nursing homes were treated with antibiotics. The mean age of these patients was 85. On a standard test for severe impairment, where scores can range from 0 to 24, with the lower scores indicating more severe impairment, three-quarters of these patients scored 0. Their ability to communicate verbally ranged from nil to minimal.

It isn't clear that using antibiotics in these circumstances prolongs life, but even if it did, how many people want their lives to be prolonged if they are incontinent, need to be fed by others, can no longer walk, and their mental capacities have irreversibly deteriorated so that they can neither speak nor recognize their children?

The interests of patients should come first, and I doubt that longer life was in the interests of these patients. Ideally, they would all have signed advanced directives indicating whether they wanted to keep living under these circumstances. When there are no such directives, however, and no way of finding out what the patient wants, and it is very doubtful that continued treatment is in the interests of a patient, it is reasonable to take account of other factors, including the views of the family, and the cost to the community. In the United States, Medicare and Medicaid costs for people with Alzheimer's disease were estimated to be $239 billion in 2021, and are expected to increase to nearly $800 billion by 2050. For comparison, in 2020 the US foreign aid budget was $51 billion. Even within the Medicare and Medicaid budgets, however, there are higher spending priorities than prolonging the lives of elderly nursing home patients with severe dementia.

D'Agata and Mitchell point out that the use of so many antibiotics by these patients carries with it a different kind of cost for the community: it exacerbates the increasing problem of antibiotic-resistant bacteria. When a dementia patient is transferred to a hospital to deal with an acute medical problem, these resistant bacteria can spread and may prove fatal to patients who otherwise would have made a good recovery and had many years of normal life ahead of them.

One may suspect that a misguided belief in the sanctity of all human life plays some role in decisions to prolong human life beyond the point where it benefits the person whose life it is. Yet on this point, some religions are more reasonable than others. The Roman Catholic Church, for instance, holds that there is no obligation to provide care that is disproportionate to the benefit it produces or unduly burdensome to the patient. In my experience, many Catholic theologians would accept a decision to withhold antibiotics from severely demented elderly patients who develop pneumonia.

Other religions are more rigid. Pneumonia has been unable to play its traditional friendly role for Samuel Golubchuk, an 84-year-old man from Winnipeg, Canada. Golubchuk suffered a brain injury that left him with limited physical and mental capacities. When he developed pneumonia and was hospitalized, his doctors proposed withdrawing life support. His children, however, said that discontinuing life support would be contrary to their Orthodox Jewish beliefs. They obtained an interim court order compelling the doctors to maintain life support.

The doctors therefore inserted a tube in Golubchuk's throat to help him breathe, and another into his stomach to feed him. He did not speak, nor get out of bed. After three months of this, the interim court order came up for review, but the court extended it until the case could be heard in full. Another three months passed. Dr. Anand Kumar, one of the hospital's doctors caring for Golubchuk, then announced that he could not ethically justify what the court was forcing him to do. "If we honestly attempt to follow the court mandate to focus on keeping Mr. Golubchuk from his natural death," he said, "we will likely have to continue to surgically hack away at his infected flesh at the bedside in order to keep the infection at bay. This is grotesque. To inflict this kind of assault on him without a reasonable hope of benefit is an abomination. I can't do it."

Two other doctors also refused to obey the court order to continue to prolong Golubchuk's life, even though by doing so they risked jail. Another physician took over, and soon after, Golubchuk died, officially from natural causes, thus rendering further legal action moot.

Normally, when patients are unable to make decisions about their treatment, the wishes of the family should be given great weight. But doctors have an ethical responsibility to act in the best interests of their patient, and the family's wishes should not override that.

From a public policy perspective, the central issue raised by the Golubchuk case is how far a publicly funded health-care system has to go to satisfy the wishes of the family, when these wishes clash with what, in the view of the doctors, is in the best interests of the patient. There has to be a limit to what a family can demand from the public purse, because to spend more money on long-term care for a patient with no prospect of recovery means that there is less money for other patients with better prospects.

In the case of a family seeking treatment that, in the professional judgment of the physicians, is futile, there is no requirement to provide expensive long-term care. If Golubchuk's children wished their father to remain on life support—and if they could have shown that keeping him alive was not causing him to suffer—they should have been told that they were free to arrange for such care, at their own expense. What the court should not have done was to order the hospital to continue to care for Golubchuk, at its own expense, and against the better judgment of its health-care professionals. Canadian taxpayers are not required to go that far in order to support the religious beliefs of their fellow citizens.

When Doctors Kill

Of all the arguments against voluntary euthanasia, the most influential is the "slippery slope": once we allow doctors to kill patients, we will not be able to limit the killing to those who want to die.

There is no evidence for this claim, even after many years of legal physician-assisted suicide or voluntary euthanasia in the Netherlands, Belgium, Luxembourg, Switzerland, and the American state of Oregon. But revelations about what took place in a New Orleans hospital after Hurricane Katrina point to a genuine danger from a different source.

When New Orleans was flooded in August 2005, the rising water cut off Memorial Medical Center, a community hospital that was holding more than 200 patients. Three days after the hurricane hit, the hospital had no electricity, the water supply had failed, and toilets could no longer be flushed. Some patients who were dependent on ventilators died.

In stifling heat, doctors and nurses were hard-pressed to care for surviving patients lying on soiled beds. Adding to the anxiety were fears that law and order had broken down in the city, and that the hospital itself might be a target for armed bandits.

Helicopters were called in to evacuate patients. Priority was given to those who were in better health and could walk. State police arrived and told staff that because of the civil unrest, everybody had to be out of the hospital by 5 p.m.

On the eighth floor, Jannie Burgess, a 79-year-old woman with advanced cancer, was on a morphine drip and close to death. To evacuate her, she would have to be carried down six flights of stairs, and would require the attention of nurses who were needed elsewhere. But if she were left unattended, she might come out of her sedation, and be in pain. Ewing Cook, one of the physicians present, instructed the nurse to increase the morphine, "giving her enough until she goes." It was, he later told Sheri Fink, who wrote a story for the *New York Times*, and subsequently published a book about these events, a "no-brainer."

According to Fink, Anna Pou, another physician, told nursing staff that several patients on the seventh floor were also too ill to survive. She injected them with morphine and another drug that slowed their breathing until they died.

At least one of the patients injected with this lethal combination of drugs appears to have otherwise been in little danger of imminent death. Emmett Everett was a 61-year-old man who had been paralyzed in an accident several years earlier, and was in the hospital for surgery to relieve a bowel obstruction. When others from his ward were evacuated, he asked not to be left behind.

But he weighed 380 pounds (173 kilograms), and it would have been extremely difficult to carry him down the stairs and then up again to where the helicopters were landing. He was told the injection he was being given would help with the dizziness from which he suffered.

In 1957, a group of doctors asked Pope Pius XII whether it is permissible to use narcotics to suppress pain and consciousness "if one foresees that the use of narcotics will shorten life." The Pope said that it was. In its Declaration on Euthanasia, issued in 1980, the Vatican reaffirmed that view.

The Vatican's position is an application of what is known as "the doctrine of double effect." An action that has two effects, one good and the other bad, may be permissible if the good effect is the one that is intended and the bad effect is merely an unwanted consequence of achieving the good effect. Significantly, neither the Pope's remarks, nor the Declaration on Euthanasia, place any emphasis on the importance of obtaining the voluntary and informed consent of patients, where possible, before shortening their lives.

According to the doctrine of double effect, two doctors may, to all outward appearances, do exactly the same thing: that is, they may give patients in identical conditions an identical dose of morphine, knowing that this dose will shorten the patient's life. Yet one doctor, who intends to relieve the patient's pain, acts in accordance with good medical practice, whereas the other, who intends to shorten the patient's life, commits murder.

Dr. Cook had little time for such subtleties. Only "a very naïve doctor" would think that giving a person a lot of morphine was not "prematurely sending them to their grave," he told Fink, and then bluntly added: "We kill 'em." In Cook's opinion, the line between something ethical and something illegal is "so fine as to be imperceivable."

At Memorial Medical Center, physicians and nurses found themselves under great pressure. Exhausted after 72 hours with little sleep, and struggling to care for their patients, they were not in the best position to make difficult ethical decisions. The doctrine of double effect, properly understood, does not justify what the doctors did; but, by inuring them to the practice of shortening patients' lives without obtaining consent, it seems to have paved the way for intentional killing.

Roman Catholic thinkers have been among the most vocal in invoking the "slippery slope" argument against the legalization of voluntary euthanasia and physician-assisted dying. They would do well to examine the consequences of their own doctrines.

Choosing Death

"I will take my life today around noon. It is time."

With these words, posted online in August 2014, Gillian Bennett, an 85-year-old New Zealander living in Canada, began her explanation of her decision to end her life. Bennett had known for three years that she was suffering from dementia. By August, the dementia had progressed to the point at which, as she put it, "I have nearly lost me."

"I want out," Bennett wrote, "before the day when I can no longer assess my situation, or take action to bring my life to an end." Her husband, Jonathan Bennett, a retired philosophy professor, and her children, supported her decision, but she refused to allow them to assist her suicide in any way, as doing so would have exposed them to the risk of a 14-year prison sentence. She therefore had to take the final steps while she was still competent to do so.

For most of us, fortunately, life is precious. We want to go on living because we have things to look forward to, or because, overall, we find it enjoyable, interesting, or stimulating. Sometimes we want to go on living because there are things that we want to achieve, or people close to us whom we want to help. Bennett was a great-grandmother; if all had been well with her, she would have wanted to see the next generation grow up.

Bennett's developing dementia deprived her of all of the reasons for wanting to continue to live. That makes it hard to deny
that her decision was both rational and ethical. By committing
suicide, she was giving up nothing that she wanted, or could
reasonably value. "All I lose is an indefinite number of years of
being a vegetable in a hospital setting, eating up the country's
money but having not the faintest idea of who I am."

Bennett's decision was also ethical because, as the reference
to "the country's money" suggests, she was not thinking only
of herself. Opponents of legal voluntary euthanasia or
physician-assisted suicide sometimes say that if the laws were
changed, patients would feel pressured to end their lives in order
to avoid being a burden to others. Baroness Mary Warnock, the
moral philosopher who chaired the British government committee responsible for the 1984 "Warnock Report," which established the framework for her country's pioneering legislation
on in vitro fertilization and embryo research, does not see this
as a reason against allowing patients to choose to end their lives.
She has suggested that there is nothing wrong with feeling that
you ought to die for the sake of others as well as for yourself. In
an interview published in 2008 in the Church of Scotland's
magazine *Life and Work*, she supported the right of those suffering intolerably to end their lives. "If somebody absolutely,
desperately wants to die because they're a burden to their family,
or the state," she argued, "then I think they too should be allowed
to die."

Because Canada's public health service provides care for
people with dementia who are unable to care for themselves,

Bennett knew that she would not have to be a burden on her family; nonetheless, she was concerned about the burden that she would impose upon the public purse. In a hospital, she might survive for another ten years in a vegetative state, at a cost she conservatively estimated to be around $50,000–$75,000 per year.

As Bennett would not benefit from remaining alive, she regarded this as a waste. She was concerned, too, about the health-care workers who would have to care for her: "Nurses, who thought they were embarked on a career that had great meaning, find themselves perpetually changing my diapers and reporting on the physical changes of an empty husk." Such a situation is, in her words, "ludicrous, wasteful and unfair."

Some will object to the description of a person with advanced dementia as an "empty husk." But, having seen this condition overtake my mother and my aunt—both vibrant, intelligent women, who were reduced to lying, unresponsive, in a bed for months or (in my aunt's case) years—it seems to me entirely accurate. Beyond a certain stage of dementia, the person we knew is gone.

If the person did not want to live in that condition, what is the point of maintaining the body? In any health-care system, resources are limited and should be used for care that is wanted by the patient, or from which the patient will benefit.

For people who do not want to live on when their mind has gone, deciding when to die is difficult. In 1990, Janet Adkins, who was suffering from Alzheimer's disease, traveled to Michigan to end her life with the assistance of Dr. Jack Kevorkian, who was widely criticized for helping her to die, because at the time of her death she was still well enough to play tennis. She chose to die nonetheless, because she could have lost control over her decision if she had delayed it.

Bennett, in her eloquent statement, looked forward to the day when the law would allow a physician to act not only on a prior "living will" that bars life-prolonging treatment, but also on one that requests a lethal dose when the patient becomes incapacitated to a specified extent. Such a change would remove the anxiety that some patients with progressive dementia have that they will go on too long and miss the opportunity to end their life at all. The legislation Bennett suggests would enable people in her condition to live as long as they want—but not longer than that.

• • •

Two years after Bennett's death, Canada legalized medical aid in dying—both physician-assisted suicide and voluntary euthanasia—for patients whose natural death is "reasonably foreseeable." The legislation was a response to a decision by the Supreme Court of Canada holding that existing prohibitions on assisted suicide and voluntary euthanasia violated the Canadian Charter of Rights and Freedoms. It is also part of a pattern of increasing acceptance of medical aid in dying, which is now legal in Australia (most states), Austria, Belgium, Canada, Colombia, Germany, Luxembourg, the Netherlands, Portugal, Spain, Switzerland, and in 11 jurisdictions of the United States, including California.

Canadians supported the legislation of medical aid in dying, but in one poll, eight out of ten respondents thought it too restrictive. In a case brought in Quebec in 2019, the province's

Superior Court ruled that the restriction of assistance in dying to patients whose natural death was foreseeable violated the Charter of Rights.

In 2021, after extensive public consultation and parliamentary debate, the Canadian parliament approved amendments making patients eligible for assistance in dying if they have a "grievous and irremediable medical condition," which is defined as "having a serious and incurable illness, disease or disability; being in an advanced state of irreversible decline in capability; and experiencing enduring physical or psychological suffering that is intolerable to them and cannot be relieved under conditions that they consider acceptable."

Although patients whose natural death is not reasonably foreseeable are now eligible for assistance in dying, requests from these patients must receive additional scrutiny, including a mandatory 90-day period in which the patient's eligibility is tested by, for example, counseling or improved palliative care that may alleviate the patient's suffering.

The 2016 legislation required a parliamentary review of the law after five years, but the review was delayed because of the pandemic and a federal election. In addition to a general overview of how the law is working, the review is considering two issues that will help to shape public discussion of assistance in dying. One is whether assistance in dying should be available to someone whose intolerable and irremediable suffering is caused by mental illness. The other is the issue that Gillian Bennett wanted discussed: whether advance requests should be permitted.

The issue of allowing advance requests for assistance in dying will become more pressing as populations age and more people develop dementia. Last year, the Dutch Supreme Court ruled that doctors cannot be prosecuted for carrying out euthanasia on patients who have given written consent, but subsequently lost the capacity to consent.

The overriding reason for permitting this is that it allows patients in the early stages of dementia to enjoy their lives, without fearing that unless they commit suicide while they are still capable of doing so, they will become, in Gillian Bennett's evocative phrase, "an empty husk."

Canada's 2021 legislation explicitly excludes mental illness as a sole ground for receiving assistance in dying, but the exclusion will automatically lapse in two years. That sets a deadline for parliament to decide what safeguards are needed to ensure that the suffering of mentally ill people who request assistance in dying is truly irremediable.

There can be little doubt that some mentally ill people are not helped by treatment, and do suffer greatly. It is hard to see why, if suffering from an incurable but non-terminal physical illness suffices for assistance in dying, suffering that is as bad or worse from incurable mental illness should not also be sufficient. Moreover, for people who are suffering from untreatable depression or other mental illnesses that do not respond to treatment, merely being judged eligible for euthanasia can in itself make life more bearable.

PUBLIC HEALTH AND PANDEMIC ETHICS

Public Health versus Private Freedom

In 2012, in contrasting decisions, a United States Court of Appeals struck down a US Food and Drug Administration requirement that cigarettes be sold in packs with graphic health warnings, and Australia's highest court upheld a law that requires not only health warnings and large images of the physical damage that smoking causes, but also that the remainder of the packs themselves be plain, with brand names in small generic type, no logos, and no color other than a drab olive-brown.

The US decision was based on America's constitutional protection of free speech. The Court accepted that the government may require factually accurate health warnings, but the majority, in a split decision, said that it could not go as far as requiring images. In Australia, the issue was whether the law implied uncompensated expropriation—in this case, of the tobacco companies' intellectual property in their brands. The High Court ruled that it did not and Australian cigarette packaging today would, one would think, be enough to scare away anyone who is not already addicted to the product.

Underlying these differences in cigarette packs in the two countries, however, is the larger issue: who decides the proper balance between public health and freedom of expression? In the United States, courts make that decision, essentially by interpreting a 225-year-old text. If that deprives the government of techniques that might reduce the death toll from cigarettes—estimated, at the time of the decision, at 443,000 Americans every year—so be it. In Australia, where freedom of expression is not given explicit constitutional protection, courts are much more likely to respect the right of democratically elected governments to strike the proper balance between freedom and public health.

There is widespread agreement that governments ought to prohibit the sale of at least some dangerous products. Countless food additives are either banned or permitted only in limited quantities, as are children's toys painted with substances that could be harmful if ingested. Many countries prohibit the sale of unsafe tools, such as power saws without safety guards.

Although there are arguments for prohibiting a variety of dangerous products, cigarettes are unique, because no other product, legal or illegal, comes close to killing the same number of people—more than traffic accidents, malaria, and AIDS combined. Cigarettes are also highly addictive. Moreover, wherever health-care costs are paid by everyone—including the United States, with its public health-care programs for the poor and the elderly—everyone pays the cost of efforts to treat the diseases caused by cigarettes.

Whether to prohibit cigarettes altogether is another question, because doing so would no doubt create a new revenue source for organized crime. It seems odd, however, to hold that the state may, in principle, prohibit the sale of a product, but may not permit it to be sold only in packs that carry graphic images of the damage it causes to human health.

After losing in Australian courts, the tobacco industry feared that the law could be copied in much larger markets, like India and China. That is, after all, where such legislation is most needed. Only about 15 percent of Australians and 20 percent of Americans smoke, but in 14 low- and middle-income countries covered in a survey published in *The Lancet*, an average of 41 percent of men smoked, with an increasing number of women taking up the habit. To prevent the spread of plain packaging legislation in those markets, tobacco-producing countries launched a complaint with the World Trade Organization (WTO), alleging that the legislation was broader than necessary to protect public health, and that it unjustifiably interfered with tobacco company trademarks on packaging.

The case against Australia's legislation was rejected by the WTO disputes panel. Two of the countries that brought the case appealed that decision, but in 2020, the Appellate dismissed the appeals. The World Health Organization hailed the decision as "a major victory for public health and tobacco control." The World Health Organization estimates that about 100 million people died from smoking in the twentieth century, and that if present patterns continue, smoking will kill up to one billion people in the twenty-first century.

Discussions of how far the state may go in promoting the health of its population often start with John Stuart Mill's principle of limiting the state's coercive power to acts that prevent harm to others. Mill could have accepted requirements for health warnings on cigarette packs, and even graphic photos of diseased lungs, if that helps people to understand the choice that they are making; but he would have rejected a ban on the sale of tobacco products.

Mill's defense of individual liberty, however, assumes that individuals are the best judges and guardians of their own interests—an idea that today verges on naiveté. The development of modern advertising techniques marks an important difference between Mill's era and ours. Corporations have learned how to sell us unhealthy products by appealing to our unconscious desires for status, attractiveness, and social acceptance. As a result, we find ourselves drawn to a product without quite knowing why. And cigarette makers have learned how to manipulate the properties of their product to make it maximally addictive.

Graphic images of the damage that smoking causes can counterbalance the power of these appeals to the unconscious, thereby facilitating more deliberative decision-making and making it easier for people to stick to a resolution to quit smoking. Instead of rejecting such laws as restricting freedom, therefore, we should defend them as ways to level the playing field between individuals and giant corporations that make no pretense of appealing to our capacities for reasoning and reflection. Requiring that cigarettes be sold in plain packs with health warnings and graphic images is equal-opportunity legislation for the rational beings inside us.

The Human Genome and the Genetic Supermarket

For a scientific discovery to be announced jointly by the president of the United States and the prime minister of the United Kingdom, it has to be something special. The completion of a "rough draft" of the human genome, announced on June 26th, is undoubtedly an important scientific milestone, but since this "most wondrous map ever produced by humankind," as President Clinton called it, does not tell us what the genes actually do, nothing much will follow from it, at least in the short run. It is as if we had learned how to read the alphabet of a foreign language, without understanding what most of the words mean. In a few years what has been done so far will be seen simply as a stepping stone on the way to the really important goal, that of understanding which aspects of human nature are genetically controlled, and by which genes. Nevertheless, the publicity accorded to gaining the stepping stone can be turned to advantage, for it may make us more ready to think seriously about the kinds of changes that could occur when we attain the further goal, a decade or two from now.

The official line is, of course, that knowing all about the human genome will enable us to discover the origins of many major diseases, and to cure them in a way that was never before possible, not by treating the symptoms, as we do now, but by eliminating the real cause—the genetic fault that gives rise to the disease or enables it to take hold of us. This will indeed be possible for some diseases. But it would be naive to think that our new knowledge of the human genome will not be put to any other use.

One indication of the kind of use to which such knowledge could be put can be seen from the advertisements that have been appearing in the last year or two in student newspapers in some of America's most prestigious universities, offering up to $50,000 for an egg from a donor who has scored extremely well in scholastic aptitude tests, and is at least 5'10" tall. Unless there are some remarkably ignorant rich people around, this sum is being offered in the knowledge that the randomness of natural human reproduction means that tall, intelligent women sometimes have short children of below average intelligence. How much would people be prepared to pay for a method that, by screening embryos, eliminated the genetic lottery, and ensured that their child would have the genetic basis for above-average intelligence, height, athletic ability, or some other desired trait?

Once this becomes technically possible, there will be pressure to prohibit it, on the grounds that it will lead to a resurgence of eugenics. But for most parents, giving their child the best possible start in life is extremely important. The desire to do so sells millions of books telling parents how to help their child achieve their potential; it causes couples to move to suburbs where the schools are better, even though they then have to spend time in daily commuting; and it stimulates saving so that the child will be able to attend a good college. Selecting the "best" genes may well benefit one's child more effectively than any of these techniques. Combine the well-known American resistance to government regulation with the fact that genetic screening could be an effective route to so widely held a goal and it seems unlikely that the US Congress will prohibit it, or if it does, that the ban will be effective.

Like it or not, then, we face a future in which eugenics will once again become an issue. Unlike earlier eugenic movements, however, it will not be state-sponsored and it will not work by coercive sterilization of the "unfit," much less by genocide. It will, instead, come about in the way that so much change comes about in America, by consumer choice, in the marketplace. That is, of course, vastly preferable to coercive eugenics, but it still raises many questions about the future of our society. Among the most troubling is: what will happen to those who cannot afford to shop at the genetic supermarket? Will their children be predestined to mediocrity? Will this be the end of the great American myth of equality of opportunity? If we do not want this to happen, we had better start thinking hard what we can do about it.

● ● ●

More than two decades have passed since I wrote the above column. In that time, genetic screening of embryos to avoid genetically based disabilities and diseases has advanced significantly. We have also learned much more about genetic influences on differences between individuals, including differences in intelligence and other factors that contribute to the abilities of individuals to succeed, in academic and economic terms. So far, these two elements have not been put together, in the way I envisaged they might be. Nevertheless, in the United States and some other countries, there are no laws against selecting embryos because they are likely to have above-average abilities in areas that are influenced by genes. I therefore continue to believe that it is only a matter of time before genetic supermarkets that screen your embryos so that you can select the one with the highest probability of qualifying to attend an elite university, or obtain a high-paying job, will be open for business.

An Ethical Pathway for Gene Editing

(with Julian Savulescu)

Ethics is the study of what we ought to do; science is the study of how the world works. Ethics is essential to scientific research in defining the concepts we use (such as the concept of "medical need"), deciding which questions are worth addressing, and what we may do to sentient beings in research.

The central importance of ethics to science is exquisitely illustrated in November 2018 by the gene editing of two healthy embryos by the Chinese biophysicist He Jiankui, resulting in the birth of baby girls, Lulu and Nana. To make the babies resistant to human immunodeficiency virus (HIV), He edited out a gene (CCR5) that produces a protein which allows HIV to enter cells. One girl has both copies of the gene modified (and may be resistant to HIV), while the other has only one (making her still susceptible to HIV).

He Jiankui invited couples to take part in this experiment where the father was HIV positive and the mother HIV negative. He offered free in vitro fertilization (IVF) with sperm washing to avoid transmission of HIV. He also offered medical insurance, expenses, and treatment capped at 280,000 RMB/CNY, equivalent to around US$40,000. The package includes health insurance for the baby for an unspecified period. Medical expenses and compensation arising from any harm caused by the research were capped at 50,000 RMB/CNY (US$7000). He said this was from his own pocket. Although the parents were offered the choice of having either gene-edited or -unedited embryos transferred, it is not clear whether they understood that editing was not necessary to protect their child from HIV, nor what pressure they felt. There has been valid criticism of the process of obtaining informed consent. The information was complex and probably unintelligible to laypeople.

The most basic ethical constraint on research involving humans is that it should not expose participants to unreasonable risk. Risks should be the minimum necessary to answer the scientific question, and the expected benefits should be proportionate to expected harms.

In deciding whether a risk is reasonable, it is important to evaluate not only the probability of achieving a benefit, but also the extent of the benefit in question. A greater expected benefit is worth greater risk than a smaller expected benefit. Avoiding HIV is certainly a benefit, but the probability that Lulu and Nana would have contracted HIV is low. In contrast, the unknown effects of the editing could cost them a normal life.

Given our ignorance of the full ramifications of changing a gene, what could justify taking the risk of a gene-editing trial in humans? The answer is, if the embryo had a catastrophic single gene disorder. Several such genetic disorders are lethal in the neonatal period, so for embryos with them, gene editing is potentially life-saving. There is a risk of off-target mutations, but the expected harm of such mutations is arguably no worse than the fate of the unedited embryos.

The geneticist George Church has defended He's research on the grounds that HIV is a public health problem for which there is no cure or vaccine. Church is right to the extent that there is no problem in principle with editing out the CCR5 gene in the future. What he fails to take into account, however, is that Lulu and Nana are being used, at great risk, and without proportionate benefit, when there are more ethical experimental designs that would meet the need for greater knowledge of the effects of editing genes.

At the conference at which He presented his experiment, George Daley, the Dean of Harvard Medical School, indicated that Huntington's disease or Tay–Sachs disease might be suitable targets for gene editing. It is not clear whether Daley is endorsing these as first-in-human trials. Huntington's disease is very different from Tay–Sachs disease. Babies with Tay–Sachs disease die in the first few years of life; people with Huntington's disease have around 40 good years. Hence Tay–Sachs disease is a better candidate for early trials, as babies with that condition have less to lose. This mirrors the rationale for experimenting with gene therapy on babies with a lethal form of ornithine transcarbamylase (OTC) deficiency rather than on adults with a mild form, such as Jesse Gelsinger, who lost his life in a badly designed gene therapy trial in 1999.

What He Jiankui did was unethical, not because it involved gene editing, but because it failed to conform to the basic values and principles that govern all research involving human participants.

Further into the future, if gene editing can be done without leading to unwanted mutations, it could be used to address genetic dispositions to common diseases, such as diabetes or cardiovascular disease. These involve tens or hundreds of genes. In principle, gene editing could be used to modify many genes accurately.

It is notable that the first human gene-edited babies were enhanced to have resistance to a disease, not to treat an existing disease. In future, perhaps gene editing will be used to engineer super-resistance to infectious threats.

At the Second International Summit on Human Genome Editing, where He revealed his research, the National Academies of Science, Engineering and Medicine called for a "translational pathway to human germ line gene editing." In our view, to be ethically justifiable, such a "translational pathway" should be: catastrophic single gene disorders (like Tay–Sachs disease), then severe single gene disorders (like Huntington's disease), then reduction in the genetic contribution to common diseases (like diabetes and cardiovascular disease), then enhanced immunity and perhaps even delaying aging.

Should the translational pathway extend to enhancing normal traits, such as intelligence? This has been the subject of almost 20 years of debate. One approach to enhancement has been to ban it. Many jurisdictions, including most in Europe and Australia, ban pre-implantation genetic diagnosis for non-disease traits. However, one US company, Genomic Prediction, has announced the use of polygenic risk scores for low normal intelligence when testing pre-implantation embryos. The company admitted the same techniques could be used to predict high normal intelligence and believe such a step is inevitable.

Further into the future, gene editing could be used for enhancement of the genetic contribution to general intelligence. China is currently funding research that is trying to unravel the genetics of high intelligence. Perhaps the best we can hope for is that wherever important enhancements, such as resistance to disease or the enhancement of intelligence (should it ever be possible) are available, they will be part of a basic healthcare plan so that everyone can benefit from them, and not only the rich.

Kidneys for Sale?

In 2009 Levy-Izhak Rosenbaum, a Brooklyn businessman, pleaded guilty to charges of having arranged the sale of three kidneys. He was sentenced to two and a half years in prison, and served more than two years before his release.

A year earlier, in Singapore, retail magnate Tang Wee Sung was sentenced to one day in jail for agreeing to buy a kidney illegally. He subsequently received a kidney from the body of an executed murderer—which, though legal, is arguably more ethically dubious than buying a kidney, since it creates an incentive for convicting and executing those accused of capital crimes.

Should selling organs be a crime? In the United States alone, 100,000 people seek an organ transplant each year, but in 2018, only 21,167 were successful. Every day, 12 Americans die from kidney failure while waiting for a transplant. Worldwide, deaths from kidney failure number in the millions.

Although buying and selling human organs is illegal almost everywhere, the World Health Organization estimates that worldwide about 10 percent of all kidneys transplanted are bought on the black market.

The most common objection to organ trading is that it exploits the poor. That view received support from a 2002 study of 350 Indians who illegally sold a kidney. Most told the researchers that they were motivated by a desire to pay off their debts, but six years later, three-quarters of them were still in debt, and regretted having sold their kidney. In contrast, when the television program *Taboo* covered the sale of body parts, it showed a slum dweller in Manila who sold his kidney so that he could buy a motorized tricycle taxi to provide income for his family. After the operation, the donor was shown driving around in his shiny new taxi, beaming happily. Should he have been prevented from making that choice? The program also showed unhappy sellers, but there are unhappy sellers in, say, the housing market as well.

To those who argue that legalizing organ sales would help the poor, Nancy Scheper-Hughes, founder of Organ Watch, pointedly replies: "Perhaps we should look for better ways of helping the destitute than dismantling them." No doubt we should, but we don't: our assistance to the poor is woefully inadequate, and leaves hundreds of millions of people living in extreme poverty.

In an ideal world, there would be no destitute people, and there would be enough altruistic donors so that no one would die while waiting to receive a kidney. Zell Kravinsky, an American who has given a kidney to a stranger, points out that donating a kidney can save a life, while the risk of dying as a result of the donation is only 1 in 4,000. Not donating a kidney, he says, thus means valuing your own life at 4,000 times that of a stranger—a ratio he describes as "obscene." But most of us still have two kidneys, and the need for more kidneys persists, along with the poverty of those we do not help.

We must make policies for the real world, not an ideal one. Could a legal market in kidneys be regulated to ensure that sellers were fully informed about what they were doing, including the risks to their health? Would the demand for kidneys then be met? Would this produce an acceptable outcome for the seller?

To seek an answer, we can turn to a country that we do not usually think of as a leader in either market deregulation or social experimentation: Iran. Since 1988, Iran has had a government-funded, regulated system for purchasing kidneys. A charitable association of patients arranges the transaction, for a set price—in 2017, equivalent to US$4600—and no one except the seller profits from it.

According to a study published in 2006 by Iranian kidney specialists, the scheme has eliminated the waiting list for kidneys in that country, without giving rise to ethical problems. A 2006 BBC television program showed many potential donors turned away because they did not meet strict age criteria, and others who were required to visit a psychologist.

If Iran's regulated system saves lives—and it seems clear that it does—then in the absence of powerful arguments against it, we should give serious consideration to following Iran's example, and improving upon it if we can. It is not obvious that the arguments against doing so are sufficiently compelling to justify the current prohibition on a regulated market in kidneys.

Deciding Who Lives
and Who Dies

You are the director of the intensive care unit in a major Austra-lian hospital. Every bed in your ICU is occupied, and every ventilator you can get your hands on is keeping alive a patient who would otherwise be dead. You get a call from the emer-gency room downstairs. A 40-year-old woman is critically ill, and likely to die unless you admit her. One of your ICU patients is over 80 years old, and others have medical conditions that, with the best care you can give them, still leave them with a life expectancy of less than five years. What do you do?

When Helga Kuhse and I were at the Monash University Centre for Human Bioethics, we ran an annual course in bio-ethics for a group of health-care professionals—often including directors of ICUs—at which we presented our participants with situations like the one I have just described. The discus-sions were lively, but, those working in ICUs told us, the sce-narios were not entirely realistic. Almost always, there was a way between the horns of the dilemma. If no ICU bed was available in the hospital to which the patient had come, a bed could usually be found in another hospital somewhere not too far away.

In March 2020, Italy had more than 40,000 confirmed cases of the novel coronavirus known as COVID-19. More than 3,000 had died. That was, in proportion to the size of Italy's population, 10 times as many cases and almost 20 times as many deaths as China had at that time.

There were not enough ICU beds and ventilators in Italy to cope with the number of patients who needed them. The situation we discussed in our bioethics course had become agonizingly real.

In normal times, the rule of allocation of ICU beds is "first come, first served." Patients already admitted to an ICU will be allowed to stay as long as they are receiving treatment that benefits them. In Italy, a working group of doctors from the Italian Society of Anaesthesia, Analgesia, Resuscitation, and Intensive Care recommended that, in the exceptional circumstances the country was facing, this rule should be suspended.

In its place, the doctors refered to the idea of triage, a term that has its origins in the need to deal with Napoleon's wounded soldiers after a battle. The word suggests sorting the injured into three classes: those who will recover without treatment, those who will die whether or not they are treated, and those for whom treatment will make the difference between life and death. Assuming that we really can determine who is in each class, it is obvious that to do the most good, we should focus our resources on those in the third class (while, one would hope, doing something to reduce the suffering of those in the other two classes).

Italy was not a battlefield, at least not in a literal sense, and so the recommendations of the working group are more nuanced, but they are equally, and quite explicitly, concerned with maximizing benefits for the greatest possible number of people. To that end, they start with the suggestion of placing an age limit on admission to the ICU, in order to admit those who have the greatest chance of survival and are likely to have the most years of life ahead of them.

Not only age, but also the broader health status of the prospective patient is relevant, the doctors say. Patients who are elderly, frail, or have other health problems in addition to the virus may occupy an ICU bed for a much longer time than younger and healthier patients. Even if the more vulnerable patients survive, the time they spent on the ventilator may have come at the cost of not using this scarce resource to save the lives of two, three, or even more younger, healthier patients. In an extreme shortage of resources, the working group says, this may mean moving out of the ICU patients who are not responding well in order to make room for others for whom there is hope of a better response.

The working group recommends taking into account the wishes of the patients, including advance declarations stating a wish not to be treated in specific circumstances.

The doctors also indicate that when patients are moved out of the ICU, this must not mean that they are simply abandoned. They must be given palliative care to reduce their suffering.

In refreshing contrast to many bioethical declarations, the working group does not shy away from bold recommendations, nor does it try to hide what it is doing in obscure or ambiguous language. It demands transparency: health-care staff should tell patients and their families exactly what is happening, and why.

The guidelines are presented in a short document, no more than twice the length of this article. They do not attempt to answer all the questions raised by the need to make life and death decisions for individual patients. How much weight should an admitting doctor give to age, which is easy to determine, as compared with life expectancy, which is arguably more significant, but always an estimate?

What about quality of life? A patient with early-onset dementia may have a longer life expectancy than a patient whose mind is still sharp: who should be preferred? Should those making admission decisions look beyond medical criteria and give priority to parents with young children over those living on their own? Or to health-care professionals, who after recovery can care for more patients?

We can hope for the best. We may never find ourselves in the desperate circumstances that Italy is in now. But it is surely wise to prepare for the worst, for if the worst does happen, we will need to act, and then we may not have time for reflection and considered discussion.

Were the Lockdowns Justified?

(with Michael Plant)

At one point in 2020 nearly four billion people, almost half the world's population, were living under government-mandated lockdowns in an effort to stop the spread of the COVID-19 coronavirus. Were the lockdowns justified?

Lockdowns have health benefits: fewer will die of COVID-19, as well as other transmissible diseases. But they also have serious costs: social isolation, unemployment, and widespread bankruptcies, to name only three of many. How should we make the trade-offs between these costs and benefits?

To get started, we need to know the size of the benefits. A group of researchers led by Olga Yakusheva, a University of Michigan economist, sought to estimate the net number of lives saved (or lost) by pandemic-mitigating policies in the United States in 2020. The team found that the lockdowns and other public-health measures saved between 913,762 and 2,046,322 lives, but also could result in an "indirect collateral loss" of 84,000 to 514,800 lives, implying that 398,962 to 1,962,322 net lives were saved. That is a wide range, but even at the low end, it still indicates that a very substantial number of lives were saved.

Yakusheva and her coauthors seek to avoid contentious ethical issues by taking into account nothing but the number of lives saved or lost. That avoids some key issues that a more adequate assessment of the costs and benefits of lockdowns should face.

First, an adequate assessment would not disregard the difference between dying at age 90 and at 20, 30, or 40. We should be counting years of life lost or saved, not simply lives.

Second, the impact of lockdowns on quality of life matters, too. Lockdowns cause widespread unemployment, for example, and that sharply reduces life satisfaction. Difficult as quality of life is to measure and quantify, a proper accounting of the costs and benefits of lockdown cannot just wave it away.

We must consider the impact of lockdowns on people who even in normal times are struggling to meet their and their families' basic needs. Governments of countries where many people live in or on the edge of extreme poverty have particularly strong reasons to avoid lockdowns, but governments of rich countries also ought not disregard the fact that a recession in the advanced economies jeopardizes the very survival of people in other countries.

Until 2020, extreme poverty had been dropping steadily for the past 20 years, hitting a low of 736 million, or less than 10% of the world's population, in 2019. According to World Bank estimates, in 2020, as a result of the pandemic, an additional 97 million people were thrust into extreme poverty. How much of that was caused by lockdowns, rather than by the virus itself, is difficult to say, but the part played by lockdowns would surely be significant.

What about the cost in terms of months or even years of education lost? According to Henrietta Fore, executive director of the United Nations Children's Fund, at the height of the pandemic, 192 countries had closed schools, leaving 1.6 billion children without in-person learning. For many, learning remotely would not have been a possibility. At least 24 million children were projected to have left school permanently. For many girls, that is likely to mean early marriage instead of the prospect of a career. School closures, combined with the economic hardship caused by the lockdowns, have caused a big increase in child labor in low-income countries.

Obviously, we are not able to provide an accurate estimate of these costs and benefits. Perhaps teams of economists and social scientists could gather the relevant data, without which we cannot say whether the lockdowns were, or were not, justified. But even if we had that data, we could not directly compare "lives saved" against "lost GDP." We need to put them into some common unit. Judging whether the benefits outweighed the costs would require converting different outcomes into a single unit of value.

One way to make progress is to consider that a lockdown, if it goes on long enough, will bring about a smaller economy that can afford fewer doctors, nurses, and medicines. In the United Kingdom, the National Health Service estimates that for about £25,000 ($30,000) it can pay for one more "quality-adjusted life year." In effect, that sum can buy a patient an extra year of healthy life.

If we then estimate how much lockdowns cost the economy, we can estimate the years of healthy life we are likely to gain now by containing the virus and compare it to how many years we are likely to lose later from a smaller economy. We have not, however, seen any sufficiently rigorous attempts to do this.

In any case, thinking solely in terms of quality-adjusted life years is too narrow. Health isn't all that matters. What we really need to do is compare the impact different policies have on our overall well-being.

To do that, we think it's best to measure well-being by using individuals' reports of how happy and how satisfied with their lives they are, an approach pioneered by academics in the World Happiness Report. Doing this means we can, in a principled way, weigh otherwise hard-to-compare considerations when deciding how to respond to COVID-19—or to any other systemic risk.

We all agree that unemployment is bad, but it's not obvious how we should trade unemployment against years of healthy life. Thinking directly in terms of well-being allows us to make this comparison. Unemployment has dire effects on well-being and has been estimated to reduce individuals' life satisfaction by 20%. With this information, we can compare the human costs of a lockdown to the well-being gained by extending lives. A broader analysis would include other impacts, such as social isolation and anxiety, and tell us when a lockdown should be lifted.

We still are not able to say whether months of government-enforced lockdowns were the right policy. We don't know, and as moral philosophers, we can't answer this question on our own. Empirical researchers need to take on the challenge of calculating the effects, not in terms of wealth or health, but in the ultimate currency, well-being.

Victims of the Unvaccinated

Novak Djokovic, the world's top-ranking tennis player at the start of 2022, was looking forward to the Australian Open, held in January. He had won it in each of the past three years. One more victory would have given him a record 21 major titles, breaking a three-way tie with Roger Federer and Rafael Nadal. The Australian government, however, requires incoming visitors to show proof of vaccination, and Djokovic had previously refused to reveal his vaccination status, calling it "a private matter and an inappropriate inquiry."

The family of Dale Weeks would disagree. Weeks, 78, was a patient at a small hospital in rural Iowa, being treated for sepsis, but the treatment was not proving effective. The hospital sought to transfer him to a larger hospital where he could have surgery, but the surge in COVID-19 patients, almost all of them unvaccinated, meant that there were no spare beds. It took 15 days for Weeks to obtain a transfer, and by then, it was too late.

Weeks was just one of the many victims of the unvaccinated. His daughter said: "The thing that bothers me the most is people's selfish decision not to get vaccinated and the failure to see how this affects a greater group of people. That's the part that's really difficult to swallow."

Around the time Weeks died, in December 2021, Rob Davidson, an emergency room physician at a hospital in Michigan, wrote an essay for the *New York Times* that provided a vivid picture of life in a hospital that had consistently been at or near capacity for several weeks. The overwhelming majority of the patients had COVID-19, and 98% of those needing acute critical care were unvaccinated.

What happened to Weeks was happening at Davidson's hospital, too: those in need of more specialized treatment could not be transferred to a larger facility because nearly every hospital in the region was already full or close to it. Davidson is unable to view the choice not to get vaccinated as a private matter. "It forces patients with ruptured appendixes and broken bones to wait for hours in my emergency department; it postpones surgeries for countless other people and burns out doctors and nurses."

That is one reason why vaccination is not a private matter; the other is that vaccinated people are less likely to spread the virus to others. That is because, first, they are less likely to get infected, and second, if they do get infected, their illness is likely to be less severe (which is why the patients needing acute critical care are, as Davidson indicated, overwhelmingly unvaccinated). Vaccinated people typically have a high load of the virus in their body for a shorter period than unvaccinated people, decreasing the amount of time in which it could spread to others.

The Australian Open is held in Melbourne, the capital of the state of Victoria, which happens to be the first jurisdiction in the world to make it compulsory to wear a seat belt in a car. The legislation was attacked as a violation of individual freedom, but

Victorians accepted it because it saved lives. Now most of the world has similar legislation. I can't recall when I last heard someone demanding the freedom to drive without wearing a seat belt.

Instead, we are now hearing demands for the freedom to be unvaccinated against the virus that causes COVID-19. Before Djokovic became the public face of unvaccinated athletes, Brady Ellison, a member of the US Olympic archery team, said that his decision not to get vaccinated before the Tokyo Olympics was "one hundred percent a personal choice," insisting that "anyone that says otherwise is taking away people's freedoms."

The oddity, here, is that laws requiring us to wear seat belts really do quite straightforwardly infringe on the freedom of the individual, whereas laws requiring people to be vaccinated if they are going to be in places where they could infect other people are restricting one kind of freedom in order to protect the freedom of others to go about their business safely.

Don't misunderstand me. I strongly support laws requiring drivers and passengers in cars to wear seat belts. In the United States, such laws are estimated to have saved approximately 370,000 lives, and to have prevented many more serious injuries. Nevertheless, these laws are paternalistic. They coerce us to do something for our own good. They violate John Stuart Mill's famous principle: "the only purpose for which power can be rightfully exercised over any member of a civilized community, against his will, is to prevent harm to others." The fact that the coercion is for the individual's own good is "not a sufficient warrant."

There is a lot to be said for this principle, especially when it is used to oppose laws against victimless crimes like homosexual relations between consenting adults, or physician aid in dying, when these acts were illegal. But Mill had more confidence in the ability of members of "civilized" communities to make rational choices about their own interest than we can justifiably have today.

Before seat belts were made compulsory, governments ran campaigns to educate people about the risks of not wearing them. These campaigns had some effect, but the number of people who wore seat belts came nowhere near the 90% or more who wear them in the United States today (with similar or higher figures in many other countries where not wearing them is an offense).

The reason is that we are not good at protecting ourselves against very small risks of disaster. Each time we get into a car, the chance that we will be involved in an accident serious enough to cause injury, if we are not wearing a seat belt, is very small. Nevertheless, given the negligible cost of wearing a belt, a reasonable calculation of one's own interests shows that it is irrational not to wear one. Car crash survivors who were injured because they were not wearing seat belts recognize and regret their irrationality—but only when it is too late, as it always is for those who were killed while sitting on their belts.

We are now seeing a very similar situation with vaccination. Brytney Cobia gave the following account of her experiences working as a doctor in Birmingham, Alabama:

> I'm admitting young healthy people to the hospital with very serious COVID infections. One of the last things they do before they're intubated is beg me for the vaccine. I hold their hand and tell them that I'm sorry, but it's too late. A few

days later when I call time of death, I hug their family members and I tell them the best way to honor their loved one is to go get vaccinated and encourage everyone they know to do the same. They cry. And they tell me they didn't know. They thought it was a hoax. They thought it was political. They thought because they had a certain blood type or a certain skin color they wouldn't get as sick. They thought it was "just the flu." But they were wrong. And they wish they could go back. But they can't.

The same reason justifies making vaccination against COVID-19 mandatory: otherwise, too many people make decisions that they later regret. One would have to be monstrously callous to say: "It's their own fault, let them die."

In any case, as we have already seen, in the COVID era, making vaccination mandatory doesn't violate Mill's "harm to others" principle. Unvaccinated Olympic athletes impose risks on others, just as speeding down a busy street does. The only "personal choice" Ellison should have had was to get vaccinated or stay at home. In a pandemic, that applies to everyone. If you are willing to stay at home, indefinitely, and not be physically close to anyone else who is not similarly isolated, fine, you should not be forced to get vaccinated. But if you are not prepared to do that, you are increasing the risk to others.

For the situation that Davidson described, and that Weeks's children believe led to their father's death, a different solution is available, one that respects the decisions of those who choose not to be vaccinated but requires them to bear the consequences of their choice. Hospitals that are at or near capacity should warn the populations they serve that, after a certain date—far enough in the future to allow ample time for people to get fully vaccinated—they will give vaccinated patients priority over unvaccinated patients with COVID-19.

After the announced date, when both a vaccinated and an unvaccinated patient with COVID-19 need the last available bed in the intensive care unit, the vaccinated patient should get it. If the last ICU bed is given to an unvaccinated patient because at the time there is no one else who needs it, and subsequently a vaccinated patient with a greater or equal need for the facility arrives, the bed should be reallocated to the vaccinated patient. The unvaccinated patient, or the family of that patient, may object; but if the move is in accord with a previously announced policy, and everyone had the opportunity to be vaccinated before the policy took effect, people must take responsibility for their own choices, especially when they have been warned that their choice could harm others, and have been told that they will be lower priority for treatment for that reason.

Hospitals with sufficient capacity should, of course, continue to treat unvaccinated patients with COVID-19 as best they can. Despite the extra strain this puts on hospital staff, everyone should have sufficient compassion to try to save lives, even when those whose lives need saving have made foolish, selfish choices.

Exceptions should be made for those few patients for whom vaccination is contra-indicated on medical grounds, but not for those who claim to have religious grounds for exemption. No major religion rejects vaccination, and if some people choose to interpret their religious beliefs as requiring them to avoid vaccination, then they, and not others, should bear the consequences.

Such a policy is likely to increase vaccination rates, which will benefit the unvaccinated as well as the vaccinated, and save lives, just as vaccine mandates have saved lives by increasing the number of vaccinated people. But even if the policy does not persuade more people to get vaccinated, at least fewer people would die from health conditions over which they have no control because others who regard vaccination as a "personal choice," and selfishly rejected it, are using scarce resources needed to save lives.

Djokovic traveled to Melbourne to play in the Australian Open, claiming that he had medical grounds for an exemption from the requirement to be vaccinated. The Australian Minister for Immigration rejected his grounds for exemption and ordered him deported, saying that his presence in the country posed a risk to public health. In a marathon five set final match, Nadal triumphed over Daniil Medvedev and became the first person ever to win 21 grand slam titles.

Ending the Taboo on Talking about Population

(with Frances Kissling and Jotham Musinguzi)

In 1968, Paul Ehrlich's bestseller *The Population Bomb* predicted that the world's population would double in less than 35 years—a frightening speed. The book had a major impact but spurred a backlash that made almost any further discussion of population radioactive.

As it turns out, Ehrlich's predictions were extreme. In 1968 the world's population was around 3.5 billion, and it only reached 7 billion in 2011, 43 years later. At today's growth rate, the next population doubling will take nearly 60 years. That slowdown gives us time to find ethical ways of sustaining ourselves and the opportunity to collaborate with stakeholders with differing perspectives on how to do so.

Still, the taboo on talking about population remains. This may be because of the controversial solutions to rapid population growth that *The Population Bomb* suggested. Ehrlich, a biologist, argued that if voluntary family planning didn't reduce population sufficiently to avoid famine and other natural disasters, then coercion and the withdrawal of food aid to some countries would be necessary and justifiable.

He had plenty of supporters, but feminists and progressives rejected such draconian solutions. When China initiated its one-child policy and reports of forced abortions emerged, feminists were in the forefront of efforts to end it. Foreign aid policies that set contraceptive targets in return for aid were condemned as violating human rights and disappeared. Feminists also contributed significantly to the taboo by urging a shift away from policies focused on population control to policies supportive of reproductive health and rights. Both feminists and population stabilization advocates now agree that providing reproductive health services to women is first and foremost a right in itself, as well as the best and most ethical way to slow population growth.

The issue of rapid population increase has not gone away. Instead, it has become regionalized. In several European countries and Japan, people are choosing to have fewer children, and there is negative or zero natural population growth. That is increasingly predicted to happen in much of Asia, including China, and the Americas. But the UN Population Division estimates that 26 African countries will at least double their present populations by 2050. By 2100, Angola, Burundi, Niger, Somalia, Tanzania, and Zambia are expected to have five times as many people as they do today. Nigeria already has an estimated population of 191 million, and women there give birth, on average, to more than five children. By 2050, Nigeria is projected to become the world's third-most populous country.

Many African family-planning advocates are concerned because society with rapid population growth means many dependent children for each adult. If fertility were reduced, there would be fewer children and more adults able to work. And if this potential workforce were adequately educated and had access to jobs, it could become the engine of economic growth, thus paying a demographic dividend to the society as a whole.

Prospects of African prosperity are also threatened by climate change. In regions that are already hot and arid, higher temperatures will make prolonged outdoor physical labor almost impossible and will also increase evaporation, further reducing already strained water resources. Yet population remains an unmentionable topic in international policy circles. None of the 17 Goals or 169 targets of the UN Sustainable Development Agenda dare to suggest that it might be desirable to slow the increase in human population, nor does this issue get much attention in World Bank documents. Researchers say they are discouraged from writing about the links between population and climate change or the survival of marine environments.

That should not be the case. The increasing recognition of reproductive health as a human right means there is less likelihood that poor countries will introduce or be coerced into draconian programs of population control. Today we should be able to safely broach the potential problems of population growth and ethical ways to respond to it.

Melinda Gates has shown one way of doing this, by focusing on making contraceptives more readily available to the 214 million women who do not want to become pregnant over the next two years but do not have effective preventive methods. Equally important is providing women with access to emergency contraception following unprotected sex and making safe abortion available to women who need it.

Finally, a central part of every discussion about population must be educating girls and women and ensuring opportunities for their participation in work and political life. Women need more options to take control of their fertility and lead fulfilling and rewarding lives.

We have learned a lot since *The Population Bomb* was published. We should not shy away from discussing what actions are ethically permissible to facilitate a stable level of population growth, nor should we leave this discussion in the hands of the affluent. The conversation about ethics, population, and reproduction needs to shift from the perspective of white donor countries to the places and people most affected by poverty, climate change, and environmental degradation.

SEX AND GENDER

Should Adult Sibling Incest
Be a Crime?

In 2014 the German Ethics Council, a statutory body that reports to the Bundestag, recommended that sexual intercourse between adult siblings should cease to be a crime. The recommendation followed a 2012 decision by the European Court of Human Rights upholding the conviction of a Leipzig man for having a sexual relationship with his sister. The man served several years in prison, owing to his refusal to abandon the relationship. (His sister was judged to be less responsible and was not jailed.)

Incest between adults is not a crime in all jurisdictions. In France, the offense was abolished when Napoleon introduced his new penal code in 1810. Consensual adult incest is also not a crime in Belgium, the Netherlands, Portugal, Spain, Russia, China, Japan, South Korea, Turkey, Côte d'Ivoire, Brazil, Argentina, and several other Latin American countries.

The Ethics Council took its investigation seriously. Its report (available only in German) begins with testimony from those in a forbidden relationship, particularly half-brothers and sisters who came to know each other only as adults. These couples describe the difficulties created by the criminalization of their relationship, including extortion demands and the threat of loss of custody of a child from a previous relationship.

The report does not attempt to provide a definitive assessment of the ethics of consensual sexual relationships between siblings. Instead, it asks whether there is an adequate basis for the criminal law to prohibit such relationships. It points out that in no other situation are voluntary sexual relationships between people capable of self-determination prohibited. There is, the report argues, a need for a clear and convincing justification for intruding into this core area of private life.

The report examines the grounds on which it might be claimed that this burden of justification has been met. The risk of genetically abnormal children is one such reason; but, even if it were sufficient, it would justify only a prohibition that was both narrower and wider than the current prohibition on incest.

The prohibition would be narrower, because it would apply only when children are possible: the Leipzig man whose case brought the issue to attention had a vasectomy in 2004, but that did not affect his criminal liability. And the goal of avoiding genetic abnormalities would justify widening the prohibition to sexual relationships between *all* couples who are at high risk of having abnormal offspring. Given Germany's Nazi past, it is difficult for Germans today to treat that goal as anything but permitting the state to determine who may reproduce.

The Council also considered the need to protect family relationships. The report notes that few families are threatened by incest between siblings, not because it is a crime, but because being brought up together in a family or family-like environment (including Israeli kibbutzim that rear unrelated children collectively) tends to negate sexual attraction. Incest between siblings is therefore a rare occurrence.

The report does recognize the legitimacy of the objective of protecting the family, however, and makes use of it to limit the scope of its recommendation to sexual relations between adult siblings. Sexual relations between other close relatives, such as parents and their adult children, are, the report argues, in a different category because of the different power relations between generations, and the greater potential for damage to other family relationships.

The taboo against incest runs deep, as the social psychologist Jonathan Haidt demonstrated when he told experimental subjects about Julie and Mark, adult siblings who take a holiday together and decide to have sex, just to see what it would be like. In the story, Julie is already on the pill, but Mark uses a condom, just to be safe. They both enjoy the experience, but decide not to do it again. It remains a secret that brings them even closer.

Haidt then asked his subjects whether it was okay for Julie and Mark to have sex. Most said that it was not, but when Haidt asked them why, they offered reasons that were already excluded by the story—for example, the dangers of inbreeding, or the risk that their relationship would suffer. When Haidt pointed out to his subjects that the reasons they had offered did not apply to the case, they often responded: "I can't explain it, I just know it's wrong." Haidt refers to this as "moral dumbfounding."

Perhaps not coincidentally, when a spokesperson for German Chancellor Angela Merkel's Christian Democrats was asked to comment on the Ethics Council's recommendation, she also said something completely beside the point, referring to the need to protect children. The report, however, made no recommendations about incest involving children, and some of those caught by the criminal law did not even know each other as children. In the case of the incest taboo, our response has an obvious evolutionary explanation. But should we allow our judgment of what is a crime to be determined by feelings of repugnance that may have strengthened the evolutionary fitness of ancestors who lacked effective contraception?

Even discussing that question has proved controversial. In Poland, a comment presenting the views of the German Ethics Council was posted online by Jan Hartman, a philosophy professor at the Jagiellonian University in Krakow. The university authorities described Hartman's statement as "undermining the dignity of the profession of a university teacher" and referred the matter to a disciplinary commission. In so quickly forgetting that the profession's dignity requires freedom of expression, a renowned university appears to have succumbed to instinct. That does not augur well for a rational debate about whether incest between adult siblings should remain a crime. Fortunately, however, after Hartman was interrogated twice by the disciplinary officer of his university, and provided evidence in support of the factual elements in his statements, the proceedings against him were discontinued.

Convincing as the reasoning of the German Ethics Council was, eight years later the German government had not acted on that recommendation.

Homosexuality Is Not Immoral

Perhaps the most remarkable change in moral attitudes of the past 20 years is the widespread acceptance, in many countries, of marriage between people of the same sex. An even wider range of countries have laws against discrimination on the basis of a person's sexual orientation, in areas like housing and employment.

When I was an undergraduate, in the 1960s, I and many other progressively minded people supported the idea that homosexuality should cease to be a crime, but we did not defend that view by arguing that it was not immoral. Instead, we followed John Stuart Mill, who in his celebrated essay *On Liberty* put forward the following principle:

> [T]he only purpose for which power can be rightfully exercised over any member of a civilized community, against his will, is to prevent harm to others. His own good, either physical or moral, is not sufficient warrant. . . . Over himself, over his own body and mind, the individual is sovereign.

Mill's principle is not universally accepted. The distinguished twentieth-century British philosopher of law, H.L.A. Hart, argued for a partial version of Mill's principle. Where Mill says that the good of the individual, "either physical or moral," is "not sufficient warrant" for state interference, Hart says that the individual's physical good *is* sufficient warrant, if individuals are likely to neglect their own best interests and the interference with their liberty is slight. For example, the state may require us to wear a seat belt when driving, or a helmet when riding a motorcycle.

But Hart sharply distinguished such legal paternalism from legal moralism. He rejected the prohibition on moral grounds of actions that do not lead to physical harm. The state may not, on his view, make homosexuality criminal on the grounds that it is immoral. That seemed right to me, and for many years I thought that Hart had provided the definitive case for abolishing the law against sodomy.

The problem with this argument, I now realize, is that it is not easy to see why legal paternalism is justified but legal moralism is not. Defenders of the distinction often claim that the state should be neutral between competing moral ideals, but is such neutrality really possible? I am not a proponent of legal moralism, but if I were, I would argue that we do, after all, appeal to a moral judgment—even if a widely shared one—when we judge that the value of riding a motorcycle with one's hair flowing free is outweighed by the risk of head injuries if one crashes.

The stronger objection to the prohibition of homosexuality is one that even Hart did not dare to make: we should object to the claim that sexual acts between consenting adults of the same sex are immoral.

Sometimes it is claimed that homosexuality is wrong because it is "unnatural," and even a "perversion of our sexual capacity," which supposedly exists for the purpose of reproduction. But we might just as well say that using artificial sweeteners is a "perversion of our sense of taste," which exists so that we can detect nourishing food. And we should always be on guard against anyone who equates "natural" with "good."

Does the fact that homosexual acts cannot lead to reproduction make them immoral? That would be a particularly bizarre ground for prohibiting sodomy in a world with eight billion people, and grave risks to biodiversity and the stability of our climate. If a form of sexual activity brings satisfaction to those who take part in it, and harms no one, what can be immoral about it?

The underlying problem with prohibiting homosexual acts, then, is not that the state is using the law to enforce private morality. It is that the law is based on the mistaken view that homosexuality is immoral.

A Private Affair?

Can a public figure have a private life? In 2007, events in three countries highlighted the importance of this question.

In the French presidential election of that year, both candidates tried to keep their domestic life separate from their campaign. The two leading candidates were Ségolène Royal and Nicolas Sarkozy. Royal was not married to François Hollande, the father of her four children. When asked whether they were a couple, Royal replied, "Our lives belong to us." Similarly, in response to rumors that Sarkozy's wife had left him, a spokesperson for Sarkozy said, "That's a private matter."

The French have a long tradition of respecting the privacy of their politicians' personal lives, and French public opinion was more broad-minded than opinion in the United States was then, where an unwed mother of four would not have been nominated for the presidency by a major party. Indeed, in that year Randall Tobias, the top foreign aid adviser in the US State Department, resigned after acknowledging that he had used an escort service described as providing "high-end erotic fantasy"—although Tobias said he only had a massage.

In Britain, Lord John Browne, the chief executive who transformed BP from a second-tier European oil company into a global giant, resigned after admitting he had lied in court about the circumstances in which he had met a gay companion (apparently, he met him through a male escort agency). In resigning, he said that he had always regarded his sexuality as a personal matter, and he was disappointed that a newspaper—*The Mail on Sunday*—had made it public.

Candidates for public office, and those holding high administrative or corporate positions, should be judged on their policies and performance, not on private acts that are irrelevant to how well they carry out, or will carry out, their public duties. Sometimes, of course, the two overlap. *The Mail on Sunday* and its sister paper, *The Daily Mail,* justified their publication of revelations by Browne's former companion on the grounds that they include allegations that Browne had allowed him to use corporate resources for the benefit of his own private business. The company denied that there was any substance to these allegations.

Tobias, as the administrator of the US Agency for International Development, implemented the Bush administration's policy that requires organizations working against HIV/AIDS to condemn prostitution if they are to be eligible for US assistance. That policy has been criticized for making it more difficult to assist sex workers who are at high risk of contracting and spreading HIV/AIDS. It's a bit of a stretch, but just possibly, the public has an interest in knowing if those who implement such policies are themselves paying for sexual services.

Where there is no suggestion that a matter of personal morality has had an impact on the performance of a business executive or government official, we should respect that person's privacy. But what about candidates for political leadership?

Since politicians ask us to entrust them with sweeping powers, it can be argued that we should know as much as possible about their morality. For example, we might reasonably ask whether they pay their fair share of taxes, or inquire about their charitable donations. Such things tell us something about their concern for the public good. Similarly, in 2004 the revelation that Mark Latham, at the time the Australian opposition leader and aspiring prime minister, had assaulted a taxi driver and broken his arm in a dispute about a fare was relevant for those who believe that a nation's leader should be slow to anger.

But does the legitimate interest in knowing more about a politician extend to details about personal relationships? It is hard to draw a line of principle around any area and determine if knowledge of it will provide relevant information about a politician's moral character. The problem is that the media have an interest in publishing information that increases their audience, and personal information, especially of a sexual nature, will often do just that.

Even so, whether people choose to marry or not, whether they are heterosexual, homosexual, bisexual, or polyamorous, whether they pay to fulfill their erotic fantasies or have fantasies they can fulfill at no cost, tells us little about whether they are good people who can be trusted with high office—unless, of course, they say one thing while doing another. If we can cultivate a wider tolerance of human diversity, politicians, business leaders, and administrators would be less fearful of "exposure," because they would realize that they have done nothing that they must hide.

Prostitution is illegal in most of the United States, including Washington, DC, and this could be one reason why Tobias had to resign. But when New Jersey Governor John Corzine was involved in a serious road accident, it became known that he violated his own state's law by not wearing his seat belt. By any sensible measure, Corzine's violation of the law was more serious than that of Tobias. Laws requiring the wearing of seat belts save many lives. Laws prohibiting prostitution do no evident good at all, and may well do harm. Yet no one suggested that Corzine should resign because of his foolish and illegal act. In the United States, at least, breaching sexual norms still brings with it a moral opprobrium that is unrelated to any real harm it may do.

How Much Should Sex Matter?

(with Agata Sagan)

Jenna Talackova reached the finals of Miss Universe Canada in 2012, before being disqualified because she was not a "natural-born" female. The tall, beautiful blonde told the media that she had considered herself a female since she was four years old, had begun hormone treatment at 14, and had sex reassignment surgery at 19. Her disqualification raised the question of what it really means to be a "Miss."

Around the same time, a question of broader significance was raised by the case of an eight-year-old Los Angeles child who is anatomically female, but dresses as, and wants to be considered, a boy. His mother tried unsuccessfully to enroll him in a private school as a boy. Is it really essential that every human being be labeled "male" or "female" in accordance with his or her sex?

People who cross gender boundaries suffer clear discrimination. In 2011, the National Center for Transgender Equality and the National Gay and Lesbian Task Force published a survey that suggested that the unemployment rate among transgender people is double that of other people. More recent surveys still report higher unemployment among transgender people, but the gap appears to have narrowed. In addition, of those respondents who were employed, 90 percent reported some form of mistreatment at work, such as harassment, ridicule, inappropriate sharing of information about them by supervisors or co-workers, or trouble with access to toilets.

Moreover, transgender people can be subject to physical violence and sexual assault as a result of their sexual identity. According to a list released for the Transgender Day of Remembrance, 375 transgender people were murdered in 2021, with 70 percent of the murders occurring in Central and South America, and one-third of them in just one country, Brazil.

Children who do not identify with the sex assigned to them at birth are in an especially awkward position, and their parents face a difficult choice. We do not yet have the means to turn young girls into biologically normal boys, or vice versa. Even if we could do it, some specialists warn against taking irreversible steps to turn them into the sex with which they identify.

Many children display cross-gender behavior or express a wish to be of the opposite sex, but when given the option of sex reassignment, only a tiny fraction undergo the full procedure. The use of hormone blocking agents to delay puberty is one option, as it offers both parents and children more time to make up their minds about this life-changing decision, but delaying puberty can have lasting effects on the child.

The broader problem remains that people who are uncertain about their gender identification, move between genders, or have both female and male sexual organs do not fit into the standard male/female dichotomy.

In 2011 the Australian government addressed this problem by providing passports with three categories: male, female, and indeterminate. The new system also allows people to choose their gender identity, which need not match the sex assigned to them at birth. The United States adopted a similar system in 2022, allowing passport applicants to use an X to indicate that their gender is "unspecified or another gender identity." Other forms of documentation will also allow the question of gender to be answered in the same manner. Such moves away from the usual rigid categorization show respect for all individuals and will save many people from the hassle of explaining to immigration officials a discrepancy between their appearance and their sex as recorded in their passport.

Nevertheless, one may wonder whether it is really necessary for us to ask people as often as we do whether they are male or female, or something else. On the Internet, we frequently interact with people without knowing that. Some people place high value on controlling what information about them is made public, so why do we force them, in so many situations, to disclose this particular piece of information about themselves?

Is the desire for such information a residue of an era in which women were excluded from a wide range of roles and positions, and thus denied the privileges that go with them? Perhaps eliminating the occasions on which this question is asked for no good reason would not only make life easier for those who can't be squeezed into strict categories, but would also help to reduce inequality for women. It could also prevent injustices that occasionally arise for men, for example, in the provision of parental leave. The same would apply to adoption, in countries in which same-sex couples are discriminated against by authorities approving adoptions. (In fact, there is some evidence that having two lesbians as parents gives a child a better start in life than any other combination.)

We do not deny that sex may be relevant in some situations. One of them is competitive sport. In 2022, Lia Thomas, a member of the University of Pennsylvania's women's swimming team, set new records in several categories. Just over a year earlier, before she came out as transgender, she had been swimming for the men's team, without being nearly as dominant. After one year of hormone replacement therapy she was eligible, under college rules, to swim as a woman. Was that fair to the competitors left in her wake, who lacked the upper body muscle development that Thomas had after going through puberty as a male? That question can only be answered by reflecting on what we are trying to achieve by the rules that govern competitive sports.

Some parents are already resisting the traditional "boy or girl" question by not disclosing the sex of their child after birth. One couple from Sweden explained that they want to avoid their child being forced into "a specific gender mold," saying that it is cruel "to bring a child into the world with a blue or pink stamp on their forehead." A Canadian couple wondered why "the whole world must know what is between the baby's legs."

Jane McCreedie, the author of *Making Girls and Boys: Inside the Science of Sex*, criticizes these couples for going too far. In the world as it is today, she has a point, because concealing a child's sex will only draw more attention to it. But if such behavior became more common—or even somehow became the norm—would there be anything wrong with it?

Many languages do not have gendered pronouns—no "he" or "she," just a single pronoun for a person. Chinese is one example. In English and some other languages that do have gendered pronouns, it has become common for people to specify, when giving their personal details, the pronouns they prefer others to use to refer to them, and if you do not wish to use "he" or "she," it has become acceptable to use the singular "they." Would it be better if everyone did that?

Ban the Burkini?

My parents came to Australia as refugees, fleeing Nazi persecution after Hitler annexed Austria. They arrived in a country eager to assimilate immigrants into its dominant Anglo-Irish culture. When they and their friends spoke German on a tram, they were told: "We speak English here!"

Assimilation of that kind has long disappeared from Australian government policy, replaced by a widely accepted form of multiculturalism that encourages immigrants to retain their distinct traditions and languages. The "burkini"—a swimsuit that covers the body from the top of the head to the feet, though not the face—is one aspect of that multiculturalism. It was invented by a Muslim woman in Sydney to enable observant Muslim girls to join their school friends and other children in the beach activities that are an important part of Australian summers.

Australians find it hard to fathom why some French seaside towns should seek to ban the burkini. Without swimming costumes that comply with their religious beliefs, observant families would not permit their daughters to go to the beach. That would reinforce, rather than reduce, ethnic and religious divides.

The burkini bans in France (some of which have since been overturned by courts) follow other French restrictions on clothing and ornamentation. Students in public schools cannot wear conspicuous religious symbols, which is usually interpreted to prohibit the headscarves worn by Islamic women, as well as the yarmulkes (skullcaps) worn by Jewish boys and large crosses worn by Christians. A full face veil—a burqa or niqab—cannot legally be worn anywhere in public.

France is often seen as a special case, because of its long history of strict separation of church and state. But in 2016, Germany's interior minister, Thomas de Maizière, proposed banning the burqa from public places such as government offices, schools, universities, and courtrooms, raising the possibility of such prohibitions spreading beyond France. It is, de Maizière said, "an integration issue," and Angela Merkel, the German Chancellor, agreed: "From my point of view, a woman who is entirely veiled has hardly any chance at integrating."

The pendulum is therefore swinging back toward assimilation, and the key question is how far that swing should go. Should a country that accepts immigrants also allow them to retain all their cultural and religious practices, even those that are contrary to values that most of the country's people consider central to their own way of life?

The right to cultural or religious practice cannot be absolute. At a minimum, that right reaches its limit when such practices may harm others. For example, children must be educated, and even if the state permits home schooling, it is entitled to set standards regarding the knowledge and skills that must be taught. In extreme cases, like forms of female genital mutilation intended to reduce sexual pleasure, almost no one supports allowing immigrants to adhere to tradition in their new country.

In France, it has been argued that allowing burkinis to be worn on beaches tacitly endorses the repression of women. To require women to cover their heads, arms, and legs when men are not similarly required is a form of discrimination. But where are we to draw a line between the widely, if not universally, accepted requirement that women must cover their breasts (also not required of men), and the greater degree of coverage of the female body required by several religions, including Islam?

It is also dubious that integration is best served by banning religious dress in public schools. This is likely to cause observant Muslims and Jews to send their children to private schools, unless private schools are also prohibited. If we really want a secular, integrated society, there is an argument for requiring every child to attend a public school; but in most Western societies, that argument has been lost.

If a society is to be more than a collection of discrete individuals or groups living within common territorial boundaries, we can reasonably want a degree of integration that enables people to mix and work together. We should reject cultural relativism—the example of female genital mutilation is enough to show that not all cultural practices are defensible. A society is justified in saying to immigrants: "You are welcome here, and we encourage you to preserve and promote many aspects of your culture, but there are some core values that you must accept."

The difficult question is to determine what these core values should be. Not harming others is a minimum, but racial and sexual equality should also be part of the core. That becomes tricky when women themselves accept restricted opportunities because of their religious beliefs. They may be the victims of a repressive ideology, but Islam is not the only religion that teaches, in at least some of its forms, that women's role in life is different from that of men.

John Stuart Mill, the great nineteenth-century liberal, thought that society should use criminal law only to prevent harm to others, but he did not think that the state had to be neutral vis-à-vis different cultures. On the contrary, he thought society has, and should use, the many means of education and persuasion available to it, in order to counter false beliefs and encourage people to find the best forms of living.

Mill would argue that if we allow sufficient time for immigrants to be exposed to the influences of education and proximity to different ways of life, they will make good choices. Given how little confidence we can have in other options, that path remains worth trying.

The Case for Legalizing Sex Work

Sex work is, as the saying goes, the world's oldest profession—except that the saying uses "prostitution" instead of "sex work." The change to a less pejorative term is warranted by a shift in attitudes toward sex workers that contributed to Amnesty International's 2016 decision to urge governments to repeal laws criminalizing the exchange of sex for money by consenting adults.

Amnesty International's appeal was met by a storm of opposition—some of it from people who were evidently failing to distinguish between the sex industry as a whole and the human trafficking that, in many countries, is a tragic part of it. No one wants to legalize coercion, violence, or fraud in the sex industry, or the use of sex workers who are not adults. But some organizations campaigning against trafficking understand that when sex work is illegal, it is much riskier for sex workers to complain to the authorities when they are enslaved, beaten, or cheated. For that reason, the International Secretariat of the Global Alliance Against Traffic in Women applauded Amnesty International for supporting decriminalization.

There was also opposition from some feminist organizations, which accused Amnesty of protecting "the rights of pimps and johns." Instead, they argued, we should "end the demand for paid sex"—but they didn't explain how this is to be done.

In species that reproduce sexually, sex is, for obvious reasons, one of the strongest and most pervasive desires. *Homo sapiens* is no exception. In every modern society, humans exchange money or other valued items for things that they desire and could not otherwise obtain. For various reasons, a significant number of people cannot get sex, or sufficient sex, or the kind of sex they want, without paying for it. Unless at least one of these conditions changes, demand for paid sex will continue. I find it hard to see how any of them will change sufficiently to eliminate that demand.

If demand for paid sex is likely to continue, what about the supply? Another response to proposals to decriminalize sex work is that we should instead change the conditions that lead people to sell their bodies. This assumes that only those who lack other means of supporting themselves would engage in sex for money.

That assumption is a myth. Leaving aside sex workers who want money because they have expensive drug habits, some could get a job in a factory or a fast-food restaurant. Faced with the prospect of monotonous, repetitive work for eight hours a day on an assembly line or flipping hamburgers, they prefer the higher pay and shorter hours that the sex industry offers. Many do not make that choice, but should we make criminals of those who do?

It's not a crazy choice. Contrary to stereotypes of paid sex, work in a legal brothel is not especially dangerous or hazardous to one's health. Some sex workers view their profession as involving greater skill and even a more human touch than alternative jobs open to them. They take pride in their ability to give not only physical pleasure, but also emotional support, to needy people who cannot get sex any other way.

If sex work is not going to disappear anytime soon, those who care about the health and safety of sex workers—not to mention their rights—should support moves to make it a fully legal industry. That is what most sex workers want as well. In the same month that decriminalization became Amnesty's official policy, the conservative government of New South Wales, Australia's most populous state, decided not to re-criminalize that state's previously legalized sex industry. Jules Kim, the CEO of Scarlet Alliance, the Australian Sex Workers Association, greeted the news with relief, saying that decriminalization had delivered "outstanding outcomes for sex workers' health and safety."

The Sex Workers Outreach Project agreed that decriminalization led to better health for sex workers, and enabled them to be covered by the standard features of the labor market, including insurance, occupational health and safety programs, and rules of fair trading. A majority of Australians now live in states that have legalized or decriminalized sex work.

This is consistent with the growing recognition in recent years that the state should be extremely reluctant to criminalize activities freely entered into by consenting adults. Laws against sodomy have been abolished in most secular countries. Physician-assisted dying is legal in an increasing number of jurisdictions. The use of marijuana is now fully legal or decriminalized in 31 US states.

The repeal of restrictive legislation has practical benefits, in addition to extending individual liberty. In Colorado, the desire to tax the marijuana industry was a major motivation for legalization. The original impetus for the legalization of the sex industry in New South Wales was an inquiry into police corruption that showed that the sex industry was a major source of police bribes. Legalization ended that in a single stroke.

Countries that criminalize the sex industry should consider the harms these laws cause, as Amnesty International has done. It is time to put aside moralistic prejudices, whether based on religion or an idealistic form of feminism, and do what is in the best interests of sex workers and the public as a whole.

DOING GOOD

Holding Charities Accountable

Suppose that, like me, you are concerned about children in Africa dying from preventable diseases. That's a bad thing, and you want to donate money to a charity that is working to reduce the toll. But there are many charities doing that. How do you choose?

The first thing that many people ask about charities is, "How much of my donation is spent on administration?" In the United States, that figure is readily available from Charity Navigator, a website that has five million users. But the information is taken from forms that the charities themselves complete and send to the tax authorities. No one checks the forms, and the proportions allocated to administration and program expenses are easily massaged with a little creative accounting.

Worse still, that figure, even if accurate, tells you nothing about the charity's impact. The pressure to keep administrative expenses low can make an organization less effective. If, for example, an agency working to reduce poverty in Africa cuts staff with expert knowledge, it is more likely to end up funding projects that fail. It may not even know which of its projects fail, because evaluating them, and learning from mistakes, requires staff—and that adds to administrative costs.

In 2006, Holden Karnofsky and Elie Hassenfeld faced the question of which charity would make the best use of their money. They were in their mid-twenties, earning six-figure incomes at an investment company—more than they needed—and were thinking about donating money to help make the world a better place. As investment advisers, they would never recommend investing in a company without detailed information about how well it was achieving its goals. They wanted to make similarly well-informed choices about the charities to which they contributed.

So Karnofsky and Hassenfeld got together with six friends who also worked in finance and divided up the field to find out which charities could be shown to be effective. They contacted organizations and received lots of attractive marketing material, but nothing that answered basic questions: what do the charities do with their money, and what evidence do they have that their activities help? They called many charities, but eventually realized something that seemed extraordinary: the information was just not there.

Some foundations said that information on their work's effectiveness was confidential. This, Karnofsky and Hassenfeld thought, is not a good way to go about charitable work. Why should information about how to help people be secret? The fact that charities were unprepared for such questions indicated to Karnofsky and Hassenfeld that other donors and foundations give more or less blindly, without the information needed to make sound decisions about whom to support.

Karnofsky and Hassenfeld now had a new goal: to obtain and publicize the information. To that end, they founded an organization called GiveWell so that other donors would not have as hard a time extracting it as they had had.

However, it soon became apparent that the task required more than part-time attention, and the following year, after raising $300,000 from their colleagues, Karnofsky and Hassenfeld left their jobs and began working full-time for GiveWell and its associated grant-making body, The Clear Fund. They invited charities to apply for grants of $25,000 in five broad humanitarian categories, with the application process demanding the kind of information that they had been seeking. In this way, a substantial part of the money they had raised would go to the most effective charity in each category, while simultaneously encouraging transparency and rigorous evaluation.

Evaluating charities can be more difficult than making investment decisions. Investors are interested in financial returns, so there is no problem about measuring distinct values—in the end it all comes down to money. It is more difficult to compare the reduction of suffering produced by restoring sight to a blind person with saving a person's life. There is no single unit of value.

In other ways, too, evaluating charities takes time, and can be expensive. Perhaps for this reason, many organizations, including some of the best-known anti-poverty organizations, did not respond to GiveWell's request for information. No doubt they calculated that a chance to get a $25,000 grant wasn't worth it.

If that was the thinking of those running the charities, they got it wrong. GiveWell has thrived, attracting support from wealthy donors and foundations, especially from Good Ventures, a philanthropic organization founded by Cari Tuna, a former journalist, and her husband, Dustin Moskovitz, one of the co-founders of Facebook. That support has enabled GiveWell to increase its staff to facilitate more research, and the amount of money that GiveWell has tracked flowing to its recommended charities has grown rapidly. In 2010, GiveWell estimated that $1.5 million had gone to its top-ranked charities as a result of its recommendations. Just five years later, in 2015, it tracked approximately $100 million in donations going to its recommended charities. In November 2021, GiveWell announced that it expected to raise at least $500 million in 2021—a sum that was, as GiveWell wrote, "a testament to our donors' trust in us and enthusiasm for our mission."

This is why the potential of GiveWell, and similar organizations, like The Life You Can Save, which grew out of a book I published in 2009, is truly revolutionary. Half a billion dollars is still only a small fraction of what could be given to highly effective charities. In the United States in 2020, $471 billion was given to charity. No one knows how effective that vast sum is in achieving the goals that donors intend to support. By giving charities an incentive to become more transparent and more focused on being demonstrably effective, GiveWell could make our charitable donations do much more good than ever before.

The current list of GiveWell's top-ranked charities is available at www.givewell.org. The Life You Can Save draws on GiveWell's recommendations along with those of other independent assessors, as well as doing some of its own research. Its recommendations are available at www.thelifeyoucansave.org.

Good Charity, Bad Charity

You are thinking of donating to a worthy cause. Good. But to which cause should you give?

If you seek help from professional philanthropy advisers, the chances are that they won't have much to say about this vital question. They will guide you, to be sure, through an array of charitable options. But the prevailing assumption in their field is that we shouldn't, or perhaps can't, make objective judgments about which options are better than others.

Take Rockefeller Philanthropy Advisors, one of the world's largest philanthropic service organizations. Its website offers a downloadable pamphlet with a chart showing areas to which a philanthropist might give: health and safety; education; arts, culture, and heritage; human and civil rights; economic security; and environment. The website then asks, "What is the most urgent issue?" and answers by saying, "There's obviously no objective answer to that question."

Is this true? I don't think so. Compare, for instance, two of the Rockefeller Philanthropy Advisors' categories: "health and safety" and "arts, culture and heritage." To me it seems clear that there are objective reasons for thinking we may be able to do more good in one of these areas than in another.

Suppose your local art museum is seeking funds to build a new wing to better display its collection. The museum asks you for a donation for that purpose. Let's say that you could afford to give $100,000. At the same time, you are asked to donate to an organization seeking to reduce the incidence of trachoma, an eye disease caused by an infectious microorganism that affects children in developing countries. Trachoma causes people to slowly lose their sight, typically culminating in their becoming blind between 30 and 40 years of age. It is preventable. You do some research and learn that each $100 you donate could prevent a person's experiencing 15 years of impaired vision followed by another 15 years of blindness. So for $100,000 you could prevent 1,000 people from losing their sight.

Given this choice, where would $100,000 do the most good? Which expenditure is likely to lead to the bigger improvement in the lives of those affected by it?

On one side we have 1,000 people spared 15 years of impaired vision followed by 15 years of blindness, with all the ensuing problems that that would cause for poor people with no social security. What do we have on the other side?

Suppose the new museum wing will cost $50 million, and over the 50 years of its expected usefulness, one million people will enjoy seeing it each year, for a total of 50 million enhanced museum visits. Since you would contribute 1/500th of the cost, you could claim credit for the enhanced aesthetic experiences of 100,000 visitors. How does that compare with saving 1,000 people from 15 years of blindness?

To answer, try a thought experiment. Suppose you have a choice between visiting the art museum, including its new wing, or going to see the museum without visiting the new wing.

Naturally, you would prefer to see it with the new wing. But now imagine that an evil demon declares that out of every 100 people who see the new wing, he will choose one, at random, and inflict 15 years of blindness on that person. Would you still visit the new wing? You'd have to be nuts. Even if the evil demon blinded only one person in every 1,000, in my judgment, and I bet in yours, seeing the new wing still would not be worth the risk.

If you agree, then you are saying, in effect, that the harm of one person's becoming blind outweighs the benefits received by 1,000 people visiting the new wing. Therefore a donation that saves one person from becoming blind would be better value than a donation that enables 1,000 people to visit the new wing. But your donation to the organization preventing trachoma will save not just one but 10 people from becoming blind for every 1,000 people it could provide with an enhanced museum experience. Hence a donation to prevent trachoma offers at least ten times the value of giving to the museum.

This method of comparing benefits is used by economists to judge how much people value certain states of affairs. It's open to criticism because many people appear to have irrational attitudes toward the small risks of very bad things happening. (That's why we need legislation requiring people to fasten their seat belts.) Still, in many cases, including the one we are now considering, the answer is clear enough.

This is, of course, only one example of how we ought to choose between areas of philanthropy. Some choices are relatively easy and others are much more difficult. In general, where human welfare is concerned, we will achieve more if we help those in extreme poverty in developing countries, as our dollars go much further there. But the choice between, say, helping the global poor directly, and helping them, and all future generations, by trying to reduce greenhouse gas emissions, is more difficult. So, too, is the choice between helping humans and reducing the vast amount of suffering we inflict on nonhuman animals.

Until recently, it wasn't even possible to find out which charities were the most effective within their own fields. But now, with independent charity evaluators like GiveWell and The Life You Can Save, we can be highly confident that a donation to, for example, the Against Malaria Foundation will save lives and reduce the incidence of malaria, and that giving to the SCI Foundation (formerly known as Schistosomiasis Control Initiative, before changing its name to something that everyone can pronounce) will, at very low cost, reduce the incidence of neglected tropical diseases, especially those caused by parasites. Or if you like the idea of giving cash and allowing the recipients to decide what to spend it on, there is GiveDirectly, which will transfer at least 90 cents of every dollar you give to an extremely low-income African family. Follow-up studies show that these cash transfers have long-term benefits for the recipients.

"Effective altruism," as this evidence-based approach to charity is known, is an international movement. Not content with merely making the world a better place, its adherents want to use their talents and resources to make the biggest possible positive difference to the world. Thinking about which fields offer the most positive impact for your time and money is still relatively new, but with more effective altruists researching the issues, we are now seeing real progress.

Heartwarming Causes
Are Nice, But . . .

If you had seen what the Make-A-Wish Foundation and the city of San Francisco did in 2013 to fulfill the superhero fantasies of a five-year-old—and not just any five-year-old, but one battling a life-threatening cancer—I'm sure you would have felt really good about it. Twenty thousand people joined in to make Miles Scott's dream to be Batkid come true. Miles got to drive with Batman in the Batmobile, and help him nab a villain and rescue a damsel in distress. Then, in front of a huge crowd, the real mayor of San Francisco awarded him the keys to the city. If that doesn't warm your heart, you must be numb to basic human emotions.

Yet we can still ask if these emotions are the best guide to what we ought to do. According to Make-A-Wish, the average cost of realizing the wish of a child with a life-threatening illness is $7,500. That sum, if donated to the Against Malaria Foundation and used to provide bed nets to families in malaria-prone regions, could save the lives of two or three children. If donated to the Fistula Foundation, it could pay for surgeries for approximately 17 young mothers who, without that assistance, will be unable to prevent their bodily wastes from leaking through their vaginas and hence are likely to be outcasts for the rest of their lives. If donated to the Seva Foundation to treat trachoma and other common causes of blindness in developing countries, it could protect 100 children from losing their sight as they grow older.

It's obvious, isn't it, that saving a child's life is better than fulfilling a child's wish to be Batkid? If Miles's parents had been offered that choice—Batkid for a day or a cure for their son's cancer—they surely would have chosen the cure.

Why then do so many people give to Make-A-Wish, when they could do so much more good with their charitable dollars? The answer lies, at least in part, in those abovementioned emotions, which, as psychological research shows, make the plight of a single identifiable individual much more salient to us than that of a large number of people we cannot identify.

In one study, people who had earned money for participating in an experiment were given the opportunity to donate some of it to Save the Children, an organization that helps poor children. One group was told things like: "Food shortages in Malawi are affecting more than three million children." A second group was shown a photo of a seven-year-old African girl, told that her name was Rokia, and urged that "her life will be changed for the better as a result of your financial gift." The second group gave significantly more. It seems that seeing a photo of Rokia triggered an emotional desire to help, whereas learning facts about millions of people in need did not.

Similarly, the unknown and unknowable children without bed nets who will be infected with malaria just don't grab our emotions like the kid with cancer we can watch on TV. That is a flaw in our emotional makeup, one that developed over millions of years when we could help only people we could see in front of us. It is not a justification for ignoring the needs of distant strangers.

Some people object that it's harder to track what happens to money sent far away. That is a concern commonly expressed by callers when I am a guest on radio programs. I remember speaking on *On Point*, a program on National Public Radio, in the United States, when Edna, clearly a generous person, told us that she volunteers one day a week at a hospital and gives to several local charities. Asked about my argument that donations go furthest when we give to impoverished people in developing countries, she said that she would do that "if I truly believed that the residents who needed that money received it, but no one's ever convinced me of that, so I give where I can see the results." Fortunately, she was followed by Meg, a family practice doctor who talked about her experiences in Haiti working with kids living on less than $2 a day. Meg pointed out that most of these children had never seen a doctor, except when they got their government vaccinations, and that $1,200 was enough to provide them with regular visits by a Haitian health-care worker for a year.

We don't have to take the word of charitable organizations that the money we give does benefit people in other countries. Technology has made it not only easier to give but easier to give effectively. Websites such as GiveWell or my own The Life You Can Save offer independent evaluations and can direct people to organizations that do not hand over money to corrupt governments but see that it gets to those who need it.

Some Americans may believe that they already do enough, through their taxes, to help poor people abroad. Polls consistently find that Americans think we spend too much on foreign aid—but when asked how much should be spent, they suggest a figure that is many times more than we actually give. In the Kaiser Family Foundation's "2013 Survey of Americans on the U.S. Role in Global Health," the median answer to the question "What percentage of the federal budget is spent on foreign aid?" was 28 percent. That result is broadly in line with a 1997 poll carried out by Kaiser, in conjunction with Harvard University and the *Washington Post*. In that poll, the median answer was 20 percent. The correct answer, both then and now, is approximately 1 percent.

Americans commonly think that the United States is a particularly generous nation, but when it comes to official foreign aid, the United States give just 17 cents in every hundred dollars that the nation earns. This is much less, as a percentage of its gross national income, than other wealthy countries. According to figures from the Organization for Economic Co-operation and Development, in 2020 Sweden, Norway, and Luxembourg gave five times as much, while Denmark, Germany, and the United Kingdom gave about four times as much, and the Netherlands, France, Switzerland, Belgium, Finland, Japan, Canada, and Ireland gave almost, or more than, twice as much. The United States, by this measure, ranks between Portugal and Poland. Charitable donations by individuals and foundations do not come anywhere near making up for this shortfall.

Perhaps if Americans knew how stingy we are when it comes to helping the world's poorest people, and were aware of opportunities to do good, we would do more. In an admittedly unscientific experiment testing this belief, The Life You Can Save offered cash to surprised strangers on street corners from

Wall Street to Santa Monica, telling them that they have a choice: keep it for themselves or donate it to the Against Malaria Foundation. Almost all of them chose to give it away—and some even added their own money to what they had just been given. Altogether, the organization gave $2,500—and the Against Malaria Foundation received back $2,421.

People who get money as a gift are likely to be more willing to give it away than those who do not receive this unexpected bounty. Nevertheless, the "giving experiment" shows not only that many Americans would like to help the global poor but also that they are genuinely happy to do so. All they need is the knowledge to be able to do so effectively.

The Ethical Cost of
High-Priced Art

In May 2014, Christie's New York salesroom sold $745 million worth of postwar and contemporary art, the highest total that it had ever reached in a single auction. Among the higher-priced works sold were paintings by Barnett Newman, Francis Bacon, Mark Rothko, and Andy Warhol, each of which sold for more than $60 million. According to the *New York Times*, Asian collectors played a significant part in boosting prices.

No doubt some buyers regard their purchases as an investment, like stocks or real estate or gold bars. In that case, whether the price they paid was excessive or modest will depend on how much the market will be willing to pay for the work at some future date.

But if profit is not the motive, why would anyone want to pay tens of millions of dollars for works like these? They are not beautiful, nor do they display great artistic skill. They are not even unusual within the artists' oeuvres. Do an image search for "Barnett Newman" and you will see many paintings with vertical color bars, usually divided by a thin line. Once Newman had an idea, it seems, he liked to work out all of the variations. Last month, someone bought one of those variations for $84 million.

A small image of Marilyn Monroe by Andy Warhol—there are many of those, too—sold for $41 million.

Ten years earlier, the Metropolitan Museum of Art in New York paid $45 million for a small *Madonna and Child* by Duccio. Subsequently, in *The Life You Can Save*, I wrote that there were better things that the donors who financed the purchase could have done with their money. I haven't changed my mind about that, but the Met's Madonna is beautifully executed and 700 years old. Duccio is a major figure who worked during a key transitional moment in the history of Western art, and few of his paintings have survived. None of that applies to Newman or Warhol.

Perhaps, though, the importance of postwar art lies in its ability to challenge our ideas. That view was firmly expressed by Jeff Koons, one of the artists whose work was on sale at the record-breaking 2014 Christie's auction. In a 1987 interview with a group of art critics, Koons referred to a work that was later sold at that auction, calling it "the 'Jim Beam' work." Koons had exhibited this piece—an oversized stainless steel toy train filled with bourbon—in an exhibition called "Luxury and Degradation," that, according to the *New York Times*, examined "shallowness, excess and the dangers of luxury in the high-flying 1980s."

In the interview, Koons said that the Jim Beam work "used the metaphors of luxury to define class structure." The critic Helena Kontova then asked him how his "socio-political intention" related to the politics of then-President Ronald Reagan. Koons answered: "With Reaganism, social mobility is collapsing, and instead of a structure composed of low, middle, and high income levels, we're down to low and high only. . . . My work stands in opposition to this trend."

Art as a critique of luxury and excess! Art as opposition to the widening gap between the rich and the poor! How noble and courageous that sounds. But the art market has no difficulty in co-opting any radical demands that a work of art makes, and turning it into another consumer good for the super-rich. When Christie's put Koons's work up for auction, the toy train filled with bourbon sold for $33 million.

If artists, art critics, and art buyers really had any interest in reducing the widening gap between the rich and the poor, they would be focusing their efforts on developing countries, where spending a few thousand dollars on the purchase of works by indigenous artists could make a real difference to the well-being of entire villages.

Nothing I have said here counts against the importance of creating art. Drawing, painting, and sculpting, like singing or playing a musical instrument, are significant forms of self-expression, and our lives would be poorer without them. In all cultures, and in all kinds of situations, people produce art, even when they are struggling to satisfy their basic physical needs.

But we don't need art buyers to pay millions of dollars to encourage people to do that. In fact, it would not be hard to argue that sky-high prices have a corrupting influence on artistic expression.

As for why buyers pay these outlandish sums, my guess is that they think that owning original works by well-known artists will enhance their own status. If so, that may provide a means to bring about change: a redefinition of status along more ethically grounded lines.

In a more ethical world, to spend tens of millions of dollars on works of art would be status-lowering, not status-enhancing.

Such behavior would lead people to ask: "In a world in which five million children die each year because they lack safe drinking water or mosquito nets, or because they have not been immunized against measles, couldn't you find something better to do with your money?"

Extreme Altruism

Fifty years ago, in an essay entitled "Famine, Affluence, and Morality," I invited readers to imagine that they are walking past a shallow pond when they see a small child who has fallen in and seems to be drowning. You could easily rescue the child, but your expensive new shoes would be ruined. Would it be wrong to ignore the child and walk on?

When I ask audiences for a show of hands on that question, they are usually unanimous in saying that it would be wrong to put one's shoes first. I then point out that by donating to a charity that protects children in developing countries from malaria, diarrhea, measles, or inadequate nutrition, we can all save a child's life.

It's a simple argument, until we realize that, having saved one child by donating to an effective charity, we have the opportunity to save another, and another, and another. Must we stop all spending on luxuries, so that we can save yet another life, giving until giving more would make us as poor as those we are helping?

My example of saving the drowning child echoes in the title of Larissa MacFarquhar's remarkable book, *Strangers Drowning*. The core of the book is a series of profiles of people who live according to a highly demanding moral standard. Let's take a glimpse at some of the people MacFarquhar profiles in her book.

Even as a child, Julia Wise felt that if each person is equally valuable, she should not care more for her own well-being than for anyone else's. If someone else could derive greater benefit from the money Julia would pay for ice cream, it would be better if she gave the money to that person. Julia started giving her savings to charities like Oxfam. When she fell in love with Jeff Kaufman, they agreed that they would both donate a large part of what they earned—currently it's about half of their income. (Wise wrote about her life at www.givinggladly.com.)

Kimberly Brown-Whale was a pastor at a church in Essex, Maryland, when she saw a news report about a young woman who needed a kidney transplant. Without a lot of thought, she called to offer one of her kidneys. Though she turned out not to be a good match for the young woman, a nurse asked her if she would be willing to donate her kidney to someone else. She agreed, joining an increasing number of people who donate their kidneys to strangers. (I know of one, Chris Croy, who was prompted to do so by a philosophy class discussion of "Famine, Affluence, and Morality.")

One rainy night, Baba Amte, the son of a wealthy Indian landowner, encountered a dying leper. Baba overcame his initial disgust and fear of catching the disease and shielded the leper from the rain. The experience stayed with him, leading him to found a leper colony. Within a few years, several thousand lepers and people with other disabilities were living there in a thriving community. After Baba died, his sons carried on his work.

Sue Hoag was 12 when she read a book about a family that adopted several needy children, and from then on, she wanted to do that, too. When she met and married Hector Badeau, they decided to have two children of their own and adopt two. They did so, but they could not shut out the knowledge that other children were in desperate need of a good home—children who were unlikely to be adopted because of a disability or their race, age, or a history of violence. Hoag and Badeau were not at all wealthy, but they ended up with a family of 20 adopted children, as well as their two biological children.

MacFarquhar interweaves these profiles with discussions of attitudes to altruism expressed by, among others, Bernard Mandeville, Adam Smith, Immanuel Kant, Charles Darwin, and Sigmund Freud. Many of these thinkers were hostile to altruism, or even denied that it exists. When MacFarquhar told her friends that she was writing a book about "do-gooders," she found that they became uncomfortable with the idea that some people not only profess, but also live by, extremely demanding moral principles. MacFarquhar found the hostility puzzling—why don't we just admire people who do so much for others, rather than dismiss them as "weird"?

The answer may be that we, too, feel that we ought to live much more ethically, and the people described in *Strangers Drowning* are a standing reproach to our own way of life. If they can live by higher moral standards, then so could we. If we could believe that all altruists are hypocrites, we would not feel so bad; but *Strangers Drowning* demonstrates that this comfortable belief is false. There are people who devote their lives to others, for no reward other than the knowledge that they are helping others and acting in accord with their own values. Many of them find their lives immensely rewarding and fulfilling. But that is not why they do it.

The Lives You Saved

In 2019, I published a new, fully revised edition of *The Life You Can Save: Acting Now to End World Poverty*, and made it available, free, as an eBook and audiobook, from www.thelifeyoucansave.org. The chapters of the audiobook are read by celebrities, including Paul Simon, Kristen Bell, Stephen Fry, Natalia Vodianova, Shabana Azmi, and Nicholas D'Agosto. Revising the book led me to reflect on the impact it has had, while the research involved in updating it made me focus on what changed during the ten years between the two editions.

The book argues that for middle-class people living in affluent countries, abiding by the traditional moral rules against lying, stealing, maiming, or killing is not enough. Living ethically in today's interconnected world involves helping people who, through no fault of their own, are suffering in ways that we could easily prevent or alleviate.

This argument influenced many readers to change their lives. Among them was Cari Tuna, who with her husband, Dustin Moskovitz, a co-founder of Facebook and Asana, created a foundation aimed at doing the most good possible with the billions of dollars they have given it. They have provided funding to GiveWell, enabling it to expand its team of researchers who are rigorously assessing charities to find those that save or improve lives the most per dollar and dramatically increasing the funds that flow through to those charities.

Charlie Bresler was at the peak of his career with a national menswear chain when he picked up a copy of *The Life You Can Save*. Reading it awoke a deep-seated dissatisfaction with work that, for all its financial rewards, did not really accord with his fundamental values. At that time, the book had spawned an organization, also called The Life You Can Save, but it had no full-time staff and wasn't accomplishing much.

Charlie contacted me with an offer: he was willing to take on the task of building up the organization into something that would effectively spread the ideas contained in the book. What made the offer too good to refuse was that he didn't want to be paid for his time—in fact, Charlie and his wife Diana have been substantial donors to The Life You Can Save. As a result, the organization is now directing many donors to the most highly effective nonprofit organizations. To date, it has been able to track $65 million in donations that have gone to those nonprofits as a result of its work.

What has happened to extreme poverty in the decade since the first edition was published? To answer this question, let's first ask what extreme poverty is. As defined by the World Bank, to be in extreme poverty is to lack sufficient income to meet one's basic needs and those of dependent family members. The 2009 edition of my book refers to 1.4 billion people living below this line. The good news is that, over the next decade, and despite a steadily increasing world population, that figure was nearly halved, to 736 million. (The pandemic pushed it up again, to 833 million, but in 2021 it started to come down once more.)

That encouraging drop in extreme poverty is paralleled by another, perhaps even more significant figure. Each year, the United Nations Children's Fund (UNICEF) publishes its estimate of the number of children dying before their fifth birthday. Most of these deaths are related to extreme poverty and its consequences, including malnutrition, lack of clean water and sanitation, diseases such as malaria, and the absence of even minimal health care. In the first edition, the most recent estimate of child deaths was 9.7 million. By 2020, it was down to 5 million.

To put that extraordinary success in perspective, suppose that an Airbus A380, with a child in every seat, is about to crash, killing everyone on board. Somehow, with great skill, the pilot manages to land the plane safely. The story would be all over the media, and the pilot would be touted as a hero.

Now, imagine that the pilots of 21 fully laden A380s have informed air controllers that they are likely to crash. As the news quickly spreads, people become aware that more than 10,000 children could be killed. We would all be glued to the latest reports, hoping that at least some of the children would be saved. What a sense of relief we would experience if, somehow, they were *all* saved!

Well, that is approximately the number of children—11,780, to be exact—whose lives have been saved, and are being saved, every day, by the reduction in child mortality over the past ten years.

Not all of this gain is the result of aid. Much of it has been brought about by economic growth, especially in China and South Asia. But aid, when it is well thought out, carefully implemented, and, most important, independently tested and verified in the field, plays an important role. It can, at extraordinarily low cost, save lives, prevent or cure blindness, improve nutrition, give children an education, and enable people to start small businesses.

HAPPINESS

Happiness, Money, and Giving It Away

Would you be happier if you were richer? Many people believe that they would be. But research conducted over many years suggests that greater wealth implies greater happiness only at quite low levels of income. People in the United States, for example, are, on average, richer than New Zealanders, but they are not happier. More dramatically, people in Austria, France, Japan, and Germany appear to be no happier than people in much poorer countries, like Brazil, Colombia, and the Philippines.

Comparisons between countries with different cultures are difficult, but the same effect appears *within* countries, except at very low income levels, such as below $12,000 annually for the United States. Beyond that point, an increase in income doesn't make a lot of difference to people's happiness. Americans are richer than they were in the 1950s, but they are not happier. Americans in the middle-income range today—that is, a family income of $50,000–$90,000—have a level of happiness that is almost identical to well-off Americans, with a family income of more than $90,000.

Most surveys of happiness simply ask people how satisfied they are with their lives. We cannot place great confidence in such studies, because this kind of overall "life satisfaction" judgment may not reflect how much people really enjoy the way they spend their time.

My former Princeton University colleague Daniel Kahneman and several co-researchers tried to measure people's subjective well-being by asking them about their mood at frequent intervals during a day. In an article published in *Science in 2006*, they reported that their data confirm that there is little correlation between income and happiness. On the contrary, Kahneman and his colleagues found that people with higher incomes spent more time in activities that are associated with negative feelings, such as tension and stress. Instead of having more time for leisure, they spent more time at and commuting to work. They were more often in moods that they described as hostile, angry, anxious, and tense.

Of course, there is nothing new in the idea that money does not buy happiness. Many religions instruct us that attachment to material possessions makes us unhappy. The Beatles reminded us that money can't buy us love. Even Adam Smith, who told us that it is not from the butcher's benevolence that we get our dinner, but from his regard for his self-interest, described the imagined pleasures of wealth as "a deception" (though one that "rouses and keeps in continual motion the industry of mankind").

Nevertheless, there is something paradoxical about this. Why do governments all focus on increasing per capita national income? Why do so many of us strive to obtain more money, if it won't make us happier?

Perhaps the answer lies in our nature as purposive beings. We evolved from beings who had to work hard to feed themselves, find a mate, and raise children. For nomadic societies, there was no point in owning anything that one could not carry, but once humans settled down and developed a system of money, that limit to acquisition disappeared.

Accumulating money up to a certain amount provides a safeguard against lean times, but today it has become an end in itself, a way of measuring one's status or success, and a goal to fall back on when we can think of no other reason for doing anything, but would be bored doing nothing. Making money gives us something to do that feels worthwhile, as long as we do not reflect too much on why we are doing it.

Consider, in this light, the life of the American investor Warren Buffett. For many years, he ranked as the second wealthiest person in the world, after Bill Gates, and in 2021 *Forbes* magazine ranks him sixth, with his fortune calculated at $96 billion. Yet his frugal lifestyle shows that he does not particularly enjoy spending large amounts of money. Even if his tastes were more lavish, he would be hard-pressed to spend more than a tiny fraction of his wealth.

From this perspective, once Buffett earned his first few millions in the 1960s, his efforts to accumulate more money might seem completely pointless. Is Buffett a victim of the "deception" that Adam Smith described, and that Kahneman and his colleagues have studied in more depth?

Coincidentally, Kahneman's article appeared the same week that Buffett announced the largest philanthropic donation in US history—$30 billion to the Bill and Melinda Gates Foundation and another $7 billion to other charitable foundations. Even when the donations made by Andrew Carnegie and John D. Rockefeller are adjusted for inflation, Buffett's is greater.

With a single stroke, Buffett gave purpose to his life. Since he is an agnostic, his gift is not motivated by any belief that it will benefit him in an afterlife. What, then, does Buffett's life tell us about the nature of happiness?

Perhaps, as Kahneman's research would lead us to expect, Buffett spent less of his life in a positive mood than he would have if, at some point in the 1960s, he had quit working, lived on his assets, and played a lot more bridge. But, in that case, he surely would not have experienced the satisfaction that he can now rightly feel at the thought that his hard work and remarkable investment skills will, through the Gates Foundation, help to cure diseases that cause death and disability to billions of the world's poorest people. Buffett reminds us that there is more to happiness than being in a good mood.

Can We Increase Gross National Happiness?

The small Himalayan kingdom of Bhutan is known internationally for two things: high visa fees, which reduce the influx of tourists, and its policy of promoting "gross national happiness" instead of economic growth. The two are related: more tourists might boost the economy, but they would damage Bhutan's environment and culture, and so reduce happiness in the long run.

When I first heard of Bhutan's goal of maximizing its people's happiness, I wondered if it really meant anything in practice, or was just another political slogan. I found out that it meant a lot when, in 2011, I was invited to Bhutan's capital, Thimphu, to speak at a conference on "Economic Development and Happiness," organized by Prime Minister Jigme Y. Thinley and co-hosted by Jeffrey Sachs, Director of The Earth Institute at Columbia University and Special Adviser to the then-United Nations Secretary-General Ban Ki-moon.

Never before have I been at a conference that was taken so seriously by a national government. I had expected Thinley to open the conference with a formal welcome, and return to his office. Instead, his address was a thoughtful review of the key issues involved in promoting happiness as a national policy. He then stayed at the conference for the entire two and a half days, and made pertinent contributions to our discussions. At most sessions, several cabinet ministers were also present.

Since ancient times, happiness has been universally seen as a good. Problems arise when we try to agree on a definition of happiness, and to measure it.

One important question is whether we see happiness as the surplus of pleasure over pain experienced over a lifetime, or as the degree to which we are satisfied with our lives. The former approach tries to add up the number of positive moments that people have, and then to subtract the negative ones. If the result is substantially positive, we regard the person's life as happy; if negative, as unhappy. So, to measure happiness defined in that way, one would have to sample moments of people's existence randomly, and try to find out whether they are experiencing positive or negative mental states.

A second approach asks people: "How satisfied are you with the way your life has gone so far?" If they say they are satisfied, or very satisfied, they are happy, rather than unhappy. But the question of which of these ways of understanding happiness best captures what we should promote raises fundamental questions of value.

On surveys that use the first approach, countries like Nigeria, Mexico, and Brazil, and the U.S. territory of Puerto Rico, do well, which suggests that the answer may have more to do with the national culture than with objective indicators like health, education, and standard of living. When the second approach is taken, it tends to be the richer countries, like Denmark and Switzerland, that come out on top. But it is not clear whether people's answers to survey questions in different languages and in different cultures really mean the same thing.

We may agree that our goal ought to be promoting happiness, rather than income or gross domestic product, but, if we have no objective measure of happiness, does this make sense? John Maynard Keynes famously said: "I would rather be vaguely right than precisely wrong." He pointed out that when ideas first come into the world, they are likely to be woolly, and in need of more work to define them sharply. That may be the case with the idea of happiness as the goal of national policy.

Bhutan has a Gross National Happiness Commission, chaired by the prime minister, which screens all new policy proposals put forward by government ministries. If a policy is found to be contrary to the goal of promoting gross national happiness, it is sent back to the ministry for reconsideration. Without the Commission's approval, it cannot go forward.

One controversial law that did go ahead—and that indicates how willing the government is to take tough measures it believes will maximize overall happiness—was a ban on the sale of tobacco. Bhutanese may bring into the country small quantities of cigarettes or tobacco from India for their own consumption, but not for resale—and they must carry the import-tax receipt with them any time they smoke in public. (The government lifted the ban during the coronavirus pandemic, to reduce cross-border travel from illegal tobacco smugglers that could spread the virus.)

As a result of a Bhutanese-initiated resolution, the United Nations General Assembly has recognized the pursuit of happiness as a fundamental human goal and noted that this goal is not reflected in GDP. The resolution invited member states to develop additional measures that better capture the goal of happiness. Bhutan also convened a panel discussion on the theme of happiness and well-being during the General Assembly's 66th session. These discussions are part of a growing international movement to re-orient government policies toward well-being and happiness.

With more scientists working on measuring happiness and understanding what increases it, the idea of happiness as a goal of public policy is gradually gaining support. We should wish the effort well, and hope that ultimately the goal becomes global, rather than merely national, happiness.

The Moral Urgency of Mental Health

(with Michael Plant)

If we can prevent great suffering at no cost to ourselves, we ought to do so. That principle is widely accepted and difficult to dispute. Yet Western governments are neglecting an opportunity to reduce the great misery caused by mental illness, even though the net cost would be nil.

The evidence for this claim comes from research by a team of economists at the London School of Economics. The team, directed by Richard Layard, drew on data from four major developed countries (Australia, Britain, Germany, and the United States) in which people were asked to indicate, on a 0–10 scale, how satisfied they were with their life.

The researchers refer to those in the bottom 10% of the population in terms of life satisfaction as being in "misery." Respondents also answered other questions designed to indicate factors affecting life satisfaction.

When Layard's team analyzed the results, they found that the biggest factors affecting misery were all non-economic: mental health, physical health, and whether someone had a partner. Mental health was the biggest predictor of all; it explained twice as much of the difference between people in terms of life satisfaction as physical health or income inequality did. (This was also true for those in the non-miserable 90% of the population.)

Overall, the researchers claim, eliminating depression and anxiety would reduce misery by 20%, whereas eliminating poverty would reduce it by just 5%—and this research was done before the COVID-19 pandemic and the resulting lockdowns, which increased the number of people with mental health problems, especially among younger people. If we want to reduce misery in the developed world, then mental health is the biggest challenge we need to overcome.

Many people will find this result surprising. After all, most of us expect that we would become happier if we were richer. So why is mental health, not poverty, the biggest cause of misery?

The answer is that people adapt to higher levels of income over time—a phenomenon known as "hedonic adaptation"—and they compare their income to that of their peers. This gives rise to the so-called Easterlin Paradox, the finding that although richer people are more satisfied with their lives than poorer people, economic growth has often not increased overall life satisfaction in the developed world. If your neighbor becomes richer, you feel poorer. If both of you become richer, neither of you is likely to be significantly happier. In contrast, people do not adapt to poor mental health; nor does your neighbor's misery make you feel better.

Given that mental health has the greatest impact on life satisfaction, we still need to ask if addressing it is the most cost-effective way for governments to reduce misery. Layard and his colleagues asked how much the British government would have to spend to tackle mental health, physical health, unemployment, or poverty. They concluded that mental health would be the cheapest of the four options: around 18 times more cost-effective in reducing misery and promoting happiness than targeting poverty.

In the United Kingdom, it costs about £650 per patient to provide psychotherapy, which is effective for about 50% of patients. That figure indicates how much governments would need to spend, but does not take into account what they might get back.

Reducing mental illness enables many people to return to work, thereby reducing the cost of unemployment benefits while increasing tax receipts. Hence, Layard and his colleagues hypothesized that treating mental health would pay for itself. In effect, the UK government would be able to reduce misery at no cost.

Further economic research, this time by Paul Frijters and his colleagues, also of the LSE, has now assessed the impact of the UK's Improving Access to Psychological Therapies program, a scheme conceived by Layard and the psychologist David Clark, which was launched in 2008. They conclude that the increase in tax receipts and the reduction in unemployment benefits pay back only about 20% of the cost of treating mental illness. However, they argue that mental health treatment still funds itself because those who receive psychotherapy demand far fewer physical health services.

In reality, the UK didn't shrink its health budget. The effect of treating mental health therefore was to free up other resources that were used for other patients. But this effect was so substantial that Frijters claims we could expand treatment to all 12% of the UK population who have mild to moderate anxiety or depression and expect the investment to pay for itself in savings in no more than two or three years.

Attitudes toward mental health have changed dramatically in the last few years; even princes and athletes now feel able to open up about it. In the UK, a study showed that mental illness affects one in four people in any year, while research carried out in 30 European countries found that 38% of the population suffered from some kind of mental or neurological illness. What has not been grasped is that this suffering is largely avoidable.

Governments in affluent countries are starting to regard mental health as seriously as they do physical health. But they could do much more. Increasing their spending on mental health could reduce an immense amount of misery—and at no cost in the long run. Moreover, as mental illness is worldwide, we need to make efforts to reduce it everywhere, including in countries where governments are unable to provide health-care services. Fortunately, charities like Strong Minds are finding that by training local people, it is possible to provide low-cost but highly effective help even to impoverished rural villagers suffering from moderate depression or anxiety, and some other forms of mental illness.

Of course, some mental illnesses are more difficult to treat than moderate depression or anxiety, and at some point higher spending may not pay for itself. But until that point has been reached, we should all agree on the moral urgency of a radical expansion in funding, both public and through non-government organizations, for mental health.

Prisoners of Pain

In 2017, an Egyptian court sentenced Laura Plummer, a 33-year-old English shop worker, to three years in prison for smuggling 320 doses of tramadol into the country. Tramadol is a prescription opioid available in the United Kingdom for pain relief. It is banned in Egypt, where it is widely abused. Plummer said that she was taking the drug to her Egyptian boyfriend, who suffers from chronic pain, and that she did not know she was breaking Egyptian law.

The UK media have been full of sympathetic stories about Plummer's plight, despite the fact that she was carrying a quantity in excess of that for which a UK doctor can write a prescription. Whatever the rights and wrongs of Plummer's conviction and sentence, however, the case illuminates an issue with much wider ramifications.

In October 2016, the *Lancet* Commission on Palliative Care and Pain Relief issued an impressive 64-page report arguing that relieving severe pain is a "global health and equity imperative." The Commission is not the first to make such a claim, but its report brings together an abundance of evidence to demonstrate the seriousness of the problem. Each year 25.5 million people die in agony for lack of morphine or a similarly strong painkiller. Only 14% of the 40 million people requiring palliative care receive it.

The report begins with a doctor's account of a man suffering agonizing pain from lung cancer. When the doctor gave him morphine, he was astonished by the difference it made; but when the patient returned the next month, the palliative-care service had run out of morphine. The man said he would return the following week with a rope; if he could not get the tablets, he would hang himself from the tree visible from the clinic's window. The doctor commented: "I believe he meant what he said."

Citizens of affluent countries are used to hearing that opioids are too easy to get. In fact, according to data from the International Narcotics Control Board and the World Health Organization, access to these drugs is shockingly unequal.

In the United States, the quantity of available opioids—that is, drugs with morphine-like effects on pain—is more than three times what patients in need of palliative care require. In India—where the man threatening to hang himself was from—the supply is just 4% of the quantity required; in Nigeria, it's only 0.2%. People in the United States suffer from over-prescription of opioids, while people in developing countries are often suffering because of under-prescription.

Although it is generally the poor who lack access to opioids, the main problem is not, for once, cost: doses of immediate-release, off-patent morphine cost just a few cents each. The *Lancet* Commission argues that an "essential package" of medicines would cost lower-middle-income countries only $0.78 per capita per year. The total cost of closing the "pain gap" and providing all the necessary opioids would be just $145 million a year at the lowest retail prices (unfairly, opioids are often more expensive for poorer countries than richer ones). In the context of global health spending, this is a pittance.

People suffer because relieving pain is not a public policy priority. There are three main explanations for this. First, medicine is more focused on keeping people alive than on maintaining their quality of life. Second, patients suffering a few months of agony at the end of life are often not well positioned to demand better treatment.

Third, and perhaps most important, is opiophobia. The misplaced fear that allowing opioids to be used in hospitals will fuel addiction and crime in the community has led to tight restrictions on their use, and clinicians are not trained to provide them when they are needed.

While opioids can be harmful and addictive, as America's current crisis demonstrates, the fact that something can be dangerous is not sufficient reason to impose extreme restrictions on its clinical use. Risks are justified when the expected benefits clearly outweigh the expected harms. Policymakers in the developing world are making a choice to impose what the WHO calls "overly restrictive regulations" on morphine and other essential palliative medicines. Low or zero access is neither medically nor morally justified.

Designing a system that provides adequate access to morphine without encouraging over-prescription or leaking drugs onto the black market is tricky but not impossible. The Lancet Commission draws attention to the Indian state of Kerala, where trained volunteers are at the center of community-based palliative care, bolstered by international collaboration with the

WHO, university researchers, and non-governmental organizations. There is no incentive to over-prescribe, and no evidence of opioid diversion.

Another model worthy of study, the Commission says, is Uganda, where a hospice run by an NGO supplies the national public health-care system with oral morphine.

Laura Plummer's smuggling of painkillers was doubtless foolish; her experience in an Egyptian jail will be a personal tragedy. But if her story is true, she is also a victim of the excessively tight restrictions on opioids that prevented her boyfriend from obtaining tramadol legally.

Plummer's case thus highlights a broader misfortune: that so many citizens of developing countries are denied effective pain relief by governments in the grip of opiophobia. This is not merely foolish; in the words of the Lancet Commission, it is also a "medical, public health, and moral failing and a travesty of justice."

No Smile Limit

If you were to walk along the streets of your neighborhood with your face up and an open expression, how many of those who passed you would smile, or greet you in some way?

Smiling is a universal human practice, although readiness to smile at strangers varies according to culture. In Australia, where being open and friendly to strangers is not unusual, the city of Port Phillip, an area covering some of the bayside suburbs of Melbourne, used volunteers to find out how often people smile at those who pass them in the street. It then put up signs that look like speed limits, but instead tell pedestrians that they are in, for example, a "10 Smiles Per Hour Zone."

Frivolous nonsense? A waste of taxpayers' money? Mayor Janet Bolitho says no, putting up the signs is an attempt to encourage people to smile or say "G'day"—the standard Australian greeting—to both neighbors and strangers as they stroll down the street. Smiling, she adds, encourages people to feel more connected with each other and safer, so it reduces fear of crime—an important element in the quality of life of many neighborhoods.

In a related effort to get its residents to know each other, the city government also facilitates street parties. It leaves the details to the locals, but offers organizational advice, lends out barbecues and sun umbrellas, and covers the public liability insurance. Many people who have lived in the same street for many years meet each other for the first time at a street party.

All of this is part of a larger program that attempts to measure changes in the city's quality of life, so that the city council can know whether it is taking the community in a desirable direction. The council wants Port Phillip to be a sustainable community, not merely in an environmental sense, but also in terms of social equity, economic viability, and cultural vitality.

Port Phillip is serious about being a good global citizen. Instead of seeing private car ownership as a sign of prosperity, the city hails a *declining* number of cars—and rising use of public transport—as a sign of progress in reducing greenhouse gas emissions while encouraging a healthier lifestyle in which people are more inclined to walk or ride a bike. The city is also seeking designs for new buildings that are more energy efficient.

Some local governments see their role as being to provide basic services like collecting the trash and maintaining the roads—and of course, collecting the taxes to pay for this. Others promote the area's economy, by encouraging industry to move to the area, thus increasing jobs and the local tax base. The Port Phillip city government takes a broader and longer-term view. It wants those who live in the community after the present generation has gone to have the same opportunities for a good quality of life as today's residents have. To protect that quality of life, it has to be able to measure all the varied aspects that contribute to it—and friendliness is one of them.

For many governments, both national and local, preventing crime is a far higher priority than encouraging friendship and cooperation. But, as Professor Richard Layard of the London School of Economics has argued in his recent book *Happiness: Lessons from a New Science*, promoting friendship is often easy and cheap, and can have big payoffs in making people happier. So why shouldn't that be a focus of public policy?

Very small positive experiences can make people not only feel better about themselves, but also be more helpful to others. In the 1970s, American psychologists Alice Isen and Paula Levin conducted an experiment in which some randomly selected people making a phone call found a ten-cent coin left behind by a previous caller, and others did not. All subjects were then given an opportunity to help a woman pick up a folder of papers she dropped in front of them.

Isen and Levin claimed that of the 16 who found a coin, 14 helped the woman, while of the 25 who did not find a coin, only one helped her. A further study found a similar difference in willingness to mail an addressed letter that had been left behind in the phone booth: those who found the coin were more likely to mail the letter.

Although later research has cast doubt on the existence of such dramatic differences, there is little doubt that being in a good mood makes people feel better about themselves and more likely to help others. Psychologists refer to it as the "glow of goodwill." Why shouldn't taking small steps that may produce such a glow be part of the role of government?

Happy, Nevertheless

Harriet McBryde Johnson | 1957–2008

I met Harriet McBryde Johnson in the spring of 2001, when I was giving a lecture at the College of Charleston. Her brand of Southern etiquette prescribed that if you're not prepared to shoot on sight, you have to be prepared to shake hands, so when I held out mine, she reached up from her powered wheelchair and took it with the three working fingers on her right hand. She added that she was attending my lecture as a supporter of Not Dead Yet, the disability rights organization that a year and a half earlier blockaded Princeton University's Nassau Hall in protest against my appointment as a professor of bioethics. I told her I looked forward to an interesting exchange.

My lecture, "Rethinking Life and Death," was a defense of the position that had aroused such vehement opposition. I pointed out that physicians routinely withdraw life support from severely disabled newborns, and I argued that this is not very different from allowing parents to decide, in consultation with their doctors, to end the life of a baby when the child has disabilities so serious that the family believes this will be best for the child or for the family as a whole.

When I finished, Johnson, who was born with a muscle-wasting disease, spoke up. I was saying, she pointed out, that her parents should have been permitted to kill her shortly after her birth. But she was now a lawyer, enjoying her life as much as anyone. It is a mistake, she said, to believe that having a disability makes life less worth living.

Our exchange of views continued for a few minutes in the lecture theater, and by e-mail afterward. Years later, when I read her autobiographical book, *Too Late to Die Young*, I wasn't surprised to see "arguing hard" listed among the pleasures of her life.

The following year, I invited her to Princeton to speak to a large undergraduate class I was teaching. She accepted but on condition that in public we avoid the informality of using first names that I had, in my Australian way, adopted over e-mail. She was also unwilling to accept the inequality implied in "Professor Singer" and "Ms. Johnson." I agreed that she could address me as Mr. Singer.

She described the visit to Princeton in "Unspeakable Conversations," her memorable cover article for *The New York Times Magazine* in 2003. She wrote beautifully, her powers of recollection were remarkable (she wasn't taking notes at the time), and she was more generous to me than I had a right to expect from someone whose very existence I had questioned. She even wrote that she found me good company, as indeed I found her.

After she spoke, I arranged for her to have dinner with a group of undergraduates who met regularly to discuss ethical questions. I sat on her right, and she occasionally asked me to move things to where she could reach them. At one point her right elbow slipped out from under her, and as she was not able to move it back, she asked me to grasp her wrist and pull it forward. I did so, and she could then again reach her food with her fork. I thought nothing of the incident, but when she told some of her friends in the disability movement about it, they were appalled that she had called on me to help her. I'm pleased that she had no difficulty with it. It suggests that she saw me not simply as "the enemy" but as a person with whom it was possible to have some forms of human interaction.

My students talked about Johnson's visit for a long time, and our conversations stayed with me, too. Her life was evidently a good one, and not just for herself, because her legal work and political activism on behalf of the disabled was valuable to others as well. I know that surveys have found that people living with disabilities show a level of satisfaction with their lives that is not very different from that of people who are not disabled. Have people with long-term disabilities adjusted their expectations downward, so that they are satisfied with less? Or do even severe disabilities really make no difference to our happiness, once we get used to them?

Over the next six years we e-mailed sporadically. If I wrote or spoke on disability issues, she would send me her criticisms, and that would lead to a flurry of e-mail messages that at least clarified the points on which we disagreed. I tried to persuade Johnson that her attribution of rights to humans with severe intellectual disabilities had implications for how we should think about animals too, since they could enjoy their lives as much as, or more than, the people whose right to life she was defending. She didn't object to the argument but felt she had enough issues to handle without getting into a new area altogether. We found it easier to agree on religion, for neither of us had any, and on our dislike for the direction the country was taking under the presidency of George W. Bush.

According to her sister, Beth, what most concerned Harriet about dying was "the crap people would say about her." And sure enough, among the tributes to her were several comments about how she can now run and skip through the meadows of heaven—doubly insulting, first because Johnson did not believe in a life after death, and second, why assume that heavenly bliss requires you to be able to run and skip?

POLITICS

The Founding Fathers' Fiscal Crises

Americans are fond of speaking in reverential tones about "the wisdom of the Founding Fathers"—that is, the men who wrote the United States Constitution. But the manner in which the House of Representatives has been able to bring the government—or, at least, its non-essential services—to a halt makes the Founding Fathers look rather foolish.

The fundamental cause of the fiscal crisis lies in the Founding Fathers' belief in the doctrine of the separation of powers. That doctrine has always been philosophically controversial.

Thomas Hobbes, writing during the English Civil War, opposed the separation of powers, believing that only a strong and unified central government could ensure peace. John Locke, for his part, was more concerned with curbing monarchical power and regarded the separation of legislative and executive powers as one way to do that.

Having fought against what they regarded as the tyranny of George III, the American revolutionaries wanted to ensure that no such tyranny could arise in the new nation that they were establishing. To do so, they wrote the doctrine of the separation of powers into its constitution.

As a result, neither the US president nor cabinet officials are members of the legislature, and they cannot be removed from office by a legislative majority. At the same time, the legislature controls the budget and the government's ability to borrow. The potential for impasse is obvious.

We might think that the Founding Fathers deserve the credit for the fact that the US government has never devolved into tyranny. But the same can be said of Britain's government, despite the absence of a constitutional separation of powers between the legislature and the executive—indeed, despite the absence of a written constitution altogether.

Nor have former British colonies like Australia, New Zealand, and Canada become tyrannies. In contrast to the United States, however, the prime minister and cabinet officials in all of these countries are members of the legislature, and governments hold office only so long as they retain the confidence of a majority of the parliament's lower house (or, in New Zealand, of its only house). If the legislature denies the executive the money that it needs to run the government, the government falls and is replaced by a new government, perhaps on a caretaker basis pending an early election.

Given the US Constitution's fundamental flaw, what seems improbable is not any particular crisis, such as that which halted parts of the government in 2013, but the fact that such impasses between the legislature and the executive have not caused chaos more often. That is testimony to most US legislators' common sense and to their willingness to compromise in order to avoid doing serious harm to the country they serve. But this common sense has been less evident over the past decade.

Constitutional amendments in the United States must be ratified by three-quarters of the states, which means that at present there is no realistic prospect of changing the constitution sufficiently to overcome the flaw that has made such crises possible. But a different factor that contributes to the hyperpartisan nature of US politics today could be changed without amending the constitution. We can best grasp this problem by asking why many members of Congress who have voted in the House of Representatives to force the government to shut down are not worried that their tactics—which will undoubtedly harm many of their constituents—will fuel an electoral backlash.

The answer is that the districts from which House members are elected are gerrymandered to an extent that citizens of most other democracies would consider preposterous. This happens because responsibility for drawing the districts' boundaries generally falls to state legislatures, where the party in control is free to draw them to its own advantage. Over the past decade, the Republicans have controlled most state legislatures, often enabling them to win a majority of House seats despite lacking the support of a majority of the American public.

The gerrymandering of US electoral districts means more than that the House of Representatives is not representative of the population as a whole; it also means that many incumbents are in no danger of losing their seat in an election. The real danger—especially in the Republican Party—comes largely from those who are further to the right than the incumbent. To be seen as a moderate is to risk defeat, not at the hands of voters as a whole, but in the Republican Party's nomination contests, in which high turnout among the party's most fervently committed members gives them disproportionate influence over outcomes.

One could imagine cool heads in both parties cutting a deal based on an understanding that it is in America's interest to establish an impartial commission to draw fair boundaries for all House electoral districts. There is no constitutional barrier to such an arrangement. In America's current environment of extreme political polarization, however, such an outcome is almost as unlikely as a constitutional amendment preventing the House of Representatives from denying the government the funds that it needs to govern.

Why Vote?

As an Australian citizen, I have voted in every federal election since I turned 18. That's not unusual. In most Australian federal elections, the turnout of registered voters is at least 95%. That figure contrasts markedly with elections in the United States, where the 62% turnout in 2020 was the highest since 1960. In congressional elections that fall in the middle of a president's term, usually fewer than 40% of eligible Americans bother to vote.

There is a reason why so many Australians vote. In the 1920s, when voter turnout fell below 60%, Parliament made voting compulsory. Since then, despite governments of varying political complexions, there has been no serious attempt to repeal the law, which polls show is supported by about 70% of the population.

Australians who don't vote receive a letter asking why. Those without an acceptable excuse, like illness or travel abroad, must pay a small fine, but the number fined is less than 1% of eligible voters.

In practice, what is compulsory is not casting a valid vote, but going to the polling place, having one's name checked off, and putting a ballot paper in the box. The secrecy of the ballot makes it impossible to prevent people leaving their ballot papers blank or, if they prefer, writing obscenities on them. While the percentage of invalid votes is a little higher where voting is compulsory, it comes nowhere near offsetting the difference in voter turnout.

Compulsory voting is not unique to Australia. Belgium and Argentina introduced it earlier, and it is practiced in many other countries, especially in Latin America, although both sanctions and enforcement vary.

Still, that isn't a full explanation of why I have voted in every federal election, because for some of them I was living in the United States, and so under no compulsion to vote. I have, of course, had my preferences regarding which party should govern Australia, but that also doesn't explain why I went to some trouble to vote, since the likelihood that my vote would decide the outcome of the election was minuscule (and, predictably, it never has).

When voting is voluntary, and the chance that the result will be determined by any single person's vote is extremely low, even the smallest cost—for example, the time it takes to stroll down to the polling place, wait in line, and cast a ballot—is sufficient to make voting seem irrational. Yet if many people follow this line of reasoning, and do not vote, a minority of the population can determine a country's future, leaving a discontented majority.

If we look around, we can find many examples of that. In the 2005 national elections in Poland, barely 40% of those eligible voted, the lowest total since the advent of free elections after the communist period. As a result, Jarosław Kaczyński was able to become prime minister with the support of a coalition of parties that gained a majority of seats in Parliament, despite receiving only six million votes, out of a total of 30 million eligible voters.

When voters in Poland were forced to go to the polls again only two years later, it became evident that many of those who had not voted in 2005 were unhappy with the outcome. Turnout rose to nearly 54%, with the increase especially marked among younger and better-educated voters.

Kaczyński's government suffered a heavy defeat.

If we don't want a small minority to determine our government, we will favor a high turnout. Yet since our own vote makes such a tiny contribution to the outcome, each of us still faces the temptation to get a free ride, not bothering to vote while hoping that enough other people will vote to keep democracy robust and to elect a government that is responsive to the views of a majority of citizens.

But there are many possible reasons for voting. Some people vote because they enjoy it, and would have nothing better to do with the time saved if they did not. Others are motivated by a sense of civic duty that does not assess the rationality of voting in terms of the possible impact of one's own ballot.

Still others might vote not because they imagine that they will determine the outcome of the election, but because, like football fans, they want to cheer their team on. They may vote because if they don't, they will be in no position to complain if they don't like the government that is elected. Or they may calculate that while the chances of their determining the outcome are only one in several million, the result is of such importance that even that tiny chance is enough to outweigh the minor inconveniences of voting.

If these considerations fail to get people to the polls, however, compulsory voting is one way of overcoming the free-rider problem. The small cost imposed on not voting makes it rational for everyone to vote and at the same time establishes a social norm of voting. Australians *want* to be coerced into voting. They are happy to vote, knowing that everyone else is voting, too. Countries worried about low voter turnout would do well to consider the Australian model.

Is Citizenship a Right?

Should your government be able to take away your citizenship?

In the United Kingdom, the government has had the legal authority to revoke naturalized Britons' citizenship since 1918. Until the terrorist bombings on the London transport system in 2005, this power was rarely exercised. Between then and the end of 2021, the British government revoked the citizenship of 175 people on national security grounds. While serving as British Home Secretary, Theresa May declared that citizenship is "a privilege, not a right."

Most of those whose citizenship has been revoked held dual nationality. Mohamed Sakr, however, did not. His parents came to Britain from Egypt, but he was not an Egyptian citizen. Therefore, by stripping him of citizenship, the UK government made him stateless.

Sakr appealed the decision from Somalia, where he was living. His case was strong, because the UK Supreme Court subsequently ruled in a different case that the government does not have the power to make a person stateless. Nevertheless, Sakr discontinued his appeal, apparently because he was concerned that the use of his cell phone was revealing his location to US intelligence services. Months later, while still in Somalia, he was killed in an American drone attack. Subsequently the British government amended legislation to state that the Home Secretary must, when revoking someone's citizenship, have a reasonable belief that this does not render the person stateless.

In the United States, citizenship can be revoked only on limited grounds, such as fraud committed in the citizenship application or service in another country's military. Arguably, joining a terrorist organization hostile to the United States is even worse than joining a foreign army, because terrorist organizations are more likely to target civilians. But one important difference is that if people who join other countries' military forces lose their US citizenship, they can presumably become citizens of the country for which they are fighting. Terrorist organizations usually have no such ties to a particular government.

The 1961 United Nations Convention on the Reduction of Statelessness, to which Britain is a signatory, does allow countries to declare their citizens stateless if it is proved that they have done something "prejudicial to the vital interests of the country." UK legislation does not require any judicial or public proof even of the weaker claim that someone's presence in the country is not conducive to the public good. Should the person whose citizenship is revoked mount an appeal, the government is not required to disclose to the appellant the evidence on which it has based its decision. Though governments are bound to make mistakes from time to time in such cases, judges or tribunals will be unable to probe the evidence put before them. Another, more sinister possibility is deliberate abuse of these powers to get rid of citizens whose presence in the country is merely inconvenient.

There is a strong case for an appeal system that allows for full and fair review of decisions to revoke citizenship. But governments will respond that to make the evidence available to a person believed to be involved with a terrorist organization could reveal intelligence sources and methods, thus jeopardizing national security.

The ability to revoke citizenship without presenting any evidence in public is one reason why a government may prefer this course to arresting and trying terrorism suspects. And yet simply revoking citizenship does not solve the problem of leaving at large a suspected terrorist, who may then carry out an attack elsewhere—unless, as with Sakr, he is killed.

The larger question raised by the UK's proposed legislation is the desirable balance between individual rights, including the right to citizenship, and the public good. Suppose that the government gets it right 19 times out of 20 when it relies on suspicion of involvement in terrorist activities to revoke people's citizenship. If that were the case with the decisions made by the UK government in 2013, there would still be a high probability that an innocent naturalized citizen was made stateless. That is a grave injustice.

Suppose, however, that the 19 people correctly suspected of involvement in terrorism were able to return to Britain, and one carried out a terrorist attack similar to the London transport bombings, which killed 52 innocent people (the four bombers also died). In the face of such atrocities, it is difficult to insist that individual rights are absolute. Is it better to have one innocent person unjustly made stateless, or to have 52 innocent people killed and many others injured?

The much greater harm done by the terrorist attack cannot be ignored; but when a democratic government starts to revoke citizenship and make people stateless, it sets a precedent for authoritarian regimes that wish to rid themselves of dissidents by expelling them, as the former Soviet Union did to the poet and later Nobel laureate Joseph Brodsky—among many others. In the absence of global citizenship, it may be best to retain the principle that citizenship is not to be revoked without a judicial hearing.

The Spying Game

Thanks to Edward Snowden, I now know that the US National Security Agency is spying on me. It uses Google, Facebook, Verizon, and other Internet and communications companies to collect vast amounts of digital information, no doubt including data about my e-mails, cell phone calls, and credit card usage.

I am not a US citizen, so it's all perfectly legal. And, even if I were a US citizen, it is possible that a lot of information about me would have been swept up anyway, though it may not have been the direct target of the surveillance operation.

Should I be outraged at this intrusion on my privacy? Has the world of George Orwell's *1984* finally arrived, three decades late? Is Big Brother watching me?

I don't feel outraged. Based on what I know so far, I don't really care. No one is likely to be reading my e-mails or listening in on my Skype calls. The volume of digital information that the NSA gathers would make that an impossible task.

Instead, computer programs mine the data for patterns of suspicious activity that intelligence analysts hope will lead them to terrorists. The process is not all that different from the data collection and analysis that many corporations use to target their ads at us more effectively, or that give us the online search results that we are most likely to want.

The question is not what information a government, or business, gathers, but what they do with it. I would be outraged if there were evidence that—for example—the US government was using the private information that it scoops up to blackmail foreign politicians into serving US interests, or if such information were leaked to newspapers in an effort to smear critics of US policies. That would be a real scandal.

If, however, nothing of that sort has happened, and if there are effective safeguards in place to ensure that it does not happen, then the remaining question is whether this huge data-gathering effort really does protect us against terrorism, and whether we are getting value for money from it. The NSA claims that communications surveillance has prevented more than 50 terrorist attacks since 2001. I don't know how to evaluate that claim, or whether we could have prevented those attacks in other ways.

The value-for-money question is even more difficult to assess. In 2010, the *Washington Post* produced a major report on "Top Secret America." After a two-year investigation involving more than a dozen journalists, the *Post* concluded that no one knows how much US intelligence operations cost—or even how many people American intelligence agencies employ.

At the time, the *Post* reported that 854,000 people held "top secret" security clearances. Just three years later, that figure was reported to be 1.4 million. (The sheer number of people does make one wonder whether misuse of personal data for blackmail or other private purposes is inevitable.)

Whatever we think of the NSA surveillance program itself, the US government has clearly overreacted to the release of information about it. It revoked Snowden's passport, and wrote to governments asking them to reject any asylum request that he might make. Most extraordinary of all, it seems that the United States was behind the apparent refusal of France, Spain, Italy, and Portugal to permit Bolivian President Evo Morales's airplane to enter their airspace en route home from Moscow, on the grounds that Snowden might have been aboard. Morales had to land in Vienna, and Latin American leaders were furious at what they took to be an insult to their dignity.

Supporters of democracy ought to think long and hard before prosecuting people like Julian Assange, Bradley Manning, and Snowden. If we think that democracy is a good thing, then we must believe that the public should know as much as possible about what the government it elects is doing. Snowden has said that he made the disclosures because "the public needs to decide whether these programs and policies are right or wrong."

He's right about that. How can a democracy determine whether there should be government surveillance of the kind that the NSA is conducting if it has no idea that such programs exist? Indeed, Snowden's leaks also revealed that National Intelligence Director James Clapper misled the US Congress about the NSA's surveillance practices in his testimony at a hearing held in March by the Senate Intelligence Committee.

When the *Washington Post* (along with *The Guardian*) published the information that Snowden provided, it asked Americans whether they support or oppose the NSA's intelligence-gathering program. Some 58% of those surveyed supported it. Yet the same poll found that only 43% supported prosecuting Snowden for disclosing the program, while 48% were opposed.

Is Marx Still Relevant?

From 1949, when Mao Zedong's communists triumphed in China's civil war, until the collapse of the Berlin Wall 40 years later, Karl Marx's historical significance was unsurpassed among thinkers. Nearly four of every ten people on Earth lived under governments that claimed to be Marxist, and in many other countries Marxism was the dominant ideology of the left, while the policies of the right were often based on how to counter Marxism.

Once communism collapsed in the Soviet Union and its satellites, however, Marx's influence plummeted. On the 200th anniversary of Marx's birth on May 5, 1818, it isn't far-fetched to suggest that his predictions have been falsified, his theories discredited, and his ideas rendered obsolete. So why should we care about his legacy in the twenty-first century?

Marx's reputation was severely damaged by the atrocities committed by regimes that called themselves Marxist, although there is no evidence that Marx himself would have supported such crimes. But communism collapsed largely because, as practiced in the Soviet bloc and in China under Mao, it failed to provide people with a standard of living that could compete with that of most people in the capitalist economies.

These failures do not reflect flaws in Marx's depiction of communism, because Marx never depicted it: he showed not the slightest interest in the details of how a communist society would function. Instead, the failures of communism point to a deeper flaw: Marx's false view of human nature.

There is, Marx thought, no such thing as an inherent or biological human nature. The human essence is, he wrote in his *Theses on Feuerbach*, "the ensemble of the social relations." It follows, then, that if you change the social relations—for example, by changing the economic basis of society and abolishing the relationship between capitalist and worker—people in the new society will be very different from the way they were under capitalism.

Marx did not arrive at this conviction through detailed studies of human nature under different economic systems. It was, rather, an application of Hegel's view of history. According to Hegel, the goal of history is the liberation of the human spirit, which will occur when we all understand that we are part of a universal human mind. Marx transformed this "idealist" account into a "materialist" one, in which the driving force of history is the satisfaction of our material needs, and liberation is achieved by class struggle. The working class will be the means to universal liberation because it is the negation of private property, and hence will usher in collective ownership of the means of production.

Once workers owned the means of production collectively, Marx thought, the "springs of cooperative wealth" would flow more abundantly than those of private wealth—so abundantly, in fact, that distribution would cease to be a problem. That is why he saw no need to go into detail about how income or goods would be distributed. In fact, when Marx read a proposed platform for a merger of two German socialist parties, he described phrases like "fair distribution" and "equal right" as "obsolete verbal rubbish." They belonged, he thought, to an era of scarcity that the revolution would bring to an end.

The Soviet Union proved that abolishing private ownership of the means of production does not change human nature. Most humans, instead of devoting themselves to the common good, continue to seek power, privilege, and luxury for themselves and those close to them. Ironically, the clearest demonstration that the springs of private wealth flow more abundantly than those of collective wealth can be seen in the history of the one major country that still proclaims its adherence to Marxism.

Under Mao, most Chinese lived in poverty. China's economy started to grow rapidly only after 1978, when Mao's successor, Deng Xiaoping (who had proclaimed that "It doesn't matter if a cat is black or white, as long as it catches mice"), allowed private enterprises to be established. Deng's reforms eventually lifted 800 million people out of extreme poverty, but also created a society with greater income inequality than any European country (and much greater than the United States). Although China still proclaims that it is building "socialism with Chinese characteristics," and under Xi Jinping has once again given more prominence to Marx, it is not easy to see what is socialist, let alone Marxist, about its economy.

If China is no longer significantly influenced by Marx's thought, we can conclude that in politics, as in economics, he is indeed irrelevant. Yet his intellectual influence remains. His materialist theory of history has, in an attenuated form, become part of our understanding of the forces that determine the direction of human society. We do not have to believe that, as Marx once incautiously put it, the hand-mill gives us a society with feudal lords, and the steam-mill a society with industrial capitalists. In other writings, Marx suggested a more complex view, in which there is interaction among all aspects of society.

The most important takeaway from Marx's view of history is negative: the evolution of ideas, religions, and political institutions is not independent of the tools we use to satisfy our needs, nor of the economic structures we organize around those tools, and the financial interests they create. If this seems too obvious to need stating, it is because we have internalized this view. In that sense, we are all Marxists now.

Should We Honor Racists?

In the Fall of 2015 I was teaching Practical Ethics at Princeton University when, in the middle of the class, several students stood up and walked out. They were joining hundreds of others in a protest led by the Black Justice League (BJL), one of many student groups that have emerged across the United States in response to police killings of unarmed African Americans.

Later that day, members of the BJL occupied the office of Princeton University President Christopher Eisgruber, vowing not to leave until their demands were met. These demands included "cultural competency training" for both academic and non-academic staff; a requirement that students take classes on the history of marginalized people; and the provision of a "cultural affinity space" on campus dedicated specifically to African American culture. But the demand that received national attention was for the university's Woodrow Wilson School of Public and International Affairs, and Wilson College, one of its residential colleges, to be renamed. The college dining hall features a large mural of Wilson, which the BJL also wanted removed. Honoring Wilson, the League said, is offensive to Black students, because Wilson was a racist.

Wilson was a progressive in domestic affairs and an idealist in foreign policy. His administration passed laws against child labor and granted new rights to workers, as well as reforming banking laws and challenging monopolies. In the aftermath of World War I, he insisted that foreign policy be guided by moral values, and advocated democracy and national self-determination in Europe.

Yet his policies for Blacks were reactionary. In 1913, when he became US president, he inherited a federal government that employed many Blacks, some working alongside whites in mid-level management positions. Under his administration, racially segregated workplaces and washrooms, which had been abolished at the end of the Civil War, were re-introduced. Black managers were demoted to more menial positions. When a delegation of Blacks protested, he told them that they should regard segregation as a benefit.

Wilson's name features prominently at Princeton not only because he is one of the university's most famous alumni (and the only one to receive the Nobel Peace Prize), but also because, before he was US president, he was Princeton's president. In the words of Anne-Marie Slaughter, a former dean of the Woodrow Wilson School, he "perhaps did more than anyone else to transform [Princeton] from a preppie gentlemen's preserve into a great research university."

Wilson is famous worldwide for the "Fourteen Points" that he proposed as the basis of a peace treaty to end World War I. He called for autonomy for the peoples of the Austro-Hungarian and Ottoman Empires, as well as an independent Polish state. No wonder, then, that there is a Wilson Square in Warsaw, that

Prague's main train station is named after him, and that there are Wilson streets in both Prague and Bratislava.

Among the other Fourteen Points are calls for open covenants—no secret treaties plotting the postwar division of another country's territory—and for a reduction in trade barriers. Perhaps most momentous is the proposal for the formation of "a general association of nations . . . for the purpose of affording mutual guarantees of political independence and territorial integrity to great and small states alike. "That call led to the founding of the League of Nations, the predecessor of the United Nations, which from 1920 until 1936 had its headquarters in the Palais Wilson, in Geneva. The building retains that name, and is today the headquarters of the UN High Commissioner for Human Rights.

History is full of deeply flawed people who did great things. In the United States, we have only to look at slave-owning Founding Fathers and early presidents like George Washington, Thomas Jefferson, and James Madison. One might plead on their behalf that, in contrast to Wilson, they were at least no worse than the standards that prevailed in their time. But is that sufficient grounds to continue commemorating them?

A New Orleans school board thought not. After adopting a resolution declaring that no school should be named after a slaveholder, it renamed George Washington Elementary School after a Black surgeon who fought for desegregation of blood transfusions. Should the name of the country's capital city be reconsidered, too?

In his book *Veil Politics in Liberal Democratic States,* Ajume Wingo describes how "political veils" gloss over a political system's historical details, creating an idealized visage. The same happens to great—or not-so-great—political leaders, who become symbolic vehicles for inculcating civic virtues.

As our moral standards shift, however, different characteristics of the historical person become more relevant, and the symbol can develop a different meaning. When Wilson's name was added to Princeton's School of Public and International Affairs in 1948, Rosa Parks's famous bus ride was still seven years away, and segregation in the American South was not under serious challenge. Now it is unthinkable. Wilson's racism therefore becomes more salient, and he ceases to embody the values that are important to Princeton University today.

Nevertheless, for nearly five years after the BJL's protests, Wilson College and the Woodrow Wilson School of Public and International Affairs retained their names, although a monument was erected outside the School acknowledging Wilson's racism. The students who led the protests had graduated, and one might have thought the matter would rest there. It was not until 2020, after the very public police murder of George Floyd, that Princeton University acknowledged that his segregationist policies made it inappropriate to have a School of Public and International Affairs named after him. It also removed his name from the college.

Wilson's contributions to the university, the United States, and the world cannot and should not be erased from history. They should, instead, be recognized in a manner that creates a nuanced conversation about changing values, and includes both his positive achievements and his contribution to America's racist policies and practices. At Princeton, one outcome of that conversation should be the education of students and faculty who would otherwise be unaware of the complexity of an important figure in the university's history.

Is Violence the Way to Fight Racism?

Should rallies by neo-Nazis and white supremacists be met with violence?

That question was raised by the tragic events in Charlottesville, Virginia, on August 12, 2017. White supremacists held a rally to protest the planned removal from a public park of a statue of Robert E. Lee, the leader of the Confederate army during the Civil War. A counter-protest was organized, and street fighting broke out. A woman was killed and 19 people injured when a white nationalist drove his car at high speed into a crowd of counter-protesters.

At a subsequent press conference, President Donald Trump said that "both sides" were to blame for what happened. Trump's apparent equation of racists and opponents of racism was condemned in the strongest terms, even by some leading Republicans. There can, of course, be no equating of neo-Nazis and white supremacists with those who oppose racism. But a close reading of the transcript of Trump's remarks suggests that a more charitable interpretation is possible.

Rather than putting the racists and anti-racists on the same footing, Trump was saying that both sides were to blame for the violence that broke out. In support of that claim, he said that some on the left "came charging with clubs in their hands, swinging clubs," and added: "Do they have a problem? I think they do."

That statement still ignores the fact that a white supremacist used his car as a weapon, with lethal results. Nothing comparable was done by any of the anti-racists.

Still, it is true that, as journalists covering the event for the *New York Times* reported, some of the counter-protesters used clubs against white nationalists, one of whom left the park bleeding from the head. The *Times* was careful to note that many of the counter-protesters were nonviolent, but in a subsequent article, the newspaper described the growth of a loose association of leftists who call themselves "antifa," a term derived from "anti-fascist," and are ready to fight neo-Nazis with sticks and fists.

In interviews, antifa activists explained their position. "You need violence to protect nonviolence," said Emily Rose Nauert. "That's what's very obviously necessary right now. It's full-on war, basically." Other antifa activists said that it is not unethical to use violence to stop white supremacists, because they have already, by stirring up hatred against minorities, caused violent attacks on individual members of those groups.

The *Times* also spoke to anti-racist activists who disavow violence. They follow the example of the strictly nonviolent forms of civil disobedience successfully used in the civil rights movement during the 1950s and 1960s under the leadership of Martin Luther King. In contrast, antifa supporters say that racists and white nationalists are not rational, so there is no point in trying to persuade them that they are wrong. Physical force is the only thing that will stop them.

Let's grant that the antifa activists are right about the irrationality of hard-core racist fanatics. It remains true that in the United States, and other countries where elections are the path to power, the far right can achieve its goals only by winning over middle-of-the-road voters. Even if many of these voters are also not completely rational—few people are—they are not likely to be won over to the anti-racist cause by seeing footage of anti-racists hitting racists with clubs or throwing urine-filled water bottles.

Such images convey, more than anything else, the idea that anti-racists are hooligans looking for a fight. Dignified nonviolent resistance and disciplined civil disobedience are more conducive to demonstrating a sincere ethical commitment to a better, non-racist society than clubbing people and hurling piss at them.

Violent resistance is particularly dangerous in the United States because some states allow anyone to carry a firearm. In Charlottesville, a large number of white supremacists paraded through the streets dressed in camouflage and carrying semi-automatic assault rifles. If the antifa activists are going to match the racists in violence, will it be possible to hold the line at clubs? How long will it be before the deadly weapons now openly on display are also used?

That last sentence was part of this essay when it was first published, in 2017. We now know the answer to the question I posed: three years. For in August 2020, Kyle Rittenhouse, a 17-year-old boy who had expressed opposition to the Black Lives Matter movement, armed himself with an assault rifle and drove for half an hour to Kenosha, Wisconsin, where a Black Lives Matter protest was taking place. There he shot and killed two people and injured a third. The person he injured had a handgun. Rittenhouse was subsequently charged with murder and pleaded self-defense. He was acquitted.

Some antifa activists trace the origin of the movement to groups that fought against fascists in Europe in the 1920s and 1930s. In Germany, in the years before Hitler came to power, the Nazis' paramilitary Stormtroopers beat up, sometimes fatally, Jews and political opponents. In self-defense, the left responded with its own militias: the Communist Party's Red Front Fighters and the Social Democrats' Iron Front.

The result was an escalation of street violence, and a sense, among the wider public, that law and order were breaking down. Many came to believe that a firm hand was required to restore order and stability. A firm hand was exactly the image that Hitler was trying to project, and as the violence worsened, the Nazi vote rose. We all know how that tragedy played out.

Is it far-fetched to think that history could repeat itself in this way? To antifa activists who see violence as the answer to the far right, it should not be. They are the ones who are drawing the historical parallels. *The Times* quotes an antifa activist: "If we just stand back, we are allowing them to build a movement whose end goal is genocide." If that is the danger, we need to find a better way of combating it than the tactic that so plainly failed in Germany.

Are Riots Justifiable?

(with Katarzyna de Lazari-Radek)

In late May and June 2020, following the brutal death of George Floyd under the knee of a police officer in Minneapolis, mass protests against systemic racism took place across the United States and around the world. Floyd's death followed many previous police killings of unarmed Blacks who were not behaving violently. Most protests were peaceful, but some turned into riots with widespread looting and vandalism. But while protesting against police brutality and racism is surely legitimate, can riots also be defended?

The most thoughtful philosophical defense of rioting is by Avia Pasternak of University College London. Pasternak defines a riot as "a public disorder in which a large group of actors, acting spontaneously and without formal organization, engages in acts of lawlessness and open confrontation with law enforcement agencies." She adds that rioters typically cause damage to public and private property, as well as harming people, often in the course of clashes with police. Pasternak wrote before Floyd's death, but her article provides a framework for assessing what took place after it.

Pasternak starts from the idea, familiar from discussions of ethics in war, that under certain conditions it is permissible to cause harm to others—even to innocent others—in order to defend oneself from an unjust attack. Commonly, three conditions are specified:

- Necessity: there is no other way of defending oneself against the unjust attack;
- Proportionality: the harm inflicted on others must be outweighed by the harm averted by stopping the unjust attack; and
- Success: the actions that inflict the harm must be part of a strategy that has a reasonable chance of stopping the unjust attack.

Pasternak argues that a justifiable riot must satisfy these conditions. Following her lead, we can ask whether the riots after Floyd's death do.

It is easy to see these riots as seeking to prevent unjust attacks on African Americans, of the kind shown with horrifying clarity in videos viewed by millions. But in democracies that offer peaceful means of bringing about change, are such riots necessary?

Such change was the goal behind Black Lives Matter, a nonviolent movement founded after George Zimmerman was acquitted of all charges in the killing of Trayvon Martin, an unarmed Black teenager, in Florida. It gained national attention in 2014 following the deaths of Michael Brown in Ferguson, Missouri and Eric Garner in New York City, both at the hands of the police. Yet police are continuing to kill people of color who pose no threat to them. It is therefore at least arguable that conventional democratic channels have failed, and that the necessity condition has been met.

Is the harm caused by the riots disproportionate to the harm caused by the unjust police killings? Damage to property ran into hundreds of millions of dollars, but how do we compare that with the loss of life that spurred the protests?

Hafsa Islam, whose family owned a restaurant that was burned down in the Minneapolis riots, gave one answer: "We can rebuild a building, but we will never reclaim the life George Floyd didn't get to live." The issue isn't quite so simple, though. The same riots also started a fire that destroyed a housing development that was being built to provide 189 affordable housing units for low-income and homeless older people. It would have been ready later this year.

Most likely, some people will remain homeless for many more months or even years than would have been the case had the riot not occurred. That is a significant human cost, as well as a financial loss. Even if we consider only loss of life, however, the balance sheet does not clearly favor the riots. Ten days after the riots began, at least 13 people had died, many of them Black. A handwritten sign posted at the memorial service for David Dorn, a Black retired police captain shot by looters at a pawn shop, read: "Y'ALL KILLED A BLACK MAN BECAUSE 'THEY' KILLED A BLACK MAN???"

Defenders of political riots may seek to disclaim responsibility for the damage caused by those who loot stores or burn down low-income housing. But even if the vast majority of participants in a political riot do not support such acts, such harms must be considered in deciding whether riots are justifiable. The very nature of riots makes them virtually impossible to control, and the foreseeable risk of serious harms makes them difficult to defend.

Finally, when peaceful protests have failed, how likely is rioting to succeed? Opinions differ, but Omar Wasow's carefully controlled study of the 1960s riots that extensively damaged many American cities suggests that they contributed to Richard Nixon's narrow victory over the more progressive Hubert Humphrey. If so, the riots helped to reinforce the power of the police and thus to perpetuate the abuses that triggered the 2020 riots.

Martin Luther King, Jr., in a speech condemning riots, nevertheless described them as "the language of the unheard." The way to reduce the damage caused by further riots is to show that we have heard. We can do that by supporting Black Lives Matter and working to ensure that police treat the health and safety of everyone, regardless of race, with the greatest possible respect.

GLOBAL PROBLEMS

The Refugee Dilemma

In July 2015, the number of migrants reaching the borders of the European Union passed 100,000. In one week in August, 21,000 migrants arrived in Greece. Tourists complained that the summer holiday they had planned on a Greek island was now in the midst of a refugee camp. Of course, the refugee crisis had far more serious implications. More than 2,500 would-be migrants drowned in the Mediterranean that year, most of them attempting to cross from North Africa to Italy.

The refugee crisis also extended beyond Europe. The civil war in Syria brought far more refugees to Turkey, Lebanon, and Jordan than to any country in Europe. Other refugees were fleeing Afghanistan, Somalia, Libya, Eritrea, the Central African Republic, South Sudan, Nigeria, and the Democratic Republic of Congo. In Asia, the persecution of the Muslim Rohingya minority in Myanmar created more refugees. At the end of 2014, UNHCR, the United Nations agency for refugees, estimated that there were 59.5 million forcibly displaced people worldwide, the highest level ever recorded. Of these, 1.8 million were awaiting a decision on their asylum applications, 19.5 million were refugees, and the rest were displaced inside their own countries.

In the midst of that situation, with nationalists and populists clamoring for borders to be closed, German Chancellor Angela Merkel said: "The fundamental right to asylum for the politically persecuted knows no upper limit." She added that this applies also to "refugees who come to us from the hell of a civil war."

Merkel followed those brave words with action. In 2015, Germany registered 890,000 asylum seekers, and over the 18-month period from September 1 of that year, accepted more than 600,000 applications for asylum. To integrate so many newcomers from very different cultural backgrounds was obviously going to be a difficult task, but Merkel famously proclaimed, "*Wir schaffen das*" (We can do it). No act by any German leader, not even Willy Brandt's spontaneous decision in 1970 to kneel before a memorial to the heroes of the Warsaw Ghetto Uprising, has more decisively distanced Germany from its racist past.

Less than two months after Merkel championed the unlimited right to asylum, however, Poland's voters put the anti-immigrant Law and Justice party in power. The following year, British voters chose to leave the EU, and Trump was elected. In 2017, Austria's snap election led to a coalition government that included the far-right Freedom Party and Germany's federal election resulted in an eight-point swing against Merkel's Christian Democratic Union. The anti-immigrant Alternative for Germany, which had never before won a seat in the Bundestag, became the country's third-largest party. In the following year Italy's general election led to a coalition government in which the far-right League party's Matteo Salvini was a dominant figure. Finally, and most predictably of all these results, Viktor Orbán, Hungary's authoritarian anti-immigrant prime minister, was returned to office with a big majority.

Migration played a role—possibly a decisive role—in every one of these results. That is tragic, not just for would-be immigrants, but for the world. Images of children separated from their parents at the Mexican border by Trump's harsh immigration policies move us all, but we cannot yet hear the cries of the children who will go to bed hungry because Trump reversed Obama's modest restrictions on greenhouse gas emissions, and climate change will alter rainfall patterns on which their parents rely to grow food for the family.

Neither those children nor their parents will be able to claim asylum in the countries responsible for climate change. The UN Convention Relating to the Status of Refugees defines refugees as those unable or unwilling to return to their country because of a well-founded fear of persecution on the grounds of "race, religion, nationality, membership of a particular social group, or political opinion." There is no requirement to take economic refugees, and those who wrote the Convention did not think about climate change refugees.

Political leaders who want to act humanely toward asylum seekers and other aspiring immigrants now face an awful moral dilemma. Either they go far enough toward stricter border control to undercut public support for far-right parties, or they risk losing not only that battle, but all the other values threatened by anti-immigration governments as well.

Merkel herself recognized this dilemma. In 2018, before a European Union summit meeting on migration, it was not Merkel the idealist, but Merkel the political realist who told the German parliament that Europe faces many challenges, "but that of migration could become one that determines the fate of the European Union." She then joined with other European leaders to agree to strengthen Europe's border controls and return people rescued at sea to the countries from which they had come. The contrast between Merkel's 2015 and 2018 statements indicates why, inspirational as the proclamation of an unlimited right to asylum may be, in the last resort, rights must have a limit.

Refugees from within Europe seems to be a different matter. In the first two weeks after Russia invaded Ukraine in February 2022, more than 2 million refugees fled the country, with 1.5 million crossing the border to Poland and others going to Hungary, Slovakia, Romania, and Moldova, as well as some going to Russia itself. The Polish and Hungarian governments, in particular, had strongly resisted pressure from the European Union to take more Syrian refugees, but welcomed the Ukrainians.

Is there a practical solution to the dilemma, as it applies to refugees who, for whatever reason, are not welcomed as the refugees from Ukraine were by their neighbors? Affluent countries have a responsibility to take refugees, and many of them can and should accept more than they do. But as the number of people seeking asylum has grown, it has become difficult for tribunals and courts to determine who is a genuine refugee, as defined by the UN Convention, and who is a well-coached migrant seeking a better life in a more affluent country.

The Convention has also given rise to the new, unscrupulous, and often lethal industry of people smuggling. If those who claim asylum in a nearby country were sent to a refugee camp, safe from persecution, and with opportunities for education and meaningful employment, supported financially by aid from affluent countries, people smuggling and the resulting deaths in transit would be eliminated. The incentive for economic migrants to seek asylum would be reduced, and affluent countries could fulfill their responsibility to accept more refugees from the camps, while maintaining control of their borders.

Turning away people who manage to reach one's country is emotionally difficult, even if they are being sent to a safe haven. But we should also have compassion for the millions of people who are waiting in refugee camps. They too need to be given hope.

Is Open Diplomacy Possible?

In 2010, WikiLeaks released a quarter million US diplomatic cables. I was reminded of Woodrow Wilson's famous "Fourteen Points" for a just peace to end World War I. The first of those fourteen points reads: "Open covenants of peace must be arrived at, after which there will surely be no private international action or rulings of any kind, but diplomacy shall proceed always frankly and in the public view."

Is this an ideal that we should take seriously? Is WikiLeaks founder Julian Assange a true follower of Woodrow Wilson ideas on international relations?

Wilson was unable to get the Treaty of Versailles to reflect his fourteen points fully, although it did include several of them, including the establishment of an association of states that proved to be the forerunner of today's United Nations. But Wilson then failed to get the US Senate to ratify the treaty, which included the covenant of the League of Nations.

Writing in the *New York Times* following WikiLeaks's release of the documents, Paul Schroeter, an emeritus professor of history, argued that open diplomacy is often "fatally flawed," and gave as an example the need for secret negotiations to reach agreement on the Treaty of Versailles. Since the treaty bears

substantial responsibility for the resurrection of German na-
tionalism that led to the rise of Hitler and World War II, it has
a fair claim to being the most disastrous peace treaty in human
history. It is hard to imagine that if Wilson's proposals had
formed the basis of the peace, and set the tone for all future
negotiations, the history of Europe in the twentieth century
would have been worse than it actually was. That makes the
Treaty of Versailles a poor example to use to demonstrate
the desirability of secrecy in international negotiations.

Open government is, within limits, an ideal that we all share.
US President Barack Obama endorsed it when he took office in
January 2009. "Starting today," he told his cabinet secretaries
and staff, "every agency and department should know that this
administration stands on the side not of those who seek to
withhold information but of those who seek to make it known."
He then noted that there would have to be exceptions to this
policy to protect privacy and national security.

Even Secretary of Defense Robert Gates has admitted, however, that while the leaks are embarrassing and awkward for the
United States, their consequences for its foreign policy are
modest.

Some of the leaked cables are just opinion, and not much more
than gossip about national leaders. But, because of the leak, we
know, for example, that when the British government set up its
supposedly open inquiry into the causes of the Iraq War, it also
promised the US government that it would "put measures in
place to protect your interests." The British government appears
to have been deceiving the public and its own parliament.

Similarly, the cables reveal that President Ali Abdullah Saleh
of Yemen lied to his people and parliament about the source of

US air strikes against al-Qaeda in Yemen, telling them that Yemen's military was the source of the bombs.

We have also learned more about the level of corruption in some of the regimes that the United States supports, like those in Afghanistan and Pakistan, and in other countries with which the United States has friendly relations, notably Russia. We now know that the Saudi royal family has been urging the United States to undertake a military attack on Iran to prevent it from becoming capable of producing nuclear weapons. Here, perhaps, we learned something for which the US government deserves credit: it has resisted that suggestion.

Knowledge is generally considered a good thing; so, presumably, knowing more about how the United States thinks and operates around the world is also good. In a democracy, citizens pass judgment on their government, and if they are kept in the dark about what their government is doing, they cannot be in a position to make well-grounded decisions. Even in non-democratic countries, people have a legitimate interest in knowing about actions taken by the government.

Nevertheless, it isn't always the case that openness is better than secrecy. Suppose that US diplomats had discovered that democrats living under a brutal military dictatorship were negotiating with junior officers to stage a coup to restore democracy and the rule of law. I would hope that WikiLeaks would not publish a cable in which diplomats informed their superiors of the plot.

Openness is in this respect like pacifism: just as we cannot embrace complete disarmament while others stand ready to use their weapons, so Woodrow Wilson's world of open diplomacy is a noble ideal that cannot be fully realized in the world in which we live.

We could, however, try to get closer to that ideal. If governments did not mislead their citizens so often, there would be less need for secrecy, and if leaders knew that they could not rely on keeping the public in the dark about what they are doing, they would have a powerful incentive to behave better.

It is therefore regrettable that the most likely outcome of the recent revelations will be greater restrictions to prevent further leaks. Let's hope that in the new WikiLeaks age, that goal remains out of reach.

Paris and the Fate of the Earth

The lives of billions of people, for centuries to come, were at stake when world leaders and government negotiators met at the United Nations Climate Change Conference in Paris in November 2015. The fate of an unknown number of endangered species of plants and animals also hung in the balance.

At the "Earth Summit" in Rio de Janeiro in 1992, 189 countries, including the United States, China, India, and all European countries, signed on to the UN Framework Convention on Climate Change (UNFCCC) and agreed to stabilize greenhouse gas emissions "at a low enough level to prevent dangerous anthropogenic interference with the climate system."

So far, however, no such stabilization has taken place, and without it, climate feedback loops could boost rising temperatures further still. With less Arctic ice to reflect sunlight, the oceans will absorb more warmth. Thawing Siberian permafrost will release vast quantities of methane. As a result, vast areas of our planet, currently home to billions of people, could become uninhabitable.

Earlier conferences of the UNFCCC signatories sought to reach legally binding agreements on emission reductions, at least for the industrialized countries that have produced most of the greenhouse gases now in the atmosphere. That strategy faltered—partly owing to US intransigence under President George W. Bush—and was abandoned when the 2009 Copenhagen conference failed to produce a treaty to replace the expiring Kyoto Protocol (which the United States never signed). Instead, the Copenhagen Accord merely asked countries for voluntary pledges to cut their emissions by specific amounts.

Those pledges came in from 154 countries, including the major emitters, and they fell far short of what is required. To fathom the gap between what the pledges would achieve and what is required, we need to go back to the language that everyone accepted in Rio.

The wording was vague in two key respects. First, what would constitute "dangerous anthropogenic interference with the climate system"? And, second, what level of safety is assumed by the term "prevent"?

The first ambiguity was resolved by the decision to aim for a level of emissions that would cap the increase in average surface temperature at 2° Celsius above the pre-industrial level. Many scientists consider even a lower increase dangerous. Consider that even with a rise of only 0.8°C so far, the planet has experienced record-high temperatures, more extreme weather events, and substantial melting of the Greenland ice sheet, which contains enough water to cause a seven-meter rise in sea levels. In Copenhagen, the pleas of representatives of small island states (some of which will cease to exist if sea levels continue to rise) for a target of 1.5°C went unheeded, essentially because world leaders thought the measures required to meet such a target were politically unrealistic.

The second ambiguity remains. The London School of Economics' Grantham Research Institute has analyzed the submissions made by all 154 countries and concluded that even if they are all implemented, global carbon emissions will rise from their current level of 50 billion tons per year to 55–60 billion tons by 2030. But, to have even a 50% chance of keeping to the 2°C limit, annual carbon emissions need to come down to 36 billion tons.

A report from Australia's National Centre for Climate Restoration is no less alarming. The level of emissions in the atmosphere today already means that we have a 10% chance of exceeding 2°C, even if we stopped adding further emissions right now (which is not going to happen).

Imagine if an airline slashed its maintenance procedures to a level at which there was a 10% chance that its planes would not safely complete their flights. The company could not claim that it had prevented dangerous planes from flying, and it would find few customers, even if its flights were much cheaper than anyone else's. Similarly, given the scale of the catastrophe that could result from "dangerous anthropogenic interference with the climate system," we ought not to accept a 10% chance—if not many times higher—of exceeding 2°C.

What is the alternative? Developing countries will argue that their need for cheap energy to lift their people out of poverty is greater than rich countries' need to maintain their often wasteful levels of energy consumption—and they will be right. That is why rich countries should aim at decarbonizing their economies as soon as possible, and by 2050 at the latest. They could start by closing down the dirtiest form of energy production, coal-fired power stations, and refuse licenses to develop new coal mines.

Another quick gain could come from encouraging people to eat more plant-based foods, perhaps by taxing meat and using the revenue to subsidize more sustainable alternatives. According to the UN Food and Agriculture Organization, the livestock industry is the second largest source of greenhouse gas emissions, ahead of the entire transport sector. This implies great scope for emission reductions, and in ways that would have a smaller impact on our lives than ceasing all fossil-fuel use. The World Health Organization and other health authorities agree that a reduction in the consumption of processed and red meat would have the additional benefit of reducing cancer deaths.

With so much at stake, how did the Paris Conference do? In contrast to the earlier Copenhagen meeting, it was not a complete failure. At the insistence of some of the countries most at risk from climate change, the text of the agreement commits the signatories to holding the increase in global temperatures to "well below" 2°C and even "to pursue efforts to limit the temperature increase to 1.5°C." More importantly, there was a consensus that all countries, developed and developing, should play their part in reducing greenhouse gas emissions. Yet, as noted above, the pledges made by all the parties to the agreement are insufficient to meet that target. In Paris, the parties agreed to ratchet up their pledges before another meeting, to be held in five years' time. That should have occurred in 2020, but it was postponed because of the COVID-19 pandemic. It was eventually held in Glasgow in November 2021. There was an agreement to reduce the use of coal, but that agreement was reached only after, at the insistence of China and India, the words "phase out" were replaced by "phase down," and it remains to be seen how much of a reduction will take place. Some, but not all, countries strengthened their pledges, but the current level of pledges is clearly insufficient to meet the targets set in Paris. Even if all the pledges in place at the end of 2021 are fully implemented, global temperatures will rise by more than 1.5°C, and quite possibly by more than 2°C.

Greta Thunberg's Moment

This is all wrong!" These words begin the most powerful four-minute speech I have ever heard. They were spoken by Greta Thunberg, the Swedish teenage climate activist, at the United Nations Climate Action Summit in September 2019, and followed a week of worldwide climate strikes and marches attended by an estimated six million people.

The marchers were predominantly the young people who will have to cope with more of the costs of climate change than the world leaders Thunberg was addressing. Her tone of moral outrage was therefore apt, as was the leitmotif of her speech: "How dare you?" She accused the world's leaders of stealing the dreams of the young with empty words. How dare they say that they are doing enough? How dare they pretend that "business as usual," coupled with yet-to-be-discovered technological solutions, will solve the problem?

Thunberg justified her outrage by pointing out that the science of climate change has been known for 30 years. World leaders have looked away while the opportunities for a timely transition to a net-zero greenhouse gas economy slipped by. Now even the heroic effort of halving emissions over the next ten years would, Thunberg pointed out, give us only a 50% chance of keeping global warming below 1.5° Celsius.

Passing that limit risks setting off uncontrollable feedback loops leading to further warming, more feedback loops, and yet more warming. Thunberg referred to the Intergovernmental Panel on Climate Change's report indicating that to reduce the risk of exceeding 1.5°C to one in three, we will need to limit global carbon dioxide emissions from now until 2050 to 350 gigatons. At the current rate, we will exceed this limit in 2028.

According to the Climate Change Performance Index, no government in the world has yet achieved a "very good" performance in protecting the world's climate. Sweden, Morocco, and Lithuania are currently doing the best, with Latvia and the United Kingdom not far behind. The United States is in the bottom five, along with Saudi Arabia, Iran, South Korea, and Taiwan.

The ethical issue is not difficult to adjudicate. For affluent countries, which are responsible for most of the CO_2 that is now in the atmosphere, there can be no ethical justification for continuing to emit greenhouse gases at far higher per capita levels than the people in low-income countries who will suffer most from climate change. To impose on them a one in three chance of warming beyond 1.5°C is playing a kind of Russian roulette, as if we had put a revolver against the heads of tens or perhaps hundreds of millions of people in low-income countries—except that to make the analogy accurate, we would have had to load our six-chambered revolver with two bullets rather than just one. Nor would the costs, for affluent countries, be in any way comparable to the risks they are imposing on low-income countries. The required switch to a clean economy would bring some transitional costs, but in the long run would save lives and benefit everyone.

How will we get there? Thunberg ended on a positive note: "We will not let you get away with this. Right here, right now is where we draw the line. The world is waking up. And change is coming, whether you like it or not."

Can young people really wake the world to the urgency of changing direction? Can they convince their parents? School strikes will trouble parents, especially parents who then need to arrange child care, but will they influence political leaders? What can be done to keep climate on the agenda until governments get serious about reducing the risk of catastrophe?

"Extinction Rebellion," an international movement that began last year with a Declaration of Rebellion in London, advocates civil disobedience. Extinction Rebellion calls for thousands of activists to block roads and shut down transport systems in major cities around the world, not just for one day, but for long enough to impose real economic costs on governments and business elites, all the while maintaining strictly nonviolent discipline even in the face of government repression.

Civil disobedience was first used as part of a mass movement by Mahatma Gandhi in South Africa and subsequently in India. In the United States, its most famous proponent was Martin Luther King, Jr., in the struggle against racial segregation. Civil disobedience played a role, along with other forms of protest, in ending the Vietnam War. In each of these examples, resorting to civil disobedience is now widely regarded as courageous and right. There are statues to Gandhi around the world, and in the United States, King's birthday is a national holiday.

The failure of governments to reduce greenhouse gas emissions is no less wrong than British rule in India, the denial of equal rights to Blacks, or the war in Vietnam—and it is likely to cause harm on a far larger scale. So, civil disobedience also would be justified if it has a chance of persuading governments to follow the science and do what is necessary to avert catastrophic climate change.

There may be other effective forms of nonviolent protest that no one has yet tried. Thunberg first became known for standing alone outside Sweden's parliament holding a sign saying, in Swedish, "School Strike for Climate." No one could have predicted that this then-15-year-old girl would start a movement supported by millions of young people and gain a platform from which to address the world's leaders. We need more innovative ideas about how best to convey the urgency of the situation and the need for a sharp change of course.

Stopping Putin

Russian President Vladimir Putin's justification for invading Ukraine was not original. As others have noted, his claim that it was necessitated by the "genocide" carried out against ethnic Russians in the Donbas region recalls Hitler's strategy for destroying democratic Czechoslovakia in the run-up to World War II.

Hitler threatened to invade Czechoslovakia in order to incorporate into the Reich border districts with a German-speaking population. He did not have to invade, because the leaders of the United Kingdom, France, and Italy, with the carnage of the Great War still in everyone's memory, acceded to his demands at the 1938 Munich conference. Within six months, however, the Nazis violated the Munich Agreement, established the Protectorate of Bohemia and Moravia in the Czech lands, and created a nominally independent Slovak puppet state. Hitler then began making claims to a slice of Poland.

Putin's attack on Ukraine began in a similar way, with the seizure of Crimea and the establishment of two Kremlin-backed statelets in the Russian-speaking eastern Donbas region in 2014. This was a flagrant violation of the Budapest Memorandum on Security Assurances, in accordance with which Ukraine, along with Belarus and Kazakhstan, gave up the nuclear arsenals they had inherited from the Soviet Union. In return, Russia, the United Kingdom, and the United States gave assurances that they would respect the sovereignty and independence of all three countries within their existing borders.

Just as the UK and France took no serious action when Hitler progressively tore up the Treaty of Versailles, so no country did anything serious enough to make Russians regret the wildly popular annexation of Crimea and encouragement of separatism in Donbas.

Hitler's claim to Czechoslovakia's Sudetenland was, he said at the time, "my last territorial claim in Europe." But anyone who had read *Mein Kampf* should have known about his ambitions to create *Lebensraum* for Germans in Eastern Europe. Similarly, we can reasonably suspect that Putin, who has described the dissolution of the Soviet Union as a disaster, wants to restore Russian dominance over former Soviet territory. If Putin can get away with occupying Ukraine and installing a puppet regime, will the ex-Soviet Baltic states, especially Estonia and Latvia, with their large Russian-speaking minorities, be next?

Putin has one great advantage that Hitler fortunately lacked: nuclear weapons. Putin has warned off countries that might attempt to interfere in Russia's "military operation" in Ukraine by testing a nuclear-capable missile shortly before launching the invasion, and saying that any country that intervenes would face "consequences that you have never seen." Four days after the invasion began, he put Russia's nuclear forces on alert.

How, then, can Putin be stopped?

Economic sanctions are already being imposed, airspace is being closed to Russian aircraft, and boycotts of Russian goods are under way. These measures, regrettably, will hurt all Russians, including those who oppose the war. But is there any other way to stop Putin from achieving his aims?

Ukrainian President Volodymyr Zelensky has bravely remained in Kyiv, rallying all Ukrainians to fight the advancing Russians. Initially, most military experts believed that a Russian military victory was inevitable, but Ukrainian resistance forced Russian forces to retreat from the areas around Kyiv and Kharkiv. Putin may have to settle for a much more limited victory, and at a heavy cost, if indeed he can achieve a victory at all.

Zelensky has called on the Russian people to stop the war. Many Russians are trying to do just that. After the invasion was announced, there were protests in 55 cities across Russia. More than one million courageous Russians put their names to a "Stop the War" petition on change.org. An independent monitoring organization said that in the first week after the invasion, 5,000 people were arrested for participating in protests without prior permission. Many more continued to protest, despite the Russian legislature increasing to 15 years the length of time to which protestors peacefully disagreeing with the government's line on the war are liable to be sentenced. Dmitry Muratov, the 2021 Nobel Peace Prize winner and editor of *Novaya Gazeta*, one of Russia's last remaining independent newspapers, posted a video in which he called for Russians to rise up against the war, saying that: "Only the anti-war movement of Russians can save life on this planet." Yelena Kovalskaya, director of the state-run

Meyerhold Theatre Center, resigned in protest against the attack on Ukraine, saying, "It is impossible to work for a murderer and receive a salary from him." More than 150 scientists and science journalists signed a letter, published on a Russian science website, lamenting that Russia has condemned itself to isolation and the status of a rogue state. A similar number of municipal deputies from many cities signed a letter condemning the attack as "an unprecedented atrocity" and adding that "Hopes for a good life in Russia are crumbling before our eyes."

What is also needed, now, is for Russian soldiers in Ukraine to stop fighting an unjust war. Both Russian and Belarussian soldiers have refused to go into Ukraine. At least at the start of the war, before Russian authorities clamped down, Russians had access to a wide range of information beyond the propaganda of their state-run media, including *Novaya Gazeta* and social media. They should have known that they were part of a war of aggression. Intentionally killing people without sufficient cause is murder, and that is what Russian soldiers are doing when they obey orders to target Ukrainians with lethal weapons. That includes not only targeting civilians, but also targeting Ukrainian soldiers, for these soldiers are engaged in the legitimate defense of their country against aggression.

Even for Russians who have been so brainwashed by Russian propaganda that they believe they are fighting a just war, at least some of them have been targeting civilians, which is a war crime. Obeying orders is no excuse for killing civilians, just as it was no excuse for those under Hitler's command.

From now on, as long as Putin remains Russia's leader, the country must be seen as an international pariah. Sanctions must be strong enough to ensure that Russians do see their hopes for a good life crumble.

This is especially unfair to those who have publicly opposed the war. But how else can they hope to replace Putin with someone who is prepared to abide by moral principles and international law? Sometimes the vanquished come to view their suffering as liberation. Just ask today's Germans.

SCIENCE AND TECHNOLOGY

A Clear Case for Golden Rice

Greenpeace, the global environmental NGO, typically leads protests. But in 2014 it became the target of one. In 2014, Patrick Moore, a spokesperson for the protests and a former Greenpeace member, accused the organization of complicity in the deaths of two million children per year. He was referring to deaths resulting from vitamin A deficiency, which is common among children for whom rice is the staple food. These deaths could be prevented, Moore claimed, by the use of "golden rice," a form of the grain that has been genetically modified to have a higher beta-carotene content than ordinary rice. Greenpeace, along with other organizations opposed to the use of genetically modified organisms (GMOs), has campaigned against the introduction of beta-carotene, which is converted in the human body into vitamin A.

Moore's mortality figures were correct for the early 1990s, but by 2014, the figures had, fortunately, dropped significantly. Still, vitamin A deficiency among children remains a major health problem, especially in parts of Africa and Southeast Asia. According to the World Health Organization, it causes blindness in about 250,000–500,000 pre-school children every year, about half of whom die within 12 months.

The deficiency also increases susceptibility to diseases like measles, still a significant cause of death in young children, although one that is declining as a result of vaccination. In some countries, lack of vitamin A is also a major factor in high rates of maternal mortality during pregnancy and childbirth.

Golden rice was first produced in 2000. It was the outcome of several years of research by Swiss scientists, specifically aimed at addressing vitamin A deficiency. The first field trials were conducted in 2004. Initially, there was a need to develop improved varieties that would thrive where they are most needed. Further field trials had to be carried out to meet the strict regulations governing the release of GMOs. That hurdle was raised higher when activists destroyed fields in the Philippines where trials were being conducted. It was not until 2021 that the Philippines became the first country to approve golden rice for farmers to grow and sell. Proponents hope that it will receive final approval in Bangladesh in 2022.

Critics have suggested that golden rice is part of the biotech industry's plans to dominate agriculture worldwide. It is true that the agribusiness giant Syngenta did assist in developing the genetically modified rice; but the company has not sought to commercialize it. Instead, Syngenta has given the right to sub-license the rice to a nonprofit organization called the Golden Rice Humanitarian Board. The board, which includes the two co-inventors, has the right to provide the rice to public research institutions and low-income farmers in developing countries for humanitarian use, as long as it does not charge more for it than the price for ordinary rice seeds. That is what is now happening in the Philippines.

When genetically modified crops were first developed in the 1980s, there were grounds for caution. Would these crops be safe to eat? Might they not cross-pollinate with wild plants, passing on the special qualities they were given, such as resistance to pests, and so create new "superweeds"? In the 1990s, as a Senate candidate for the Australian Greens, I was among those who argued for strong regulations to prevent biotech companies putting our health, or that of the environment, at risk in order to increase their profits.

Genetically modified crops are now grown on about one-tenth of the world's cropland, and none of the disastrous consequences that we Greens feared have come to pass. There is no reliable scientific evidence that GM foods cause illness, despite the fact that they have received more intense scrutiny than "natural" foods.

Although cross-pollination between GM crops and wild plants can occur, so far no new superweeds have emerged. We should be pleased about that—and perhaps the regulations that were introduced in response to the concerns expressed by environmental organizations played a role in that outcome. Regulations to protect the environment and the health of consumers should be maintained. Caution is reasonable. What needs to be rethought, however, is blanket opposition to the very idea of GMOs.

With any innovation, risks need to be weighed against possible benefits. Where the benefits are minor, even a small risk may not be justified; where those benefits are great, a more significant risk may well be worth taking.

Regulations should, for instance, be sensitive to the difference between releasing a GM crop that is resistant to the herbicide glyphosate (making it easier for farmers to control weeds) and releasing GM crops that can resist drought and are suitable for drought-prone regions of low-income countries. Similarly, a GM crop that has the potential to prevent blindness in a half-million children would be worth growing even if it does involve some risks. The irony is that glyphosate-resistant crops are grown commercially on millions of hectares of land, whereas golden rice (which has not been shown to pose any risk at all to human health or the environment) still cannot be released.

In some environmental circles, blanket opposition to GMOs is like taking a loyalty oath—dissidents are regarded as traitors in league with the evil biotech industry. It is time to move beyond such a narrowly ideological stance. Some GMOs may have a useful role to play in public health, and others in fighting the challenge of growing food in an era of climate change. We should consider the merits of each genetically modified plant on a case-by-case basis.

Life Made to Order

In the sixteenth century, the alchemist Paracelsus offered a recipe for creating a living being that began with putting sperm into putrefying *venter equinus.* This is usually translated as "horse manure," but the Latin *venter* means abdomen or uterus.

So occultists may appreciate the fact that Craig Venter was the driving force behind the team of scientists that in 2010 announced that they had created a synthetic form of life: a bacterium with a genome designed and created from chemicals in a laboratory.

The new bacterium, nicknamed "Synthia," replicates and produces proteins. By any reasonable definition, it is alive. Although it is very similar to a natural bacterium from which it was largely copied, the creators put distinctive strings of DNA into its genome to prove that it is not a natural object. These strings spell out, in code, a website address, the names of the researchers, and apt quotations, such as Richard Feynman's "What I cannot build, I cannot understand."

For some years now, synthetic biology has been looming as the next big issue in bioethics. The scientists at the J. Craig Venter Institute expected to be told that they were "playing God," and they were not disappointed. If one believes that life was created by God, then this comes as close to "playing God" as humans have come, so far.

Well-known University of Pennsylvania bioethicist Art Caplan says that the achievement ranks as a discovery of historic significance, because it "would seem to extinguish the argument that life requires a special force or power to exist." Asked about the significance of what the team had done, Venter described it as bringing about "a giant philosophical change in how we view life."

Others have pointed out that, although the team produced a synthetic genome, they put it into a cell from another bacterium, replacing that cell's DNA. We have yet to build a living organism entirely from bottles of chemicals, so anyone who believes in a "life force" that only a divine being could imbue into inert matter will no doubt claim that the life force was already in the cell and survived the replacement of the cell's DNA.

At a more practical level, Venter said, the team's work has produced "a very powerful set of tools" for redesigning life. He has been criticized for the fact that the research was funded by Synthetic Genomics, a company that he co-founded, which will hold the intellectual property rights resulting from the research—and has already filed for 13 patents related to it. But the work has taken 20 scientists a decade to complete, at an estimated cost of $40 million, and commercial investors are an obvious source for such funds.

Others object that living things should not be patented. That battle was lost in 1980, when the US Supreme Court decided that a genetically modified microorganism designed to clean up oil spills could be patented. Patenting life was taken a step further in 1984, when Harvard University successfully applied for a patent on its "oncomouse," a laboratory mouse specifically designed to get cancer easily, so that it would be more useful as a research tool. There are good grounds for objecting to turning a sentient being into a patented laboratory tool, but it is not so easy to see why patent law should not cover newly designed bacteria or algae, that presumably can feel nothing and may be as useful as any other invention.

Indeed, Synthia's very existence challenges the distinction between living and artificial that underlies much of the opposition to "patenting life"—though pointing this out is not to approve the granting of sweeping patents that prevent other scientists from making their own discoveries in this important new field.

As for the likely usefulness of synthetic bacteria, the fact that Synthia's birth had to compete for headlines with news of the world's worst-ever oil spill made the point more effectively than any public relations effort could have done. One day, we may be able to design bacteria that can quickly, safely, and effectively clean up oil spills. The most exciting prospect held out by Venter, however, is a form of algae that can absorb carbon dioxide from the atmosphere and use it to create diesel fuel or gasoline. Synthetic Genomics entered into a $600 million agreement with ExxonMobil to obtain fuel from algae. In 2018, ExxonMobil announced that it was anticipating producing 10,000 barrels of algae biofuel per day by 2025.

Synthetic biology has expanded rapidly in the years since 2010, but not by using the methods Venter's team used. Just six years after the dramatic announcement of the creation of Synthia, the emergence of newer techniques led Sarah Richardson and Nicola Patron, researchers in the field, to suggest that using Venter's methods for creating synthetic organisms would be "as appealing as buying monochrome cathode ray tube monitors."

Obviously, the release of any synthetic organism must be carefully regulated, just like the release of any genetically modified organism. But any risk must be weighed against other grave threats that we face. Climate change is obviously one. In such circumstances, the risks of synthetic biology may be outweighed by the hope that it will enable us to avert a looming environmental catastrophe.

A Dream for the Digital Age

Fifty years ago, Martin Luther King dreamed of an America that would one day deliver on its promise of equality for all of its citizens, Black as well as white. Facebook founder Mark Zuckerberg has a dream, too: he wants to provide Internet access to everyone on our planet.

Zuckerberg's vision may sound like a self-interested push to gain more Facebook users. But the world currently faces a growing technological divide, with implications for equality, liberty, and the right to pursue happiness that are no less momentous than the racial divide against which King preached.

When Zuckerberg began talking about universal Internet access, only two billion people were living in the Digital Age. They were able to access a vast universe of information, communicate at little or no cost with their friends and family, and connect with others with whom they can cooperate in new ways. The other five billion were still stuck in the Paper Age in which my generation grew up.

In the Paper Age, if you wanted to know something but did not own an expensive encyclopedia (or your encyclopedia was no longer sufficiently up-to-date to tell you what you wanted to know), you had to go to a library and spend hours searching for what you needed. To contact friends or colleagues overseas, you had to write them a letter and wait at least two weeks for a reply. International phone calls were prohibitively expensive, and the idea of actually seeing someone while you talked to them was the stuff of science fiction.

Internet.org, a global partnership launched by Zuckerberg in 2013, aimed to bring the five billion people without Internet access into the Digital Age. The partnership consisted of seven major information-technology companies, as well as nonprofit organizations and local communities. Knowing that you cannot ask people to choose between buying food and buying data, the partnership sought new, less expensive means of connecting computers, more data-efficient software, and new business models.

Internet access did increase dramatically over the following decade, although not exactly in the way that Zuckerberg's partnership had envisaged. By 2021, 4.6 billion people, or nearly 60% of the world's population, were accessing the Internet, mostly through mobile devices. The problem was not so much access to the Internet as the ability to afford the service.

Microsoft founder Bill Gates has suggested that Internet access is not a high priority for the poorest countries. It is more important, he says, to tackle problems like diarrhea and malaria. I have nothing but praise for Gates's efforts to reduce the death toll from these diseases, which primarily affect the world's poorest people. Yet his position seems curiously lacking in big-picture awareness of how the Internet could transform the lives of the very poor. For example, if farmers could use it to get more accurate predictions of favorable conditions for planting, or to obtain higher prices for their harvest, they would be better able to afford sanitation, so that their children do not get diarrhea, and bed nets to protect themselves and their families against malaria.

A friend working to provide family planning advice to poor Kenyans recently told me that so many women were coming to the clinic that she could not spend more than five minutes with each. These women have only one source of advice, and one opportunity to get it, but if they had access to the Internet, the information could be there for them whenever they wanted it.

Moreover, online consultations would be possible, sparing women the need to travel to clinics. Internet access would also bypass the problem of illiteracy, building on the oral traditions that are strong in many rural cultures and enabling communities to create self-help groups and share their problems with peers in other villages.

What is true for family planning is true for a very wide range of topics, especially those that are difficult to speak about, like homosexuality and domestic violence. The Internet is helping people to understand that they are not alone, and that they can learn from others' experience.

Enlarging our vision still more, it is not absurd to hope that putting the world's poor online would result in connections between them and more affluent people, leading to more assistance. Research shows that people are more likely to donate to a charity to help the hungry if they are given a photo and told the name and age of a girl like those the charity is aiding. If a mere photo and a few identifying details can do that, what might Skyping or Zooming with the person do?

Providing universal Internet access does have its risks, and sensitive ethical issues. Online scammers will have access to a new and perhaps more gullible audience. Breaches of copyright will become even more widespread than they are today (although they will cost the copyright owners very little, because the poor would be very unlikely to be able to buy books or other copyrighted material).

Perhaps more seriously, the distinctiveness of local cultures may be eroded, which has both a good and a bad side, for such cultures can restrict freedom and deny equality of opportunity. On the whole, though, it is reasonable to expect that giving poor people access to knowledge and the possibility of connecting with people anywhere in the world will be socially transforming in a very positive way.

The Tragic Cost of Being Unscientific

Throughout his tenure as South Africa's president, from 1999 to 2008, Thabo Mbeki rejected the scientific consensus that AIDS is caused by a virus, HIV, and that antiretroviral drugs can save the lives of people who test positive for it. Instead, he accepted the views of a small group of dissident scientists who suggested other causes for AIDS, continuing to embrace this position even as the evidence against it became overwhelming. When anyone publicly questioned Mbeki's views, Mbeki's supporters viciously denounced them. That happened even to Nelson Mandela, the heroic resistance fighter against apartheid who became South Africa's first Black president, and was Mbeki's immediate predecessor.

While Botswana and Namibia, South Africa's neighbors, provided antiretrovirals to the majority of its citizens infected by HIV, South Africa under Mbeki failed to do so. A team of Harvard University researchers has now investigated the consequences of this policy. Using conservative assumptions, it estimates that, had South Africa's government provided the appropriate drugs, both to AIDS patients and to pregnant women who were at risk of infecting their babies, it would have prevented 365,000 premature deaths.

That number is a revealing indication of the staggering costs that can arise when science is rejected or ignored. It is roughly comparable to the loss of life from the genocide in Darfur, and close to half of the toll from the massacre of Tutsis in Rwanda in 1994.

One of the key incidents in turning world opinion against South Africa's apartheid regime was the 1961 Sharpeville massacre, in which police fired on a crowd of Black protesters, killing 69 and wounding many more. Mbeki, like Mandela, was active in the struggle against apartheid. Yet the Harvard study shows that he is responsible for the deaths of 5,000 times as many Black South Africans as the white South African police who fired on the crowd at Sharpeville.

How are we to assess a man like that?

In Mbeki's defense, it can be said that he did not intend to kill anyone. He appears to have genuinely believed that antiretrovirals are toxic.

We can also grant that Mbeki was not motivated by malice against those suffering from AIDS. He had no desire to harm them, and for that reason, we should judge his character differently from those who do set out to harm others, whether from hatred or to further their own interests.

But good intentions are not enough, especially when the stakes are so high. Mbeki is culpable, not for having initially entertained a view held by a tiny minority of scientists, but for having clung to this view without allowing it to be tested in fair and open debate among experts. When Professor Malegapuru Makgoba, South Africa's leading Black immunologist, warned that the president's policies would make South Africa a laughingstock in the world of science, Mbeki's office accused him of defending racist Western ideas.

After Mbeki's ouster, his successor, Kgalema Motlanthe, moved quickly to implement effective measures against AIDS. Mbeki's health minister, who notoriously suggested that AIDS could be cured by the use of garlic, lemon juice, and beetroot, was promptly fired. It is tragic that the African National Congress, South Africa's dominant political party, was so much in thrall to Mbeki that he was not deposed many years earlier.

Mbeki must have known that, if his unorthodox views about the cause of AIDS and the efficacy of antiretrovirals were wrong, his policy would lead to a large number of unnecessary deaths. That knowledge put him under the strongest obligation to allow all the evidence to be fairly presented and examined without fear or favor. Because he did not do this, Mbeki cannot escape responsibility for hundreds of thousands of deaths.

The lessons of this story are applicable wherever science is ignored in the formulation of public policy. In October 2021, a Brazilian Senate inquiry into the government's response to the COVID-19 pandemic recommended bringing criminal charges against president Jair Bolsonaro and others in his administration for promoting, against all the evidence, the use of hydroxychloroquine and ivermectin as remedies for COVID-19. The inquiry also discussed recommending that Bolsonaro and others be charged with "murder by omission" for delaying vaccine purchases, but this recommendation was not in the final report. The recommendations were not expected to lead to any actual charges, as the prosecutor was a political ally of the president.

In the United States—the only country in the world to have more deaths from COVID-19 than Brazil—national policy supported the development and delivery of vaccines, under both President Trump and President Biden. But many people were misled by claims that vaccines were part of some perfidious plot to control the population, or to make them sterile. Instead of looking at the scientific evidence, many people with large followings on social media spread this misinformation. Those who did so caused innocent people to die. In the United States, in just six months, from June 1 to November 30, 2021, 163,000 more people died than would have died if the population had been fully vaccinated, according to a Kaiser Family Foundation study.

I am not saying that whatever view has the support of a majority of scientists is always true. The history of science clearly shows the contrary. Scientists are human and can be mistaken. They, like other humans, can be influenced by a herd mentality, and the fear of being marginalized. We may disagree with scientists, but we must not reject science as a method of inquiry. Whether we are government leaders, corporate heads, or social media influencers, there are many areas in which we cannot know what we ought to do without assessing a body of scientific evidence. Especially when lives are at stake, to act without doing so, as carefully and as objectively as possible, is grossly irresponsible.

FREEDOM AND
RESPONSIBILITY

Free Speech, Muhammad, and the Holocaust

The timing of Austria's conviction and imprisonment of David Irving for denying the Holocaust could not have been worse. Coming after the deaths of at least 30 people in Syria, Lebanon, Afghanistan, Libya, Nigeria, and other Islamic countries during protests against cartoons ridiculing Muhammad, the Irving verdict makes a mockery of the claim that in democratic countries, freedom of expression is a basic right.

We cannot consistently hold that cartoonists have a right to mock religious figures but that to deny the existence of the Holocaust is a crime. I believe that we should stand behind freedom of speech. And that means that David Irving should not have been imprisoned.

Before you accuse me of failing to understand the sensitivities of victims of the Holocaust, or the nature of Austrian anti-Semitism, I should say that I am the son of Austrian Jews. My parents escaped Austria in time, but my grandparents did not. The Nazi regime sent my father's parents to the Lodz ghetto, in Poland, and murdered them with carbon monoxide piped into the back of trucks at the extermination site at Chełmno. My mother's parents were deported to Theresienstadt, in what is now the Czech republic, where my maternal grandfather died from the diseases caused by overcrowding, underfeeding, and terrible sanitation. My mother's mother was one of the few who managed to survive long enough to be liberated and eventually join us in Australia.

So I have no sympathy for David Irving's absurd denial of the Holocaust. I support efforts to prevent any return to Nazism in Austria or anywhere else. But how is the cause of truth served by prohibiting Holocaust denial? If there are still people crazy enough to deny that the Holocaust occurred, will they be persuaded by imprisoning people who express that view? On the contrary, they will be more likely to think that people are being imprisoned for expressing views that cannot be refuted by evidence and argument alone.

In his classic defense of freedom of speech in *On Liberty*, John Stuart Mill wrote that if a view is not "fully, frequently, and fearlessly discussed," it will become "a dead dogma, not a living truth." The existence of the Holocaust should remain a living truth, and those who are skeptical about the enormity of the Nazi atrocities should be confronted with the evidence for it.

In the aftermath of World War II, when the Austrian republic was struggling to establish itself as a democracy, it was reasonable, as a temporary emergency measure, for Austrian democrats to suppress Nazi ideas and propaganda. But that danger is long past. Austria is a democracy and a member of the European Union. Despite the occasional resurgence of anti-immigrant and racist views—an occurrence that is, lamentably, not limited to countries with a fascist past—there is no longer a serious threat of any return to Nazism in Austria.

By contrast, freedom of speech is essential to democratic regimes, and it must include the freedom to say what everyone else believes to be false, and even what many people find offensive. We must be free to deny the existence of God, and to criticize the teachings of Jesus, Moses, Muhammad, and Buddha, as reported in texts that millions of people regard as sacred. Without that freedom, human progress will always run up against a basic roadblock.

Article 10 of the European Convention on Human Rights and Fundamental Freedoms states: "Everyone has the right to freedom of expression. This right shall include freedom to hold opinions and to receive and impart information and ideas without interference by public authority and regardless of frontiers." To be consistent with that clear statement, countries with laws against Holocaust denial should repeal them, while maintaining or strengthening their efforts to inform their citizens about the reality of the Holocaust and why the racist ideology that led to it should be rejected. Laws against incitement to racial, religious, or ethnic hatred, in circumstances where that incitement is intended to—or can reasonably be foreseen to—lead to violence or other criminal acts, are different, and are compatible with maintaining freedom to express any views at all.

Free Speech and Fake News

About a week before the US presidential election of November 2016, someone claimed on Twitter that Hillary Clinton was at the center of a pedophilia ring. The rumor spread through social media, and Alex Jones, a right-wing talk show host, repeatedly stated that she was involved in child abuse and that her campaign chairman, John Podesta, took part in satanic rituals. In a YouTube video (since removed), Jones referred to "all the children Hillary Clinton has personally murdered and chopped up and raped." The video, posted four days before the election, was watched more than 400,000 times.

Emails released by WikiLeaks showed that Podesta sometimes dined at a Washington, DC, pizza restaurant called Comet Ping Pong. Apparently for that reason the child-sex-ring accusations focused on the pizza restaurant and used the hashtag #pizzagate. The allegations were frequently retweeted by bots—programs designed to spread certain types of messages—contributing to the impression that many people were taking "Pizzagate" seriously. The story, amazingly, was also retweeted by General Michael Flynn, who after the election was appointed by Donald Trump as his national security adviser.

Even after Trump's election—and despite debunking by the *New York Times* and the *Washington Post*—the story continued to spread. Comet Ping Pong was harassed by constant, abusive, and often threatening phone calls. When the manager approached the DC police, he was told the rumors were constitutionally protected speech.

Edgar Welch, a Christian who has Bible verses tattooed on his back, was one of Jones's listeners. On December 4, he drove 350 miles from his home in North Carolina to Comet Ping Pong, armed with an assault rifle, a revolver, and a knife. He allowed guests and staff to leave while he searched for enslaved children supposedly hidden in tunnels. He fired his rifle at least once, to open a locked door. After finding no children, he surrendered to police.

Fake news—"active misinformation" that is packaged to look as if it comes from a serious news site—is a threat to democratic institutions. There have been less absurd examples, including a fake report of a nuclear threat by Israel's defense minister that misled his Pakistani counterpart into retweeting the report and warning Israel that Pakistan, too, is a nuclear power.

Whether or not fake news cost Clinton the presidency, it plainly *could* cause a candidate to lose an election and it can upset international relations. It is also contrary to one of the fundamental premises on which democracy rests: that voters can make informed choices between contending candidates.

The First Amendment to the US Constitution states that "Congress shall make no law . . . abridging the freedom of speech, or of the press." By 1919, the Supreme Court's interpretation of those words had led to the doctrine that Congress could prohibit speech only if it posed "a clear and present danger" of serious harm.

That position was further refined in what is perhaps the greatest defense of freedom of speech by an American judge: Louis Brandeis's concurring opinion in the 1927 case of *Whitney v. California.* Brandeis described freedom of speech and assembly as "functions essential to effective democracy." He appealed to "courageous, self-reliant men, with confidence in the power of free and fearless reasoning applied through the processes of popular government." On that basis, for speech to pose a clear and present danger that could justify prohibiting it, the harm the speech would cause must be so imminent that it could preclude any opportunity to discuss fully what had been said. If, Brandeis insisted, there is "time to expose through discussion the falsehood and fallacies, to avert the evil by the processes of education, the remedy to be applied is more speech, not enforced silence."

Today, it is difficult to have so much confidence in the power of "free and fearless reasoning," especially if it is supposed to be "applied through the processes of popular government"— which presumably requires that it influence elections. Similarly, Brandeis's belief that "more speech, not enforced silence" is the remedy for "falsehood and fallacies" seems naïve, especially if applied in an election campaign.

What, though, is the alternative? What Jones said about Clinton is surely defamation, and she could bring a civil suit against him; but that would be costly and time-consuming, most likely taking years to move through the courts. In any case, civil defamation lawsuits are effective only against those who have the assets to pay whatever damages are awarded.

What about criminal libel? In the United Kingdom, "defamatory libel" was for many centuries a criminal offense, but it fell into disuse and was abolished in 2010. In the United States, criminal libel is not a federal offense. It continues to be a crime in some states, but few cases are brought. A 2015 report by A. Jay Wagner and Anthony L. Fargo for the International Press Institute describes many of the recent cases as "petty" and regards the civil libel law as a better recourse for "personal grievances." The report concludes that criminal libel has become "redundant and unnecessary." That conclusion may have been premature. To accuse, during an election campaign, a US presidential candidate of personally murdering children is not petty, and civil libel law provides no adequate remedy. In the Internet age, is it time for the legal pendulum to swing back toward the offense of criminal libel?

Why Google Was Wrong

James Damore, a software engineer at Google, wrote a memo in which he argued that there are differences between men and women that may explain, in part, why there are fewer women than men in his field of work. For this, Google fired him.

Google's CEO, Sundar Pichai, sent Google employees a memo saying that "much of what was in that memo is fair to debate," but that portions of it cross a line by advancing "harmful gender stereotypes in our workplace."

Pichai did not specify which sections of the memo discussed issues that are fair to debate and which portions cross the line. That would have been difficult to do, because the entire memo is about whether certain gender stereotypes have a basis in reality. Damore argues that there is evidence to show that women, when compared to men, tend to:

- be more interested in people
- be less interested in analyzing or constructing systems
- have higher anxiety and lower tolerance of stress
- have a lower drive for status
- be more interested in balancing life and work

Damore is careful to point out that the evidence for these claims does not show that all women have these characteristics to a higher degree than men. He says that many of these differences are small, that there is significant overlap between men and women, and that "you can't say anything about an individual given these population level distributions." He shows this with a graph, too. He says that to reduce people to their group identity is bad.

There is scientific research supporting the views Damore expresses. There are also grounds for questioning some of this research. In assessing Google's action in firing Damore, it isn't necessary to decide which side is right, but only whether Damore's view is one that a Google employee should be permitted to express.

I think it is. First, as I've said, it is not some twisted, crazy view. There are serious articles, published in leading peer-reviewed scientific journals, supporting it.

Second, it addresses an important issue. Google is rightly troubled by the fact that its workforce is largely male. Sexism in many areas of employment is well-documented. Employers should be alert to the possibility that they are discriminating against women, and should take steps to prevent such discrimination. Some orchestras now conduct blind auditions—the musician plays from behind a screen, so that those making the appointment do not know if they are listening to a man or a woman. That has led to a dramatic increase in the number of women in orchestras. More businesses should look at the possibilities of similarly blinding themselves, when hiring, to the gender of applicants.

But once such anti-discrimination measures have been taken, to the greatest extent feasible, does the fact that a workforce in a particular industry is predominantly male prove that there has been discrimination? Not if the kind of work on offer is likely to be attractive to more men than women.

If the view Damore defends is right, that will be true of software engineering. If it is, then moving beyond the avoidance of discrimination in hiring and promotion to a policy of giving preference to women over men would be questionable. That is not to say that it would be impossible to justify. For example, in some professions, having female role models is important, and a valid reason for giving preference to qualified women applicants. There may also be other reasons, specific to different industries and professions, for thinking it desirable to have a more even balance of men and women. But the case would need to be made for this in the particular area of employment in which such a policy was suggested.

So: On an issue that matters, Damore put forward a view that has reasonable scientific support, and on which it is important to know what the facts are. Why was he fired?

Pichai, Google's CEO, says that "To suggest a group of our colleagues have traits that make them less biologically suited to that work is offensive and not OK." But Damore explicitly, and more than once, made it clear that he was not reducing individuals to a group, and so was not saying that women employed by Google as software engineers are less biologically suited to their work than men. Google is a very selective employer, and so it is highly probable that Google's selection processes have led to Google employing women who are, in specific traits, uncharacteristic of women as a whole. The target of Damore's memo was the idea that we should expect women to make up half the software engineering workforce, and that Google should take measures directed toward achieving that outcome.

Pichai also quotes Google's Code of Conduct, which expects "each Googler to do their utmost to create a workplace culture that is free of harassment, intimidation, bias and unlawful discrimination." Damore's memo did not harass or intimidate anyone, and in a society that protects freedom of expression, there was nothing unlawful about it. Was it biased? To show that it was, it would need to be demonstrated that Damore was biased in selecting certain scientific studies that supported his view while disregarding others that went against it. Perhaps that case could—and should—be made, but to do so would take some time and research. Pichai does not attempt, in even the most cursory way, to make a case for that.

Ironically, what Pichai has done, in firing Damore, is precisely contrary to the passage that he quotes. He has created a workplace culture in which those with opinions like Damore's will be intimidated into remaining silent.

In an ironic aftermath to Google's decision to fire Damore because of his memo about women, in 2021 a court allowed four lead plaintiffs to bring a class action against Google on behalf of 10,800 women, seeking $600 million in damages for violations of California's Equal Pay Act. The case is expected to be heard in 2023. The suit alleges that Google paid women "less base salary, smaller bonuses, and less stock than men in the same job code and location."

Keeping Discussion Free

In April 2021, the *Journal of Controversial Ideas*—of which I am a co-editor—published its first issue. The journal is a response to the shrinking boundary, even in liberal democracies, of acceptable discourse. It is specifically designed to provide a forum in which authors can, if they wish, use a pseudonym to avoid running the risk of receiving personal abuse, including death threats, or of irrevocably harming their careers.

There was a time when the threat to academic freedom in democratic countries came primarily from the right. The free speech *cause célèbre* of the early-twentieth-century United States featured Scott Nearing, a left-leaning economist at the University of Pennsylvania who was dismissed because his activism for social justice did not sit well with the bankers and corporate leaders on the university's board of trustees.

Fifty years later, in the McCarthy era, many people were blacklisted or dismissed because of their support for leftist ideas. When I came to Princeton in 1999, Steve Forbes (who was then campaigning for the Republican nomination for president) called for my appointment to be rescinded because he objected to my critique of the traditional doctrine of the sanctity of human life.

Today, however, most of the opposition to freedom of thought and discussion comes from the left. One exemplary instance occurred in 2017, when Rebecca Tuvel published "In Defense of Transracialism" in *Hypatia*, a journal of feminist philosophy. Tuvel's article asked why people who strongly support the right to choose one's gender deny a similar right to choose one's race. More than 800 people, mostly academics, signed a letter demanding that *Hypatia* retract the article. There were also calls for Tuvel, a young female academic without tenure, to be dismissed.

Shannon Winnubst, a feminist philosopher and member of the collective that wrote the letter, has explained that she did so because of her knowledge "of the damage this kind of scholarship does to marginalized groups, especially black and trans scholars." Winnubst does not attempt to refute Tuvel's argument, but only to show that it may be damaging to some — although without specifying the nature and severity of the damage.

It would be difficult to imagine a clearer contrast with John Stuart Mill's classic defense of freedom of thought and discussion in *On Liberty*. Mill considers the objection that allowing free speech will cause offense. But "there is no parity," he responds, "between the feeling of a person for his own opinion, and the feeling of another who is offended at his holding it; no more than between the desire of a thief to take a purse, and the desire of the right owner to keep it."

Whether we accept or reject the parallel Mill draws, it is at least not obvious that the fact that a view may offend some people is a sufficient reason for suppressing it. Taking that seriously would drastically narrow the scope for freedom of expression on a wide range of ethical, political, and religious questions.

The *Journal of Controversial Ideas* is a peer-reviewed interdisciplinary academic journal. Submissions must pass an initial check that excludes articles that an editor judges have no chance of receiving favorable recommendations from reviewers. Those that are not summarily rejected are sent for review to experts on the article's topic.

Reviewers then consider whether a submission is discussing a controversial idea, and if it is, what is the strength of the evidence, or the rigor of the argument, for that idea. Only submissions that make a well-argued case for their conclusions will be accepted. Other criteria for publication are that articles should not be polemical in character and must criticize only ideas and arguments, rather than the people who are the sources of those ideas and arguments.

All of this, apart from the special focus on controversial ideas, is true of most academic journals. What is distinctive about the *Journal of Controversial Ideas,* however, is authors' option of using a pseudonym, thus protecting them from the various forms of intimidation that they may otherwise fear if they advocate controversial ideas. If, at a later date, they want to be acknowledged as the authors of their articles, their identities can be confirmed. Three of the ten articles in the first issue were published under a pseudonym.

Another important aspect of the journal is that anyone with an Internet connection can read it, free and without paid advertising. The editors have pledged not to bow to public pressure to retract an article, unless it is subsequently shown to contain false data or to involve plagiarism. Because the journal is online only, the editors are not beholden to any institution or publisher. We have received financial support from a wide range of donors who share our concerns about restrictions on free speech, so we are not reliant on the favor of any particular donor or group of donors.

In seeking to protect authors from the hindrances to freedom of thought we have described, we should not forget that in much of the world, expressing controversial ideas, especially those critical of governments or a dominant religion, comes at an even higher cost. The Academic Freedom Monitoring Project of the Scholars at Risk Network reports that for the 12 months leading up to May 27, 2022, there were 241 attacks on scholars, students, and universities, including 98 killings, acts of violence, or disappearances, and 54 cases of imprisonment, while 30 scholars lost their position. China, Russia, Turkey, Iran, and Myanmar are responsible for the majority of these cases.

Yet expressing ideas can lead to long jail sentences even in countries that we do not think of as repressive dictatorships. In Thailand in 2021, a woman known only as Anchan was sentenced to 43 years in prison for posting on social media audio clips from a podcast criticizing the monarchy.

We invite people who face prison, threats, harassment, intimidation, or harm to their careers for publishing their ideas under their own name to send them to us under a pseudonym. Well-argued ideas can stand and be judged on their own, without the author's real name.

LIVING, WORKING, PLAYING

Why Pay More?

When the Polish Minister of Foreign Affairs, Radosław Sikorski, went to the Ukraine in 2013 for a talk, his Ukrainian counterparts reportedly laughed at him because he was wearing a Japanese quartz watch that cost only $165. A Ukrainian newspaper reported on the preferences of Ukrainian ministers. Several of them have watches that cost more than $30,000. Even a Communist Member of Parliament was shown wearing a watch retailing at more than $6,000.

The laughter should have gone in the other direction. Wouldn't you laugh (maybe in private, to avoid being impolite) at someone who pays more than 200 times as much as you do, and ends up with an inferior product? That's what the Ukrainians have done. They could have bought an accurate, lightweight, maintenance-free quartz watch that can run for five years, telling the time accurately without ever being moved or wound. Instead they paid far more for clunkier watches that can lose minutes every month, that will stop if you forget to wind them for a day or two (or if they have an automatic mechanism, they will stop if you don't move them). The quartz watches also have integrated alarm, stopwatch, and timer functions that the other watches either lack, or have only as design-spoiling, hard-to-read attempts to keep up with the competition.

Why would any wise shopper accept such an extremely bad bargain? Out of nostalgia, perhaps? A full-page ad for Patek Philippe has Thierry Stern, the president of the company, saying that he listens to the chime of every watch with a minute repeater that his company makes, as his father and grandfather did before him. That's all very nice, but since the days of Mr. Stern's grandfather, we have made progress in timekeeping. Why reject the improvements that human ingenuity has provided us? I have an old fountain pen that belonged to my grandmother, and I treasure it as a nice memento, but I wouldn't dream of using it to write this column.

Thorstein Veblen knew the answer. In his classic *Theory of the Leisure Class*, published in 1899, he argued that once the basis of social status became wealth itself—rather than, say, wisdom, knowledge, moral integrity, or skill in battle—the rich needed to find ways of spending money that had no other objective than the display of wealth itself. He termed this "conspicuous consumption." Veblen wrote as a social scientist, refraining from making moral judgments, although he left the reader in little doubt of his attitude to such expenditure, in a time when many lived in poverty.

Wearing a ridiculously expensive watch to proclaim that one has achieved an elevated level of social standing seems especially bad for someone who is in public office, paid by the taxpayers, in a country that still has a significant portion of its population living in real poverty. These officials are wearing the equivalent of four or five years' average Ukrainian salary on their wrists. That suggests either "You poor benighted taxpayers are paying me too much" or "Although my official salary would not permit me to afford this watch, I have other ways of getting such an expensive watch."

The Chinese government knows what those "other ways" might be. One aspect of Beijing's campaign against corruption is a clampdown on expensive gifts. As a result, according to Jon Cox, an analyst at Kepler Capital Markets, "it's no longer acceptable to have a big chunky watch on your wrist." The Chinese market for expensive watches is in steep decline. Ukrainians, take note.

Wearing a watch that costs 200 times more than one that does a better job of keeping the time says something else, even when the watch is worn by people who are not governing a relatively poor country. Andrew Carnegie, the richest man of Veblen's era, was blunt in his moral judgments. "The man who dies rich," he is often quoted as saying, "dies disgraced." We can adapt that judgment to the man or woman who wears a $30,000 watch, or buys similar luxury goods, like a $12,000 handbag. Such a person may be telling us: "I am too ignorant to know that children are dying from diarrhea or malaria because they don't have safe drinking water, or a mosquito net, and what I have spent on this ostentatiously expensive item would have been enough to help several of them survive." Alternatively, they may be saying: "I know that I could have saved several children's lives with the money I spent on this ostentatiously expensive item, but I care so little about them that I would rather let them die than buy something less expensive." It's hard to see any third possibility.

To laugh at someone for having a sensible watch at a modest price puts pressure on others to join the race to greater and greater extravagance. That pressure should be turned in the opposite direction, and we should celebrate those with modest tastes and higher priorities than conspicuous consumption.

Sikorski had the last laugh. Less than a year after his visit to Ukraine, the corruption symbolized by the expensive watches on the wrists of Ukrainian ministers was a key issue in the protests that led to the ousting of President Viktor Yanukovych and his cronies. As this book goes to press, however, a very different Ukrainian president, Volodymyr Zelensky, is risking his own life as he inspires his fellow citizens to fight for the survival of Ukraine as a democratic independent country.

Beyond the Traditional Family

(with Agata Sagan)

Early in 2019, Pope Francis traveled to Abu Dhabi, where he met Ahmed el-Tayeb, the Grand Imam of Al-Azhar (Al-Azhar University is the leading Sunni institution for the study of Islamic law). The two religious leaders signed a "Document on Human Fraternity for World Peace and Living Together," calling on their adherents, as well as world leaders, to spread tolerance and peace and to end "the moral and cultural decline that the world is presently experiencing."

One aspect of this supposed moral and cultural decline concerns the family: "To attack the institution of the family, to regard it with contempt or to doubt its important role," the Pope and the Grand Imam state, "is one of the most threatening evils of our era." The document asserts that the family is the "fundamental nucleus of society and humanity" and "is essential in bringing children into the world, raising them, educating them, and providing them with solid moral formation and domestic security."

Their anxiety is understandable: in many countries today, the traditional family consisting of a heterosexual married couple with children is becoming less dominant. But is this really a bad thing?

The United Nations predicts that the world's population will exceed 11 billion by the end of the century, with the fastest growth occurring in some of the world's poorest countries. In these circumstances, if some people choose not to bring children into the world, they should not be disparaged.

The proportion of people who are legally married is declining in some regions, for a variety of reasons. As the stigma once attached to "living in sin" fades, many couples see little reason to get married, whether or not they have children. In some countries, the legal difficulties and costs associated with divorce are a deterrent to marriage.

Such couples may, of course, establish families that are just as strong as those established by couples that have gone through a legal marriage ceremony. Similarly, "blended" or "patchwork" families that bring together children from previous relationships can provide everything that a traditional family offers. In many countries, same-sex couples may now marry and form families, although both Francis and el-Tayeb oppose such families and presumably do not regard them as providing children with "solid moral formation." The trend among single women to have children, often using artificial insemination or in vitro fertilization, no doubt also disturbs supporters of the traditional family.

Perhaps the most significant change, however, is the growing number of people who choose to be single. In the United States, 45% of adults are either divorced, widowed, or have never been married. In some places, like New York City, the majority of people are single.

Contrary to the stereotype that single people are lonely and unhappy, research shows that single people are actually more engaged in a wide network of friends and acquaintances than married people. They do more for the community and for others, and are more likely to help their parents, siblings, or neighbors, than married people.

This shouldn't really come as a surprise. Married couples are likely to put their spouse first, at least until they have children, and then the children often take priority. The tendency to care for a wider circle than one's own family is, we would argue, ethically preferable, especially in affluent societies, where other family members are likely to be far better off than more distant strangers in low-income countries. Both the Bible and the Koran recognize this more universal view as ethically superior.

We are not denying that there is great value in dividing society into small units in which adults have specific responsibility for the children living with them. This is in harmony with our evolved instinctive feelings, which we can observe in other social mammals as well. Alternative arrangements, such as the collective child-rearing in an Israeli kibbutz, have not been successful, although informal experiments in co-parenting, in which groups of adults bring up the children of some of them together, appear to be spreading.

A well-functioning family provides a more loving and more stable environment for children than any other model devised so far, but that does not mean that it must be based on a traditional marriage. In fact, despite the apparent agreement of the Pope and the Grand Imam on the importance of the family, the Christian and Muslim traditions have different conceptions of what a family is, with the latter allowing men to have more than one wife. If, despite these differences, Francis and el-Tayeb are ready to accept each other's support for "the family," they should be able to accept other models, too, as long as there is no solid evidence that they are harmful to those involved, including the children.

It is curious that a "Document on Human Fraternity for World Peace and Living Together" should assert that to doubt the importance of the family is one of the most threatening evils of our era. From a global perspective, it is not helpful to limit ourselves to such small units. Travel and the Internet are enabling new friendships beyond the home and beyond the borders of our countries. If we are really concerned with "human fraternity," then maybe we should place more emphasis on building relationships that span the globe, rather than condemn those who see the traditional family as unduly constricting.

Tiger Mothers or Elephant Mothers?

Many years ago, my wife and I were driving somewhere with our three young daughters in the back, when one of them suddenly asked: "Would you rather that we were clever or that we were happy?"

I was reminded of that moment when I read Amy Chua's *Wall Street Journal* article, "Why Chinese Mothers Are Superior," a promotional piece for her book, *Battle Hymn of the Tiger Mother,* which became an instant bestseller.

Chua's thesis is that, when compared to Americans, Chinese children tend to be successful because they have "tiger mothers," whereas Western mothers are pussycats, or worse. Chua's daughters, Sophia and Louise, were *never* allowed to watch television, play computer games, sleep over at a friend's home, or be in a school play. They had to spend hours every day practicing the piano or violin. They were expected to be the top student in every subject except gym and drama.

Chinese mothers, according to Chua, believe that children, once they get past the toddler stage, need to be told, in no uncertain terms, when they have not met the high standards their parents expect of them. (Chua says that she knows Korean,

Indian, Jamaican, Irish, and Ghanaian mothers who are "Chinese" in their approach, as well as some ethnic Chinese mothers who are not.) Their egos should be strong enough to take it.

But Chua, a professor at Yale Law School (as is her husband), lives in a culture in which a child's self-esteem is considered so fragile that children's sports teams give "Most Valuable Player" awards to every member. So it is not surprising that many Americans react with horror to her style of parenting.

One problem in assessing the tiger-mothering approach is that we can't separate its impact from that of the genes that the parents pass on to their children. If you want your children to be at the top of their class, it helps if you and your partner have the brains to become professors at elite universities. No matter how hard a tiger mom pushes, not every student can finish first (unless, of course, we make everyone "top of the class").

Tiger parenting aims at getting children to make the most of what abilities they have, and so seems to lean toward the "clever" side of the "clever or happy" choice. That's also the view of Betty Ming Liu, who blogged in response to Chua's article: "Parents like Amy Chua are the reason why Asian-Americans like me are in therapy."

Stanley Sue, a professor of psychology at the University of California, Davis, has studied suicide, which is particularly common among Asian American women (in other ethnic groups, more males commit suicide than females). He believes that family pressure is a significant factor.

Chua would reply that reaching a high level of achievement brings great satisfaction, and that the only way to do it is through hard work. Perhaps, but can't children be encouraged to do things because they are intrinsically worthwhile, rather than because of fear of parental disapproval?

I agree with Chua to this extent: a reluctance to tell a child what to do can go too far. One of my daughters, who now has children of her own, tells me amazing stories about her friends' parenting styles. One of them let her daughter drop out of three different kindergartens, because she didn't want to go to them. Another couple believes in "self-directed learning" to such an extent that one evening they went to bed at 11 p.m., leaving their five-year-old watching her ninth straight hour of Barbie videos.

Tiger mothering might seem to be a useful counterbalance to such permissiveness, but both extremes leave something out. Chua's focus is unrelentingly on solitary activities in the home, with no encouragement of group activities, or of concern for others, either in school or in the wider community. Thus, she appears to view school plays as a waste of time that could be better spent studying or practicing music.

But to take part in a school play is to contribute to a community good. If talented children stay away, the quality of the production will suffer, to the detriment of the others who take part (and of the audience that will watch it). Children whose parents bar them from such activities miss the opportunity to develop social skills that are just as important and rewarding—and just as demanding to master—as those that monopolize Chua's attention.

We should aim for our children to be good people, and to live ethical lives that manifest concern for others as well as for themselves. This approach to child-rearing is not unrelated to happiness: there is abundant evidence that those who are generous and kind are more content with their lives than those who are not. But it is also an important goal in its own right.

Tigers lead solitary lives, except for mothers with their cubs. We, by contrast, are social animals. So are elephants, and elephant mothers do not focus only on the well-being of their own offspring. Together, they protect and take care of all the young in their herd, running a kind of day-care center.

If we all think only of our own interests, we are headed for collective disaster—just look at what we are doing to our planet's climate. When it comes to raising our children, we need fewer tigers and more elephants.

How Honest Are We?

You have lost your wallet. Its contents include your business cards with your e-mail address. How likely is it that you will receive a message telling you that it has been found? If the wallet has money in it, does that improve or reduce the odds that you will get it back, with its contents intact?

To ask these questions is also to ask to what extent most people are basically honest, or care about strangers. Some evolutionary psychologists argue that altruism is limited to our kin and to those who can reciprocate whatever help we give them. Is that too cynical? Last month, researchers from the United States and Switzerland shed some light on that question when they published the results of a huge and ingenious study involving more than 17,000 "lost" wallets in 40 countries.

At banks, theaters, museums, hotels, and public offices in 355 different cities, research assistants handed in a wallet, telling the person at the counter that they had found it on the street, but were in a hurry. The assistant then asked that person to "please take care of it" and left without providing contact details or asking for a receipt.

All the wallets were made of transparent plastic, and three identical business cards with an e-mail address were immediately visible. The wallets also contained a grocery shopping list, written in the local language. Some wallets contained no money, while others had $13.45, or its purchasing power equivalent in local currency, and some—in a trial limited to the United States, the United Kingdom, and Poland—contained $94.15 or its equivalent. Most wallets also contained a key. The researchers recorded the number of messages reporting the wallet found that were received at the e-mail address on the business cards. To enable the researchers to study factors that led to reporting, each wallet contained cards with a unique e-mail address.

As one might expect, the reporting rate tended to be higher in more affluent countries. Switzerland, Norway, the Netherlands, Denmark, and Sweden topped the list, with more than 65% of presumed wallet owners notified. Poland and the Czech Republic were close behind—and ahead of wealthier countries like Australia, Canada, and the United States.

Some people think that religious believers are more likely to obey moral rules than non-believers, but the study does not support this view, at least if we can judge the extent of religious belief by the proportion of people in a country who say that religion is important to them. In Sweden, Denmark, Norway, and the Czech Republic, at least 75% of the population say that religion is not important to them, yet all these countries have high reporting rates. On the other hand, more than 80% of the population in Peru and Morocco say that religion is very important to them, yet both countries have reporting rates below 25%.

Women were roughly 2% more likely to report a wallet than men. This study thus adds to previous research suggesting that women tend to be more ethical than men.

The most striking result of the study, however, is that wallets containing money were more likely to be reported to their presumed owners than wallets with no money. That finding was consistent across 38 of the 40 countries—the exceptions were Mexico and Peru, where the presence of money made no statistically significant difference to the (low) reporting rate. Moreover, in the three countries where the wallets containing $94.15 were "found," they were reported at a higher rate than those with only $13.45.

The researchers considered various possible explanations for this outcome, including fear of being punished for keeping the money, expectation of a reward for reporting it, and the possibility that even when the found wallet was reported, it would be returned without the cash. But when reported wallets were collected, 98% of the money in them was returned. Other evidence suggested that neither fear of punishment nor hope of reward was likely to be the primary motivation for reporting the finding of the wallet.

Why, then, would people be more likely to report a wallet that has more money in it? The researchers propose four factors that determine whether someone with the opportunity to return a wallet will do so: the economic payoff from keeping it, the effort of reporting it, altruistic concern for the owner, and an aversion to seeing oneself as a thief. According to this model, although the presence of money increases the economic payoff of keeping the wallet (and the more money the higher the payoff), that economic gain is outweighed by the combination of altruistic concern and the desire to see oneself as an honest person.

The evidence that altruistic concern plays some role in the decision to report the wallet comes from comparing return rates for wallets with and without a key. The key is presumably important to the owner, but, in contrast to money, is of no use to the person in possession of the wallet. Hence, it is unlikely to be relevant to that person's self-image as an honest person rather than a thief. Yet wallets with a key and money in them were more likely to be reported to the owner than those with money and no key, suggesting that it was not only concern for one's self-image that motivated the reports.

We should all be encouraged by these findings. It is common to hear people complain that we live in an era in which self-interest prevails, moral standards have collapsed, few care about others, and most people would steal if they thought they could get away with it. This study provides solid evidence that the world is not nearly so bad.

Is Doping Wrong?

I first wrote about drugs in sport in 2007. The topic came up every July, when the Tour de France was held. So many leading cyclists tested positive for drugs, or admitted, from the safety of retirement, that they had used them, that many people doubted that anyone could be competitive in major endurance cycling race without taking drugs.

In the United States, the debate was fueled by the baseball player Barry Bonds' march toward the all-time record for home runs in a career. Bonds is widely believed to have been helped by drugs and synthetic hormones. He is frequently booed and mocked by fans, and many thought that baseball's commis sioner, Bud Selig, should not attend games at which Bonds might tie or break the record.

The most prominent international doping scandal began in 2016 when a Russian whistleblower revealed that members of the Russian Olympic team had been taking performance-enhancing drugs for many years, including at least 15 medal winners from the 2014 winter Olympics. Russia received a two-year ban from the World Anti-Doping Agency, but that became less significant when Russian athletes were allowed to compete at the 2021 summer and winter Olympics, under the auspices of the Russian Olympic Committee, but not as officially representing Russia.

The problem will not go away, because at the elite level, the difference between being a champion and an also-ran is so minuscule, and yet matters so much, that athletes are pressured to do whatever they can to gain the slightest edge over their competitors. In many sports, it is now unclear whether gold medals now go, not to those who are drug-free, but to those who most successfully refine their drug use for maximum enhancement without detection.

Professor Julian Savulescu, who directs the Uehiro Centre for Practical Ethics at Oxford University and holds degrees in both medicine and bioethics, has proposed a radical solution: drop the ban on performance-enhancing drugs, and allow athletes to take whatever they want, as long as it is safe for them to do so.

Savulescu proposes that instead of trying to detect whether an athlete has taken drugs, we should focus on measurable indications of whether an athlete is risking their health. So, if an athlete has a dangerously high level of red blood cells as a result of taking erythropoietin (EPO), they should not be allowed to compete. The issue is the red blood cell count, not the means used to elevate it.

To those who say that this will give drug users an unfair advantage, Savulescu replies that those with the best genes already have an unfair advantage. They must still train, of course, but if their genes produce more EPO than ours, they are going to beat us in the Tour de France, no matter how hard we train. Unless, that is, we take EPO to make up for our genetic deficiency.

Setting a maximum level of red blood cells actually levels the playing field by reducing the impact of the genetic lottery. Effort then becomes more important than having the right genes.

Some argue that taking drugs is "against the spirit of sport." It is difficult to defend the current line between what athletes can and cannot do in order to enhance their performance. In the Tour de France, cyclists may use overnight intravenous nutrition and hydration to restore their bodies. Training at high altitude is permitted, though it gives those athletes who can do it an edge over competitors who must train at sea level. The World Anti-Doping Code no longer prohibits caffeine. In any case, performance enhancement is, Savulescu says, the very spirit of sport. We should allow athletes to pursue it by any safe means.

Anyway, there is no single spirit of sport. People play sports to socialize, for exercise, to keep fit, to earn money, to become famous, to prevent boredom, to find love, and for the sheer fun of it. They may strive to improve their performance, but often they do so for its own sake, for the sense of achievement.

Popular participation in sport should be encouraged. Physical exercise makes people not only healthier, but also happier. To take drugs will usually be self-defeating. I swim for exercise, and time myself over a set distance to give myself a goal that leads me to work harder. I am pleased when I swim a good time, but I would get no sense of achievement if an improvement came out of a bottle.

Yet elite sport, watched by millions but participated in by few, is different. For the sake of fame and glory now, athletes will be tempted to risk their long-term health if they can get away with it. So, while Savulescu's bold suggestion may reduce illegal drug use, because fewer drugs will be illegal, it will not end it.

The problem is not with the athletes, but with us. If we stopped making such a fuss over the winners, doping would stop. But that doesn't seem likely to happen anytime soon.

Is It OK to Cheat at Football?

Shortly before halftime in the 2010 World Cup knockout match between England and Germany, the English midfielder Frank Lampard had a shot at goal that struck the crossbar and bounced down onto the ground, clearly over the goal line. The goalkeeper, Manuel Neuer, grabbed the ball and put it back into play. Neither the referee nor the linesman, both of whom were still coming down the field—and thus were poorly positioned to judge—signaled a goal, and play continued.

After the match, Neuer gave this account of his actions: "I tried not to react to the referee and just concentrate on what was happening. I realized it was over the line and I think the way I carried on so quickly fooled the referee into thinking it was not over."

To put it bluntly: Neuer cheated, and then boasted about it.

By any normal ethical standards, what Neuer did was wrong. But does the fact that Neuer was playing football mean that the only ethical rule is "Win at all costs"?

In soccer, that does seem to be the prevailing ethic. The most famous of these incidents was Diego Maradona's goal in Argentina's 1986 World Cup match against England, which he later described as having been scored "a little with the head of Maradona and a little with the hand of God." Replays failed to show divine intervention, and left no doubt that it was the hand of Maradona that scored the goal. Twenty years later, he admitted in a BBC interview that he had intentionally acted as if it were a goal, in order to deceive the referee.

Something similar happened last November, in a game between France and Ireland that decided which of the two nations went to the World Cup. The French striker Thierry Henry used his hand to control the ball and pass to a teammate, who scored the decisive goal. Asked about the incident after the match, Henry said: "I will be honest, it was a handball. But I'm not the ref. I played it, the ref allowed it. That's a question you should ask him."

But is it? Why should the fact that you can get away with cheating mean that you are not culpable? Players should not be exempt from ethical criticism for what they do on the field, any more than they are exempt from ethical criticism for cheating off the field—for example, by taking performance-enhancing drugs.

Sports today are highly competitive, with huge amounts of money at stake, but that does not mean it is impossible to be honest. In cricket, if a batsman hits the ball and one of the fielders catches it, the batsman is out. Sometimes when the ball is caught behind the batsman, the umpire cannot be sure if it touched the edge of the bat as it passed through. The batsman usually knows and traditionally should "walk"—leave the ground—if he knows that he is out.

Some still do. The Australian batsman Adam Gilchrist "walked" in the 2003 World Cup semi-final against Sri Lanka, although the umpire had already declared him not out. His decision surprised some of his teammates but won applause from many cricket fans.

There are a few cases of footballers doing something equivalent to a batsman walking. Morten Wieghorst was captaining Denmark against Iran in 2003 when someone in the stands blew a whistle. An Iranian defender thought it was the referee blowing half-time, and picked up the ball inside the penalty area. Wieghorst was given the penalty, but deliberately put it wide. There are a few other examples of players who were awarded penalties telling the referee that they were not fouled.

More often, though, a culture of excessive partisanship trumps ethical values. Fans don't seem to mind if members of their own team cheat successfully; they only object when the other side cheats. That is not an ethical attitude. (Though, to their credit, many French football followers, from President Nicolas Sarkozy down, expressed their sympathy for Ireland after Henry's handball.)

Yes, we can deal with the problem to some extent by using modern technology or video replays to review controversial refereeing decisions. That reduces the opportunity for cheating, but it won't eliminate it, and it isn't really the point. We should not make excuses for intentional cheating in sports. In one important way, it is much worse than cheating in one's private life. When what you do in a World Cup football match will be seen by millions, revisited on endless video replays, and dissected on television sports programs, that makes it especially important to do what is right.

How would football fans have reacted if Neuer had stopped play and told the referee that the ball was a goal? The initial reaction would no doubt have been a surprise. Some German fans might have been disappointed. But the world as a whole—and every fair-minded German fan too—would have had to admit that he had done the right thing.

Neuer missed a rare opportunity to do something noble in front of millions of people. He could have set a positive ethical example to people watching all over the world, including those who are young and impressionable. Who knows what difference that example might have made to the lives of some of those watching? Neuer could have been a hero, standing up for what is right. Instead, he is just another footballer who is clever at cheating.

Why Climb Mount Everest?

In 1953, when Edmund Hillary and Tenzing Norgay became the first people to reach the summit of Mount Everest, I was seven years old. I immersed myself in the stories of the epic climb. It seemed like an achievement for all of humankind, like reaching the South Pole. Would there still be any frontiers left, I wondered, by the time I grew up?

A photo of the southern summit ridge of Everest has brought these memories back to me. But what a different Everest this is! The splendid isolation of the top of the world has gone. Instead, there is a long line of climbers waiting their turn to stand briefly on the summit.

It's not hard to see why. As the expedition company Seven Summit Treks advertises: "If you want to experience what it feels like to be on the highest point on the planet and have strong economic background to compensate for your old age and your fear of risks you can sign up for the VVIP Mount Everest Expedition Service." You need the "strong economic background" because it will cost you $130,000. There are less expensive ways to climb Everest, but they all start with the $11,000 fee that the Nepalese government charges for a permit.

We shouldn't object to the government of a low-income country seeking revenue from wealthy foreign climbers. But even with the best support money can buy, in the thin air above 8,000 meters, people die—12 in 2019 alone. There are at least 200 bodies still on the mountain, some in crevasses, others buried by avalanches. Still others have been described as "familiar fixtures on the route to Everest's summit."

It used to be taken for granted that if a climber was in danger, others would help, even if that meant abandoning their own plans. No longer. In 2006, it was reported that David Sharp, who had chosen to climb Everest without Sherpa support, slowly froze to death while about 40 climbers passed him on their way to the summit. Edmund Hillary found it "horrifying." Later reports suggested that most of the 40 did not notice Sharp, or were unaware that he needed help. But some climbers, like the Australian Brad Horn, have been quite explicit in saying that they are on the mountain only to get to the top, and will not stop to help anyone else until they have achieved that goal.

I've used the example of rescuing a child drowning in a shallow pond to explore questions about our obligation to save the lives of strangers. When I ask my students if they would wade into a shallow pond to save a drowning child, even if doing so would ruin their favorite, and most expensive, pair of shoes, they tell me that you can't compare a child's life with a pair of shoes, so of course they would save the child. What if the only way to save a child from being struck and killed by a runaway train is to divert it down a siding where it will destroy your most precious possession, a vintage Bugatti, into which you have sunk most of your savings? Never mind, most still say, you have to save the child.

If that's right, then why does climbing Everest allow one to refrain from saving the life of a fellow climber? Is it because, as Horn says in defending his attitude, "Everyone knows the risk"? That may be true, but, as Immanuel Kant argued, our obligation to help strangers is grounded by our own desire to be helped when in need. Hence, we cannot will, as a universal law, that people pass by strangers in need. Horn would need to reply that, had he needed to be rescued, other climbers would have been justified in leaving him to die as they headed to the summit.

In any case, even if you are lucky enough to get to the top of Everest without passing a climber in need of help, you are still choosing to reach the summit rather than to save a life. That's because the cost of the climb would be enough to save the lives of several people, if given to an effective charity.

I enjoy hiking, and being in wild places. I like hikes that take me to a summit, especially one with a view. So I can understand why Hillary wanted to climb Mount Everest. But I have trouble understanding why anyone would see that as a worthwhile goal today. It does not require great mountaineering skill, and it is very far from a wilderness experience. Arnold Coster, a Dutch mountaineer who organizes Everest climbs, says that many of his customers are more like trophy hunters than mountaineers. Tim Macartney-Snape, who climbed Everest in 1984, says that today's climbers are "more interested in talking about it at a cocktail party than actually being in the mountains. It's a status-enhancing thing."

If that is right, one can only regard it as a pity that the desire for status leads us to set goals that involve pointless or even harmful activities rather than goals that have value independent of status, like helping those in need and making the world a better place.

A Surfing Reflection

For me, as for most Australians, summer holidays have always meant going to the beach. I grew up swimming and playing in the waves, eventually moving on to a body board, but somehow missing out on learning to stand on a surfboard.

I finally made up for that omission when I was in my fifties—too old ever to become good at it, but young enough for surfing to give me a decade of fun and a sense of accomplishment. This southern summer, I'm back in Australia and in the waves again.

At the beach where I surfed today, I heard about a ceremony that had taken place there earlier in the season—a farewell to a local surfer who had died at a ripe old age. His fellow surfers paddled out into the ocean and formed a circle, sitting on their boards, while his ashes were scattered over the surface. Other friends and family stood and watched from the beach and cliff top. I was told that he was one of the best surfers around, but at a time when there was no money in it.

Was it his bad luck, I wondered, to be born too early to take part in today's lucrative professional surfing circuit? Or was it his good luck to be part of a surfing scene that was less about stardom and more about enjoying the waves?

This is not a general rant against the corrupting influence of money. Having money opens up opportunities that, if used well, can be very positive. Surfers have created environmental organizations like the Surfrider Foundation, which has a special concern for the oceans; and SurfAid, which tries to spread some of the benefits of surfing tourism in developing countries to the poorest of the local people. Still, the spirit of surfing's early days (think of the harmony of wave and human action portrayed in the 1971 movie *Morning of the Earth*) contrasts sharply with the razzamatazz of today's professional circuit.

Some sports are inherently competitive. Tennis fans may admire a well-executed backhand; but watching players warm up on court would soon become dull if no match followed. The same is true of soccer: who would go to watch a group of people kicking a ball around a field if it wasn't all about winning or losing? Players of these sports cannot exhibit the full range of their skills without being pushed by a competitive opponent.

Surfing is different. It offers opportunities to meet challenges that call on a variety of skills, both physical and mental; but the challenges are intrinsic to the activity and do not involve beating an opponent. In that respect, surfing is closer to hiking, mountaineering, or skiing than to tennis or football: the aesthetic experience of being in a beautiful natural environment is an important part of the activity's attractiveness; there is satisfaction to be found in the sense of accomplishment; and there is vigorous physical exercise without the monotony of running on a treadmill or swimming laps. An artificial wave pool may enable you to improve your technique, but it won't give you the kind of experience I'm talking about either.

To make surfing competitive requires contriving ways to measure performance. The solution is to judge certain skills displayed in riding a wave. There is nothing wrong with surfers competing to see who can do the most difficult maneuvers on a wave—just as there is nothing wrong with seeing who can pull off the most difficult dive from the ten-meter platform.

But when we make surfing competitive, a recreational activity in which millions of people can happily participate is transformed into a spectator sport to be watched, for most, on a screen. It would be highly regrettable if the competitive sport's narrow focus on point-scoring were to limit our appreciation of the beauty and harmony we can experience riding a wave without fitting as many turns as possible into our time on it.

Many of the highlights of my surfing have more to do with experiencing the splendor and power of the waves than with my ability to ride them. In fact, at the time of my single most magical surfing moment, I wasn't on a wave at all. At Byron Bay, Australia's easternmost point, I was paddling out to where the waves were breaking. The sun was shining, the sea was blue, and I was aware of the Pacific Ocean stretching ahead thousands of miles, uninterrupted by land until it reached the coast of Chile.

A pulse of energy generated in that vast expanse of water neared a submerged line of rocks and reared up in front of me in a green wall. As the wave began to break, a dolphin leapt out ahead of the foam, its entire body clear of the water.

It was a sublime moment, but not such an unusual one. As many of my fellow wave riders know, we are the only animal that plays tennis or football, but not the only animal that enjoys surfing.

THE FUTURE

Should We Live to 1,000?

On which problems should we focus research in medicine and the biological sciences? There is a strong argument for tackling the diseases that kill the most people—diseases like malaria, measles, and diarrhea, which kill millions in developing countries but very few in the developed world.

Developed countries, however, devote most of their research funds to the diseases from which their citizens suffer, and that seems likely to continue for the foreseeable future. Given that constraint, which medical breakthrough would do the most to improve our lives?

If your first thought is "a cure for cancer" or "a cure for heart disease," think again. Aubrey de Grey, who founded the SENS Research Foundation and was for a time the world's most prominent advocate of anti-aging research, argues that it makes no sense to spend the vast majority of our medical resources on trying to combat the diseases of aging without tackling aging itself. If we cure one of these diseases, those who would have died from it can expect to succumb to another in a few years. The benefit will be modest. (SENS parted with de Grey in 2021 after two scientists made complaints of improper conduct against him, and de Grey then attempted to exert influence over one of the complainants.)

In developed countries, aging is the ultimate cause of 90 percent of all human deaths; thus, treating aging is a form of preventive medicine for all of the diseases of old age. Moreover, even before aging leads to our death, it reduces our capacity to enjoy our own lives and to contribute positively to the lives of others. So, instead of targeting specific diseases that are much more likely to occur when people have reached a certain age, wouldn't a better strategy be to attempt to forestall or repair the damage done to our bodies by the aging process?

De Grey believes that even modest progress in this area over the coming decade could lead to a dramatic extension of the human life span. All we need to do is reach what he calls "longevity escape velocity"—that is, the point at which we can extend life sufficiently to allow time for further scientific progress to permit additional extensions, and thus further progress and greater longevity. Speaking at Princeton University in 2012, de Grey said: "We don't know how old the first person who will live to 150 is today, but the first person to live to 1,000 is almost certainly less than 20 years younger."

What most attracts de Grey about this prospect is not living forever, but rather the extension of healthy, youthful life that would come with a degree of control over the process of aging. In developed countries, enabling those who are young or middle-aged to remain youthful longer would attenuate the looming demographic problem of an historically unprecedented proportion of the population reaching advanced age—and often becoming dependent on younger people.

On the other hand, we still need to pose the ethical question: Are we being selfish in seeking to extend our lives so dramatically? And, if we succeed, will the outcome be good for some but unfair to others?

People in rich countries already can expect to live about 30 years longer than people in the poorest countries. If we discover how to slow aging, we might have a world in which the poor majority must face death at a time when members of the rich minority are only one-tenth of the way through their expected life spans.

That disparity is one reason to believe that overcoming aging will increase injustice in the world. Another is that if people continue to be born, while others do not die, the planet's population will increase at a faster rate than it does now, which will likewise make life for some much worse than it would have been otherwise. Rather than seeking to discover how we can live to 1,000, wouldn't it be much better to support existing research on preserving health and enabling everyone to retain their full capacities, or as close to that as possible, for their entire life?

Whether we can overcome these objections depends on our degree of optimism about future technological and economic advances. Often innovations are expensive initially, but the price then drops sharply, as it has for computers and for the drugs that prevent the development of AIDS. If the world can continue to develop economically and technologically, people will become wealthier, and, in the long run, anti-aging treatment will benefit everyone. So why not get started and make it a priority now?

As for the second objection, contrary to what most people assume, success in overcoming aging could itself give us breathing space to find solutions to the population problem, because it would also delay or eliminate menopause, enabling women to have their first children much later than they can now. If economic development continues, fertility rates in developing countries will fall, as they have in developed countries. In the end, technology, too, may help to overcome the population objection, by providing new sources of energy that do not increase our carbon footprint.

The population objection raises a deeper philosophical question. If our planet has a finite capacity to support human life, is it better to have fewer people living longer lives, or more people living shorter lives? One reason for thinking it better to have fewer people living longer lives is that only those who are born know what death deprives them of; those who do not exist cannot know what they are missing.

What is still not clear, however, is whether the initial optimism about overcoming aging, shown by de Grey and others, was justified. It is now a decade since de Grey suggested that the first person to live to 150 is already alive, and that the first person to live to 1,000 would not be more than 20 years younger. Despite the lack of major anti-aging breakthroughs since he made that claim, I don't find it too difficult to believe that there is a ten-year-old alive now who will live to 150. But research over the past decade has produced nothing to suggest that living to 1,000 will be achievable in the next century or two.

Rights for Robots?

(with Agata Sagan)

Robots today are performing many functions, from serving in restaurants to defusing bombs. Children and adults play with toy robots, while vacuum-cleaning robots are sucking up dirt in a growing number of homes and—as evidenced by YouTube videos—entertaining cats. There is even a World Cup in soccer for robots, part of a project that aims, by 2050, to have a team of robots winning a game against the human players who won the most recent World Cup. If the standard of the latest RoboCup, held in Sydney in 2019, is any guide, footballers have no need to feel threatened just yet. (Chess and Go, of course, are different matters.)

Robots have been used in elder care for more than a decade, and the demand for them is growing, because in some affluent societies, elderly people make up an increasing proportion of the population, and there is a shortage of people willing to work in homes for them. They perform simple tasks like fetching food and water, and more sophisticated ones like playing games, reminding people of their appointments, and even engaging with people socially.

Is there something wrong with people conversing with a robot, rather than a human being? What about parents employing robots as babysitters? Noel Sharkey, professor of artificial intelligence and robotics at the University of Sheffield, has asked what spending a lot of time with a machine that cannot express genuine empathy, understanding, or compassion, will do to a child.

In his book *Love and Sex with Robots*, David Levy goes further, suggesting that we will fall in love with warm, cuddly robots, and even have sex with them. (If the robot has multiple sexual partners, just remove the relevant parts, drop them in disinfectant, and, voilà, no risk of sexually transmitted diseases!) But what will the presence of a "sexbot" do to the marital home? How will we feel if our spouse starts spending too much time with an inexhaustible robotic lover?

A more ominous question is familiar from novels and movies: Will we have to defend our civilization against intelligent machines of our own creation? Some consider the development of superhuman artificial intelligence inevitable, and expect it to happen no later than 2070. If that happens, the crucial question for the future of civilization is: Will the super-intelligent computers be friendly? A good deal of thought is now going into ways in which we can prevent our own creations from becoming hostile to us, or more positively, to ensure that any machines that rival or surpass our intelligence are also aligned with our values.

We have focused less, however, on the opposite question: not that robots will harm us, but that we will harm them. At present, robots are mere items of property. But what if they become sufficiently complex to have feelings? After all, isn't the human brain just a very complex machine?

If machines can and do become conscious, will we take their feelings into account? The history of our relations with the only nonhuman sentient beings we have encountered so far—animals—gives no ground for confidence that we would recognize sentient robots not just as items of property, but as beings with moral standing and interests that deserve consideration.

Powerful new technologies, once they are available at reasonable cost, tend to spread rapidly, in an uncontrolled way. The development of a conscious robot that (who?) was not widely perceived as a member of our moral community could therefore lead to mistreatment on a large scale.

The hard question, of course, is how we could tell that a robot really was conscious, and not just designed to mimic consciousness. Understanding how the robot had been programmed would provide a clue—did the designers write the code to provide only the appearance of consciousness? If so, we would have no reason to believe that the robot was conscious.

But if the robot was designed to have human-like capacities that might incidentally give rise to consciousness, we would have a good reason to think that it really was conscious. What moral status should it have? In 2021, Jamie Harris and Jacy Reese Anthis reviewed the literature on this topic and found 294 relevant items. In this extensive literature, they reported, there is widespread agreement that, in future, some artificial entities will warrant moral consideration.

Can Artificial Intelligence Be Ethical?

Last month, AlphaGo, a computer program specially designed to play the game Go, caused shockwaves among aficionados when it defeated Lee Sidol, one of the world's top-ranked professional players, winning a five-game tournament by a score of 4–1.

Why, you may ask, is that news? Twenty years have passed since the IBM computer Deep Blue defeated world chess champion Garry Kasparov, and we all know computers have improved since then. But Deep Blue won through sheer computing power, using its ability to calculate the outcomes of more moves to a deeper level than even a world champion can. Go is played on a far larger board (19 by 19 squares, compared to 8 by 8 for chess) and has more possible moves than there are atoms in the universe, so raw computing power was unlikely to beat a human with a strong intuitive sense of the best moves.

Instead, AlphaGo was designed to win by playing a huge number of games against other programs and adopting the strategies that proved successful. You could say that AlphaGo evolved to be the best Go player in the world, achieving in only two years what natural selection took millions of years to accomplish.

Eric Schmidt, executive chairman of Google's parent company, the owner of AlphaGo, is enthusiastic about what artificial intelligence (AI) means for humanity. Speaking before the match between Lee and AlphaGo, he said that humanity would be the winner, whatever the outcome, because advances in AI will make every human being smarter, more capable, and "just better human beings."

Will it? Around the same time as AlphaGo's triumph, Microsoft's "chatbot"—software named Taylor that was designed to respond to messages from people aged 18–24—was having a chastening experience. "Tay," as she called herself, was supposed to be able to learn from the messages she received and gradually improve her ability to conduct engaging conversations. Unfortunately, within 24 hours, people were teaching Tay racist and sexist ideas. When she starting saying positive things about Hitler, Microsoft turned her off and deleted her most offensive messages.

I do not know whether the people who turned Tay into a racist were themselves racists, or just thought it would be fun to undermine Microsoft's new toy. Either way, the juxtaposition of AlphaGo's victory and Taylor's defeat serves as a warning. It is one thing to unleash AI in the context of a game with specific rules and a clear goal; it is something very different to release AI into the real world, where the unpredictability of the environment may reveal a software error that has disastrous consequences.

Nick Bostrom, the director of the Future of Humanity Institute at Oxford University, argues in his book *Superintelligence* that it will not always be as easy to turn off an intelligent machine as it was to turn off Tay. He defines superintelligence as an intellect that is "smarter than the best human brains in practically every field, including scientific creativity, general wisdom, and social skills." Such a system may be able to outsmart our attempts to turn it off.

Some doubt that superintelligence will ever be achieved. Bostrom, together with Vincent Müller, asked AI experts to indicate dates corresponding to when there is a one in two chance of machines achieving human-level intelligence and when there is a nine in ten chance. The median estimates for the one in two chance were in the 2040–2050 range, and 2075 for the nine in ten chance. Most experts expected that AI would achieve superintelligence within 30 years of achieving human-level intelligence.

We should not take these estimates too seriously. The overall response rate was only 31%, and researchers working in AI have an incentive to boost the importance of their field by trumpeting its potential to produce momentous results.

The prospect of AI achieving superintelligence may seem too distant to worry about, especially given more pressing problems. But there is a case to be made for starting to think about how we can design AI to take into account the interests of humans, and indeed of all sentient beings (including machines, if they are also conscious beings with interests of their own).

With driverless cars already on California roads, it is not too soon to ask whether we can program a machine to act ethically. As such cars improve, they will save lives, because they will make fewer mistakes than human drivers do. Sometimes, however, they will face a choice between lives. Should they be programmed to swerve to avoid hitting a child running across the road, even if that will put their passengers at risk? What about swerving to avoid a dog? What if the only risk is damage to the car itself, not to the passengers?

Perhaps there will be lessons to learn as such discussions about driverless cars get started. But driverless cars are not superintelligent beings. Teaching ethics to a machine that is more intelligent than we are, in a wide range of fields, is a far more daunting task.

Bostrom begins *Superintelligence* with a fable about sparrows who think it would be great to train an owl to help them build their nests and care for their young. So they set out to find an owl egg. One sparrow objects that they should first think about how to tame the owl; but the others are impatient to get the exciting new project underway. They will take on the challenge of training the owl (for example, not to eat sparrows) when they have successfully raised one.

If we want to make an owl that is wise, and not only intelligent, let's not be like those impatient sparrows.

Do You Want to Be a Cyborg?

(with Agata Sagan)

Have you ever wished you could add extra memory to your brain? Elon Musk may be able to help you with that.

Musk heads the company best known for making Tesla, the industry-leading electric car, and is the CEO of SpaceX, which is building rockets so that humans can live on Mars. He is also the founder and chief executive of Neuralink, a startup seeking to create cerebral implants that will turn computers into a direct extension of our brains and thus enhance our intelligence and memory.

Musk's various projects have a single overarching aim: to safeguard the future of our species. Electric cars improve our chances of preventing dangerous levels of global warming. A permanent settlement on Mars would reduce the risk of climate change—or a nuclear war, bioterrorism, or asteroid collision— wiping out our species.

Neuralink serves this goal, too, because Musk is among those who believe that to build a machine smarter than yourself is, as Nick Bostrom, the author of *Superintelligence*, puts it, "a basic Darwinian error." Yet, given rapid progress on development of artificial intelligence, and the multiple incentives for making computers even smarter, Musk sees no way of preventing that from happening. His favored strategy to save us from being eliminated by superintelligent machines is therefore to hook us into computers, so that we become as clever as state-of-the-art artificial intelligence, however intelligent that may be.

There is nothing new about people having electronic devices implanted in their bodies. The artificial cardiac pacemaker has been in use for nearly 60 years. Since 1998, scientists have been implanting devices in the brains of people who are paralyzed, enabling them to move a cursor on a screen with their thoughts, or in more advanced versions, to move an artificial hand that can grasp things.

Such devices don't extend our abilities beyond those of a normal healthy person. The artist Neil Harbisson, however, had an antenna implanted in his skull that enables him to hear frequencies corresponding not only to colors we can see—Harbisson has an extreme form of colorblindness—but also to infrared and ultraviolet light, which are invisible to us. Harbisson claims that he is a cyborg, that is, an organism with technologically enhanced capacities.

To move from these useful but limited devices to the kind of brain–machine interactions that Musk is seeking would require major scientific breakthroughs. Most of the research on brain implants uses nonhuman animals, and the decades of harm inflicted on monkeys and other animals make it ethically dubious.

In any case, for Musk's plan to succeed, experimenting on humans as well as animals will be unavoidable. Incurably disabled or terminally ill patients may volunteer to participate in medical research that offers them hope where otherwise there would be none. Neuralink will begin with research designed to assist such patients, but to achieve its grand aim, it will need to move beyond them.

In the United States, Europe, and most other countries with advanced biomedical research, strict regulations on the use of human subjects would make it extremely difficult to obtain permission to carry out experiments aimed at enhancing our cognitive abilities by linking our brains to computers. US regulations drove Phil Kennedy, a pioneer in the use of computers to enable paralyzed patients to communicate by thought alone, to have electrodes implanted in his own brain in order to make further scientific progress. Even then, he had to go to Belize, in Central America, to find a surgeon willing to perform the operation. In the United Kingdom, cyborg advocate Kevin Warwick and his wife had data arrays implanted in their arms to show that direct communication between the nervous systems of separate human beings is possible.

Musk has suggested that the regulations governing the use of human subjects in research could change. That may take some time. Meanwhile, freewheeling enthusiasts are going ahead anyway. Tim Cannon doesn't have the scientific or medical qualifications of Phil Kennedy or Kevin Warwick, but that hasn't stopped him from co-founding a Pittsburgh company that implants bionic devices, often after he has first tried them out on himself. His attitude is, as he said at an event billed as "The world's first cyborg-fair," held in Düsseldorf in 2015, "Let's just do it and really go for it."

People at the Düsseldorf cyborg fair had magnets, radio frequency identification chips, and other devices implanted in their fingers or arms. The surgery is often carried out by tattoo-ists and sometimes veterinarians, because qualified physicians and surgeons are reluctant to operate on healthy people.

Are the doctors right? Should healthy people be discouraged, if not prevented, from implanting devices in themselves?

Warwick says that scientific research has benefited from what the cyborg enthusiasts have done. "It's their call," he says, and that seems right—so long as people are properly informed of the risks and freely consent to take them. If we do not prevent people from smoking, or from climbing K2 in winter, it isn't easy to see why we should be more paternalistic when people volunteer to contribute to advances in science. Doing so may add meaning to their lives, and if Musk is right, it could ultimately save us all.

Preventing Human Extinction

(with Nick Beckstead and Matt Wage)

Many scientists believe that a large asteroid impact caused the extinction of the dinosaurs. Could humans face the same fate? It's a possibility. NASA has tracked most of the large nearby asteroids and many of the smaller asteroids. If a large asteroid were found to be on a collision course with Earth, that could give us time to deflect the asteroid. NASA has analyzed multiple options for deflecting an asteroid in this kind of scenario, including using a nuclear strike to knock the asteroid off course, and it seems that some of these strategies would be likely to work. The search is, however, not yet complete. The B612 Foundation is working on tracking the remaining asteroids in order to "protect the future of civilization on this planet." Finding one of these asteroids could be the key to preventing a global catastrophe.

Fortunately, the odds of an extinction-sized asteroid hitting the Earth this century are low, on the order of one in a million. Unfortunately, asteroids aren't the only threats to humanity's survival. If the threat of nuclear war had receded since the end of the Cold War, it was raised again in 2022 when Vladimir

Putin warned Western nations against interfering with his invasion of Ukraine, and to make his threat unmistakable, announced that he was raising the level of alert for Russia's nuclear arsenal. Other potential threats stem from bioengineered diseases, extreme climate change, and dangerous future technologies.

Given that there is some risk of humanity going extinct over the next couple of centuries, the next question is whether we can do anything about it. We will first explain what we can do about it, and then ask the deeper ethical question: How bad would human extinction be?

The first point to make here is that if the risks of human extinction turn out to be "small," this shouldn't lull us into complacency. No sane person would say, "Well, the risk of a nuclear meltdown at this reactor is only 1 in 1,000, so we're not going to worry about it." When there is some risk of a truly catastrophic outcome and we can reduce or eliminate that risk at an acceptable cost, we should do so. In general, we can measure how bad a particular risk is by multiplying the probability of the bad outcome by how bad the outcome would be. Since human extinction would, as we shall shortly argue, be extremely bad, reducing the risk of human extinction by even a very small amount would be very good.

Humanity has already done some things that reduce the risk of premature extinction. We've made it through the Cold War and scaled back our reserves of nuclear weapons. We've tracked most of the large asteroids near Earth. We've built underground bunkers for "continuity of government" purposes, which might help humanity survive certain catastrophes. We've instituted disease surveillance programs that track the spread of diseases, so that the world could respond more quickly in the event of a large-scale pandemic. (We need to learn from our experience with the virus that causes COVID-19, and do much better next time, because the next novel virus could be equally contagious, but much more lethal.) We've identified climate change as a potential risk and developed some plans for responding, even if the actual response so far has been lamentably inadequate. We've also built institutions that reduce the risk of extinction in subtler ways, such as decreasing the risk of war or improving the government's ability to respond to a catastrophe.

One reason to think that it is possible to further reduce the risk of human extinction is that all these things we've done could probably be improved. We could track more asteroids, build better bunkers, improve our disease surveillance programs, reduce our greenhouse gas emissions, encourage nonproliferation of nuclear weapons, and strengthen world institutions in ways that would probably further decrease the risk of human extinction. There is still a substantial challenge in identifying specific worthy projects to support, but it is likely that such projects exist.

Since the beginning of the 21st century, a few books have sought to raise awareness about existential risks: Martin Rees's *Our Final Century,* Toby Ord's *The Precipice,* and Will MacAskill's *What We Owe to the Future* are among the most prominent. The organization Open Philanthropy has done some thoughtful work on possible interventions for reducing these risks, but we know of no in-depth, systematic analysis of the different strategies for reducing these risks, and their costs and likelihood of achieving their objectives. Such analyses would be a reasonable first step toward deciding on the actions that we should be taking to increase the probability of our survival.

If what we've said is correct, then there is some risk of human extinction and we probably have the ability to reduce this risk. There are a lot of important related questions, which are hard to answer: How high a priority should we place on reducing the risk of human extinction? How much should we be prepared to spend on doing so? Where does this fit among the many other things that we can and should be doing, like helping the global poor? Does the goal of reducing the risk of extinction conflict with ordinary humanitarian goals, or is the best way of reducing the risk of extinction simply to improve the lives of people alive today and empower them to solve the problem themselves?

We won't try to address those questions here. Instead, we'll focus on this question: How bad would human extinction be?

One very bad thing about human extinction would be that billions of people would likely die painful deaths. But in our view, this is, by far, not the worst thing about human extinction. The worst thing about human extinction is that there would be no future generations.

We believe that future generations matter just as much as our generation does. Since there could be so many generations in our future, the value of all those generations together greatly exceeds the value of the current generation.

Considering a historical example helps to illustrate this point. About 70,000 years ago, there was a supervolcanic eruption known as the Toba eruption. Many scientists believe that this eruption caused a "volcanic winter" which brought our ancestors close to extinction. Suppose that this is true. Now imagine that the Toba eruption had eradicated humans from the Earth. How bad would that have been? Some 3,000 generations and 100 billion lives later, it is plausible to say that the death and suffering caused by the Toba eruption would have been small in comparison with the loss of all the human lives that have been lived from then to now, and everything humanity has achieved since that time.

Similarly, if humanity goes extinct now, the worst aspect of this would be the opportunity cost. Civilization began only a few thousand years ago. Yet Earth could remain habitable for another billion years. And if it is possible to colonize space, our species may survive much longer than that.

Some people would reject this way of assessing the value of future generations. They may claim that bringing new people into existence cannot be a benefit, regardless of what kind of life these people have. On this view, the value of avoiding human extinction is restricted to people alive today and people who are already going to exist, and who may want to have children or grandchildren.

Why would someone believe this? One reason might be that if people never exist, then it can't be bad for them that they don't exist. Since they don't exist, there's no "them" for it to be bad for, so causing people to exist cannot benefit them.

We disagree. We think that causing people to exist can benefit them. To see why, first notice that causing people to exist can be bad for those people. For example, suppose a woman knows that if she conceives a child during the next few months, the child will suffer from multiple painful diseases and die before their third birthday. It would obviously be bad for her child if she decided to conceive during the next few months. In general, it seems that if a child's life would be brief and miserable, existence is bad for that child.

If you agree that bringing someone into existence can be bad for that person and if you also accept the argument that bringing someone into existence can't be good for that person, then this leads to a strange conclusion: being born could harm you but it couldn't help you. If that is right, then it appears that it would be wrong to have children, because there is always a risk that they will be harmed, and with no compensating benefit to outweigh the risk of harm.

Pessimists like the nineteenth-century German philosopher Arthur Schopenhauer or the contemporary South African philosopher David Benatar accept this conclusion. But if parents have a reasonable expectation that their children will have happy and fulfilling lives, and having children would not be harmful to others, then it is not bad to have children. More generally, if our descendants have a reasonable chance of having happy and fulfilling lives, it is good for us to ensure that our descendants exist, rather than not. Therefore we think that bringing future generations into existence can be a good thing.

The extinction of our species—and quite possibly, depending on the cause of the extinction, of all life—would be the end of the extraordinary story of evolution that has already led to (moderately) intelligent life, and has given us the potential to make much greater progress still. We have made great progress, both moral and intellectual, over the last couple of centuries, and there is every reason to hope that, if we survive, this progress will continue and accelerate. If we fail to prevent our extinction, we will have blown the opportunity to create something truly wonderful: an astronomically large number of generations of human beings living rich and fulfilling lives, and reaching heights of knowledge and civilization that are beyond the limits of our imagination.

Should We Colonize Outer Space?

(with Agata Sagan)

On April 10, 2019, scientists produced the first image of a black hole, a century after Einstein's work had implied the existence of such extraordinary objects. You didn't need to know a lot of physics to be impressed by the image. The black hole it showed was some 55 million light-years distant from us, and had a diameter about 3 million times that of the Earth. Like the famous "Earthrise" photograph taken by William Anders during the 1968 Apollo 8 mission, showing the Earth rising over the surface of the moon, the image of the black hole calls on us to assess our place in the universe, but the two images pull us in different directions. "Earthrise" allowed us to see our planet as a sphere in space and emphatically displays the importance of making that sphere sustainable. Seeing the black hole, in contrast, forces us to grapple with the strangeness of the universe of which we are such a tiny part.

In the same week that we marveled at the black hole, a private Israeli lunar probe, Beresheet, experienced a technical glitch and crashed onto the surface of the moon. Its venture into space, like Elon Musk's SpaceX venture which plans to colonize Mars, raises ethical issues about humans' exploration and use of the universe beyond their own planet. Is the solar system, and the entire universe beyond, now open for everyone to colonize, for whatever purpose they wish, if they have the means to do so?

One outcome of both public and private ventures beyond our planet is already evident: the vast quantity of debris circling the planet. Space Surveillance Networks are tracking 22,300 entities, and the European Space Agency estimates that at the start of 2022, there were more than a million objects larger than 1cm, including 36.500 larger than 10cm, and 130 million larger than 1mm. In 2007, a single event—China's deliberate destruction of one of its own satellites in order to test an anti-satellite rocket—added 3,400 new trackable entities, and two years later another 2,300 were created by the accidental collision of two satellites.

At low orbit levels where most of the debris is, we can predict that the more objects there are, the more collisions there will be, and the more collisions there are, the more debris there will be, creating a vicious spiral that will eventually make frequently used orbits dangerous places to occupy. The debris could also be a hazard for traffic between Earth and the Moon, or Earth and Mars, which some think could increase significantly in decades to come.

In February 2022, NASA wrote to the US Federal Communications Commission about SpaceX's plan to put 30,000 Starlink satellites into orbit (in addition to the 1,800 already there). The safety of spaceflight was, not surprisingly, one of NASA's concerns, but the agency also referred, in a phrase that could portend a different way of looking at space, to "the long-term sustainability of the space environment."

The European Space Agency is also concerned about space debris because "modern life depends on the uninterrupted availability of space infrastructures" that are being destroyed by collisions with debris. There is also a risk to people on the ground from re-entering space entities.

These concerns are reason enough to avoid the creation of more space debris, and they also suggest that removing some of the junk already in orbit is a moral imperative. That is, however, such a difficult task that Space Force—the newest branch of the US military—is offering substantial prizes for anyone who can come up with the technology to do it.

The risks that space debris pose imply there is something wrong with littering the atmosphere. In debates about environmental ethics, it is common to distinguish between those who think that protecting the environment is important only because of the benefits it brings to humans and those who think that the preservation of wilderness is important for its own sake. A similar distinction can be applied to the extraterrestrial environment. Should we protect it because doing so will benefit humans? Or is there some intrinsic value in preserving places beyond our own planet as they were prior to human contact?

André Galli and Andreas Losch, from the physics institute and the faculty of theology, respectively, at the University of Bern, have discussed the implications of extending the idea of sustainable development to space. One way of doing this that fits within an anthropocentric ethical framework is to recognize that a time may come when humanity is able to survive only because it has expanded beyond the Earth. That thought lies behind both Elon Musk's desire to colonize Mars, and Jeff Bezos's Blue Origin, which envisages a day when Earth's resources will be insufficient to sustain humanity and we will need to draw on the Moon or other objects in space.

But what if our foray into space posed a threat to life—possibly even sentient life—outside our orbit? The biological contamination of extraterrestrial environments may be of greater concern than littering space with pieces of metal or plastic. After all, Europeans have a terrible record of contaminating the parts of the world they colonized, introducing not only diseases, but also plants and animals that have forever changed the ecology of previously isolated regions such as Australia and New Zealand. Are we about to repeat the same mistakes when we explore space?

The Industrial Revolution and everything that has followed it, including our growing population, has undoubtedly damaged ecosystems around the world and polluted the atmosphere. Indeed, the electricity that we are using to write these words has made the nights less dark and dimmed the stars. Still, technological advances have made our lives much more comfortable. Ultimately, the awe we experience when confronted with the immensity of the universe is not in itself a compelling ethical argument against leaving our traces in those parts of space we are able to reach.

There are, however, many good reasons why, even without attributing value to the stars themselves, we should strive to avoid treating our corner of space as nothing more than a quarry, a rubbish dump, and a lawless frontier. Here the idea of sustainable development is key.

We can start with concern for our own safety and the sustainability of our environment. We can extend this by recognizing that we should not discount the interests of future generations, who seem likely to travel at least to our nearer planets. Nor can we exclude the possibility of other sentient or intelligent life outside our orbit. And if we fail to respect the extraordinary and still mysterious universe in which we live, then perhaps one day our descendants, or these other forms of life, will regret that failing, as we now regret the damage we have done to Earth.

Do Aliens Have Rights?

On a pleasant summer day I was walking with my granddaughter along a beach near Melbourne when we noticed several people gathered around a rock pool, peering into the water. Wondering what had attracted their attention, we went over and saw that it was an octopus. It seemed to reciprocate the spectators' interest, coming to the edge of the pool, directing one of its eyes at the people above, and stretching a tentacle out of the water, as if offering to shake hands. No one took up the offer, but at least no one tried to capture the animal or turn it into dinner. That was pleasing because, as Peter Godfrey-Smith says in *Other Minds: The Octopus, the Sea, and the Deep Origins of Consciousness*, an octopus is "probably the closest we will come to meeting an intelligent alien."

If we do ever meet an intelligent alien, even a tasty one, I hope we have sufficient ethical awareness to think of more than pleasing our palates or filling our stomachs. That leads to a deeper question: What moral status would extraterrestrials have? Would we have obligations to them? Would they have rights? And would our answers depend on how intelligent they are?

Take, for example, E.T., from Steven Spielberg's celebrated 1982 movie *E.T. the Extra-Terrestrial*, which features a friendly extraterrestrial who lands on Earth with some colleagues on a botanical research expedition and is accidentally left behind. E.T. is befriended by Elliott, a ten-year-old boy, and soon shows that he has a full range of human-like feelings, including home-sickness. He also has greater compassion for other species than most humans do. In one memorable scene, Elliott, moved by feelings that come from E.T., liberates the frogs in his biology class.

I use E.T. as a thought experiment to challenge students to reconsider their speciesism—the still widely held assumption that the boundary of our species is also the boundary of beings with rights, or with interests that we ought to take seriously. So far, the only nonhumans we have encountered are animals, plants, fungi, and microscopic living things such as protozoans, bacteria, algae, and spirochetes. When we consider the moral status of these organisms, our thinking is likely to be biased by our own interests in using them, especially as sources of food, or in avoiding being made ill by them.

E.T. challenges the moral significance of the species boundary both because we recognize in him a being with feelings very like ours, and because we have no prejudice against him based on a history of eating his kind, putting them in circuses for our amusement, or using them as beasts of burden. So if I ask my students, "Would it have been ethically permissible for scientists to kill E.T. and dissect him for the purposes of what would surely be extremely interesting scientific research?," they unanimously reject that idea. Some things that we could do to harm aliens, they concede, are wrong. If they accept that, then they must also accept that the sphere of proper ethical concern is not limited to members of the species *Homo sapiens*.

Accepting that it would be wrong to kill and dissect E.T. is a first step in exploring our ethical obligations to extraterrestrial life, but it does not take us very far. Perhaps we have ethical obligations only to beings who have a high level of intelligence, self-awareness, or communicative ability, and if we ever discover extraterrestrial life lacking in these qualities, we will have no obligations to them.

Once the species barrier has been breached, however, it is not so easy to fall back on the requirement that a being pass some threshold for cognitive abilities in order to have rights. For then we have to consider human beings who fail that test—as both human infants, and humans with profound intellectual disability, do. Surely they have interests that need to be considered, whether or not they possess, or have the potential to develop, higher cognitive capacities.

Most of us now accept that we have at least some obligations to avoid inflicting suffering on nonhuman animals, and the same would surely hold for any extraterrestrial beings who we discover to be capable of suffering. Pain and suffering are equally bad, no matter what the species, or planetary origins, of the being suffering. The only thing that matters is the intensity and duration of the suffering, and the same applies to pleasure and happiness. We can think of this as a form of equality—equal consideration for similar amounts of suffering or happiness.

It might, however, be difficult to tell whether extraterrestrial life-forms are capable of suffering or experiencing happiness. We recognize the suffering of other beings by analogy with our own. Where there is a nervous system sufficiently like ours, and behavior similar to our responses to pain, it is reasonable to assume that a nonhuman animal is experiencing pain. This reasoning is strengthened by our knowledge that we and nonhuman animals have a common evolutionary origin, because it is plausible that the mechanisms we share with other animals work in similar ways.

The further back our evolutionary divergence from another being was, the more difficult it is to establish whether consciousness is present. That is why an encounter with an octopus is so fascinating. The behavioral evidence, not only for consciousness but also for intelligence, is very strong—just go to YouTube and search for "octopus intelligence" and you will find many videos of octopuses solving novel problems as well as learning how to do things by observing how another, more experienced, octopus goes about it. Yet our last common ancestor with the octopus was a worm-like creature living 600 million years ago, which is presumably long before there were any minds at all on this planet. So mind has evolved twice—at least—on this planet. Perhaps if we do encounter extraterrestrial organisms that might have minds, we can use behavioral tests, as we do with the octopus and other cephalopods, to determine whether it is probable that they really are conscious.

If there are reasonable grounds for believing that a being may be capable of suffering, we should, wherever possible, give that being the benefit of the doubt. That means applying the principle of equal consideration, but with a discount for uncertainty.

Albert Schweitzer famously advocated an ethic of "reverence for life," and some deep ecologists hold that rivers and mountains have intrinsic value. We don't need to go to those lengths in order to see that the existence of another mind—another center of consciousness—places moral demands on us. If there is something that it is like to be another being, then we have a moral responsibility to avoid harming that conscious being, and, insofar as it is within our power and a reasonable use of our resources, to make that being's life go as well as possible.

SOURCES

Note that most essays have been updated for the 2022 edition.

CHAPTER TITLE	SOURCE
A Pale Blue Dot at the Hinge of History	A new essay, drawing on "The Value of a Pale Blue Dot," Project Syndicate, May 14, 2009, and "The Hinge of History," Project Syndicate, October 8, 2021
Does Anything Matter?	Project Syndicate, June 13, 2011
Is There Moral Progress?	A new essay drawing on "Is There Moral Progress," Project Syndicate, April 14, 2008, and "Is Violence History?," a review of Steven Pinker's *The Better Angels of Our Nature*, New York Times, October 6, 2011
The God of Suffering	*Free Inquiry*, October/November 2008
Do You Have a Moral Plan? (with Agata Sagan)	Project Syndicate, December 30, 2020
Are We Ready for a "Morality Pill"? (with Agata Sagan)	*New York Times*, January 28, 2012
The Empathy Trap	Project Syndicate, December 12, 2016

Can Ethics Be Taught?	Project Syndicate, August 9, 2019
Thinking about the Dead	*Free Inquiry*, Summer 2003
Should This Be the Last Generation?	*New York Times*, June 6, 2010
The Case for Going Vegan	Based on an article that appeared in *Free Inquiry*, April/May 2007, with additional material
Why Loving Our Animals Is Not Enough (with Agata Sagan)	Project Syndicate, June 7, 2018
Learning from Europe's More Ethical Eggs	Project Syndicate, January 17, 2012
If Fish Could Scream	Project Syndicate, September 13, 2010
The Nation of Kangaroos	Project Syndicate, March 13, 2018
Who Is a Person?	*New York Daily News*, October 21, 2014
The Cow Who . . .	Project Syndicate, February 5, 2016
The Measure of Moral Progress	Project Syndicate, June 9, 2021
Are Insects Conscious?	Project Syndicate, May 17, 2017
Plant Liberation?	Project Syndicate, February 4, 2022
The Real Abortion Tragedy	Project Syndicate, August 13, 2012
Abortion, Democracy, and the Reversal of *Roe*	Project Syndicate, June 28, 2022
Treating (or Not) the Tiniest Babies	*Free Inquiry*, June/July 2007
Pulling Back the Curtain on the Mercy Killing of Newborns	*Los Angeles Times*, March 11, 2005

Should Children Have the Right to Die?	Project Syndicate, October 7, 2016
No Diseases for Old Men	Project Syndicate, March 14, 2008
When Doctors Kill	Project Syndicate, November 13, 2009
Choosing Death	A new essay drawing on "Choosing Death," Project Syndicate, September 9, 2014, and "Extending the Right to Die," April 6, 2021
Public Health versus Private Freedom	Project Syndicate, September 6, 2012
The Human Genome and the Genetic Supermarket	*Free Inquiry*, Winter 2001
An Ethical Pathway for Gene Editing (with Julian Savulescu)	*Bioethics*, January 29, 2019
Kidneys for Sale?	Project Syndicate, August 14, 2009
Deciding Who Lives and Who Dies	*Sydney Morning Herald*, March 21, 2020
Were the Lockdowns Justified? (with Michael Plant)	This essay draws on "When Will the Pandemic Cure Be Worse than the Disease," published in Project Syndicate on April 6, 2020 (co-authored with Michael Plant) and "To Lock Down or Not to Lock Down," Project Syndicate, October 7, 2020
Victims of the Unvaccinated	A new essay based on "Why Vaccination Should Be Compulsory," Project Syndicate August 4, 2021 and "Victims of the Unvaccinated," Project Syndicate, January 5, 2022

Ending the Taboo on Talking about Population (with Frances Kissling and Jotham Musinguzi) — *Washington Post*, June 18, 2018

Should Adult Sibling Incest Be a Crime? — Project Syndicate, October 8, 2014

Homosexuality Is Not Immoral — Project Syndicate, October 16, 2006

A Private Affair? — Project Syndicate, May 14, 2007

How Much Should Sex Matter? (with Agata Sagan) — Project Syndicate, April 13, 2012

Ban the Burkini? — Project Syndicate, September 8, 2016

The Case for Legalizing Sex Work — Project Syndicate, November 14, 2016

Holding Charities Accountable — Project Syndicate, February 14, 2008

Good Charity, Bad Charity — *New York Times*, August 10, 2013

Heartwarming Causes Are Nice, But . . . — *Washington Post*, December 19, 2013

The Ethical Cost of High-Priced Art — Project Syndicate, June 4, 2014

Extreme Altruism — Project Syndicate, March 15, 2016

The Lives You Saved — Project Syndicate, December 11, 2019

Happiness, Money, and Giving It Away — Project Syndicate, July 12, 2006

Can We Increase Gross National Happiness? — Project Syndicate, September 13, 2011

The Moral Urgency of Mental Health (with Michael Plant)	Project Syndicate, November 15, 2017
Prisoners of Pain	Project Syndicate, January 8, 2018
No Smile Limit	Project Syndicate, April 16, 2007
Happy, Nevertheless	*The New York Times Magazine,* December 28, 2008
The Founding Fathers' Fiscal Crises	Project Syndicate, October 2, 2013
Why Vote?	Project Syndicate, December 14, 2007
Is Citizenship a Right?	Project Syndicate, May 6, 2014
The Spying Game	Project Syndicate, July 5, 2013
Is Marx Still Relevant?	Project Syndicate, May 1, 2018
Should We Honor Racists?	Project Syndicate, December 11, 2015
Is Violence the Way to Fight Racism?	Project Syndicate, August 23, 2017
Are Riots Justifiable? (with Katarzyna de Lazari-Radek)	Project Syndicate, July 9, 2020
The Refugee Dilemma	A new essay drawing on "Escaping the Refugee Crisis," Project Syndicate, September 1, 2015 and "The Migration Dilemma," Project Syndicate, July 6, 2018
Is Open Diplomacy Possible?	Project Syndicate, December 13, 2010
Paris and the Fate of the Earth	Project Syndicate, November 11, 2015
Greta Thunberg's Moment	Project Syndicate, October 7, 2019

Stopping Putin	Project Syndicate, March 1, 2022
A Clear Case for Golden Rice	Project Syndicate, February 17, 2014
Life Made to Order	Project Syndicate, June 11, 2010
A Dream for the Digital Age	Project Syndicate, September 9, 2013
The Tragic Cost of Being Unscientific	Project Syndicate, December 15, 2008
Free Speech, Muhammad, and the Holocaust	Project Syndicate, March 1, 2006
Free Speech and Fake News	Project Syndicate, January 6, 2017
Why Google Was Wrong	*New York Daily News*, August 10, 2017
Keeping Discussion Free	Project Syndicate, May 10, 2021
Why Pay More?	Project Syndicate, May 9, 2013
Beyond the Traditional Family (with Agata Sagan)	Project Syndicate, March 5, 2019
Tiger Mothers or Elephant Mothers?	Project Syndicate, February 11, 2011
How Honest Are We?	Project Syndicate, July 5, 2019
Is Doping Wrong?	Project Syndicate, August 14, 2007
Is It OK to Cheat at Football?	Project Syndicate, June 29, 2010
Why Climb Mount Everest?	Project Syndicate, September 5, 2019
A Surfing Reflection	Project Syndicate, January 15, 2015
Should We Live to 1,000?	Project Syndicate, December 10, 2012
Rights for Robots? (with Agata Sagan)	Project Syndicate, December 14, 2009

Can Artificial Intelligence Be Ethical?	Project Syndicate, April 12, 2016
Do You Want to Be a Cyborg? (with Agata Sagan)	Project Syndicate, May 16, 2017
Preventing Human Extinction (with Nick Beckstead and Matt Wage)	http://www.effective-altruism.com/ea/50/preventing_human_extinction/, August 19, 2013
Should We Colonize Outer Space? (with Agata Sagan)	*New Statesman*, May 20, 2019
Do Aliens Have Rights?	*Nautilus*, April 6, 2017

INDEX

abortion, 97–104; contraception as reducing, 97–98; in democracies around the world, 104; in developing world, 97–98; and *Dobbs v. Jackson Women's Health Organization*, 101–4; forced, 165; medical, 98–99; and personal choice, 99–100; with pills, 98–99; and "pro-life" groups/stance, 99, 109; and right to life, 99–100; *Roe v. Wade* and its reversal, 101–4; safe, 98–99, 166; unsafe, 97–98; in the US, 98–104. *See also* reproductive health/rights

abstract reasoning, 15–16

Abu Dhabi, 349

academic freedom, 174, 338, 341

Academic Freedom Monitoring Project of the Scholars at Risk Network, 341

active misinformation. *See under* misinformation: active

Adam and Eve, 19, 86

Adkins, Janet, 126–27

administrative expenses, of charitable organizations, 197

adoption, 184–85, 215–16

adults, consenting, 160, 176, 191, 193

advance directives, 117, 127, 151

affluence. *See* developed countries; wealth

Afghanistan, 283, 290, 327

Africa: abortion in, 97–98; and animal protection laws, 83; and family planning, 97, 165–66, 319; future effects of climate change in, 166; population growth in, 165–66; refugees from, 283; vitamin A deficiency among children in, 309–10. *See also* developing countries; *by topic, e.g.,* malaria; *specific regions and countries*

African Americans: Black Justice League, 268, 271; Black Lives Matter, 274–75, 277–78; discrimination against (*see* racism); police killings of unarmed, 268, 271, 276–79; progress toward racial equality for, 13–14; Woodrow Wilson's policies for, 269, 271. *See also* civil rights movement; Civil War, US; King, Martin Luther, Jr.; segregation; slavery

African National Congress (South Africa), 323

Against Empathy (Bloom), 30, 32–33

Against Malaria Foundation, 204–6

age, chronological and mental, 114

age limits, 114. *See also* consenting adults